POVERTY OF NATIONS

REMEDIAL MEASURES

DR SUBHRENDU BHATTACHARYA

authorHOUSE®

AuthorHouse™
1663 Liberty Drive
Bloomington, IN 47403
www.authorhouse.com
Phone: 1-800-839-8640

Published by AuthorHouse   01/14/2015

ISBN: 978-1-4969-4250-0 (sc)
ISBN: 978-1-4969-4251-7 (e)

Library of Congress Control Number: 2014917372

To
My Parents

Mr. K. R. Bhattacharya
Mrs. Jaya Bhattacharya

Who inspired me to be kind hearted to family and people

Acknowledgments

My acknowledgements go to numerous academics, public policy makers and researchers, who dealt the issues of poverty, in different parts of the world. My acknowledgements go to my respected parents, who motivated me, all through my life to serve humanity and pursue learning. They constantly inspired me, when I was studying graduation, to pay enormous attention, to the studies and emphasized that education helps, in personality development, as well as in professional progress. With their inspiration, I could join the top administrative job, in the Government of India, which gave me the opportunities, to work closely with the poor. I learnt from my parents, how inclusive one needs to be, with the poor. I feel happy to have practiced inclusiveness, to this day, to the public at large, duly touching their lives, in whichever assignments, I had the opportunity to work. Family and community welfare, according to them, were priorities that I should focus, when I hold positions.

My acknowledgements, go to all the academics, who shared their ideas, on the topic of poverty, in all its ramifications. These include academics, from India and also globally, who have either academically worked with poverty, or have been associated with poverty reduction measures, in different economies. Through interface with the officials of the World Bank and the Asian development bank, who visited India, on a number of missions, I had the details of what causes poverty and how successful has been the steps of the multilateral institutions, to help the nations reduce them. Interface with official supplementing bilateral aid institutions, also has been quite rewarding, such as British Aid and agencies of the Dutch bilateral assistance. I owe a great deal of learning from the learned authors, in the areas of globalization, international trade, market economies, role of democracy, in the reduction of poverty. During the course of my career, as public policy maker and development administrator, taking up schemes of poverty reduction, in the districts of India I have had, the first hand experience of the problems that the poor face and the areas that challenge them, and how the poverty can be reduced considerably, with bottom up initiatives, of course, not without the rural level village leadership. I have witnessed, how the dedication of the district administration and the poverty reduction aiming, development projects, for improvement of labor castes and the tribes, can achieve considerable economic progress. I have valued both the top down efforts, emulation, from the trickle down effects and projects targeted to the poor welfare measures and consider each one of the positive moves add on.

My acknowledgements go to the thinkers and the scholars in different fields, including engineering, health, women and child welfare, business administration, police and the judiciary, from whom I learnt about the role of different aspects of life, which either accentuate poverty or reduce it. For example, I firmly believed and I also noticed that education plays, a very important role, in steering up desire, to come up in life and opens globally, a lot of economic opportunities. I have also learnt how in India, the desire of parents, to be family focused and caring for the education of children, have catapulted the poor, to a level, where they could forget poverty, for themselves and their parents.

The duties that I addressed included, assigning the agricultural land to the landless poor; training the poor farmer, in modernized scientific agriculture, to get increased productivity, through agricultural expertise in the districts; the small economic support schemes, which were implemented to help rural poor, improve their economic activities, with my advice, in coordination with the loans assistance from the banks; who were motivated to help the poor, as much as possible, to supervise the hostels, where the poor students lived and studied in all its micro details. The children and their poor parents, enriched my knowledge, about the happiness, they derive from the little things they have, following simple Indian way of life. It was interesting to observe how even in the poor families, how important for them, is their lifetime spouse and children and how involved, they usually are with their family, no matter how challenging, are their finances or their workplaces. The poor, who experienced poverty a decade ago, could be seen on a path of economic progress. The elders nurture high ambitions for their children, that they would become professionals such as doctors, engineers, university professions, or administrators.. I only wish the global poor in Africa or America, learn from their self-confidence, patience and their values of family and education, besides engaged participation in their democracy, to make improvements happen in their lives. The base level of poverty in developed world, is nice, but in transition for the Indian poor, is way ahead from the poor in America or in EU.

My acknowledgments go to Shona, my wife who has been, a tremendous help and support to motivate me, to write the book, even sharing some of her valued thoughts, on poverty and its reduction. Abhijeet, our very scholarly son never failed to remind me of the deadline, which is getting crossed, if the book is not completed. His informing his own acquaintances that I am writing a book, on poverty of nations, put an indirect pressure, on me, to write the book and complete the same, as his friends asked me, how far the book came to be completed. Being an economist, with excellent education in the US, he shared a lot of his considered views, with me, on related topics that added value, to my book.

My acknowledgments go to my poor brethren, in different economies, with whom I talked in caring manner, to understand why they landed in poverty and if I had a solution on some occasions, I felt happy to advise them, how best they could pull themselves away from the indigent atmosphere, giving them hope that sunshine will come in their lives, given the discipline, to educate themselves, take their jobs seriously and leading a disciplined social life.

Contents

Chapter 1

Colonization and Poverty of the Colonies

Another change after industrial revolution, was the colonization of different parts of the world, leveraging the naval expertise that some of the European powers, like the British the French and the Dutch, had acquired in recent centuries. Spain and Portugal were however pioneers in naval expeditions that made them, stay ahead of other countries, in the world in setting up colonies.

Most of the colonies were set up, in Asia and Africa, for the purpose of the trade and these establishments, were located near the coasts in the colonized countries. The monopoly trade companies, started trading some goods, mostly primary products and raw materials, were imported into Europe and finished goods, were exported to the colonized countries. The labor in colonized countries, was paid very small amounts, with which nothing but poverty could be multiplied and prosperity earned, for the mother countries. Finished goods were priced high, to gouge higher profit margins. Thus level playing fields that are so much talked about, in modern business parlance, of the late 20th and early 21st century, was complied with more in its violation, during the period of colonization, by the European naval and industrial countries. In so doing, it has been established, both by the researchers and by the intelligentsia of the mother countries and colonies that through the process of colonization, prosperity by the route of trade, travelled to the goods exporting countries, particularly to a cliché of the business owners. The business owners also paid slightly higher taxes, which governments could use, to spruce up their infrastructure, modernizing and beautifying the cities and laying fine metal roads, connecting rural areas with the cities. Colonization though hollowed wealth out the colonies. Hence poverty in a large measure, came to be imported into the colonies, year through year. Economic activities, in the colonies, were neglected or discouraged by higher rates of taxation and the goods made by the colonies, were discouraged, to be exported, as they were competing with the goods makers, of the mother countries. So industries suffered. Only a part of the taxes collected in the colonies, was spent in the colony's welfare. Most went to meet the administrative costs, and was also transferred to the mother countries. Small farmers were made to pay the taxes and the tax collection being delegated, to the local landlords in India, their landlordism worked against the peasants, who were further impoverished, paying to two masters, one to the landowner and another to the new foreign ruler. Army was raised very cheaply, from places like India and deployed in Europe, to fight wars that saved Britain, a lot of wealth and in turn deprived India, a lot of wealth. These armies, which were to be used, for the defense of India and also relief works, in times of natural calamities, were asked to protect British economic and financial interests, in foreign lands. The British fought the Russians in the Afghan war, deputing the Indian troops to Afghanistan. Similarly, in the First World War and the Second World War, millions of troops recruited in India and paid half the wages, paid to the British soldiers, were sent to Europe, to fight the world wars. There were lot of causalities, in these wars and many Indian troops died. A conservative estimate indicates that about 2 million Indian troops died, fighting on behalf of the British, in the global wars, in the first half of the 20th century. Thus, 2 million families were deprived of the income earner and astonishingly no pensions, were given to the spouse of the Indian origin soldiers. How much poverty was inflicted, in this manner can be gauged, from a combination of wrong decisions of the British administration, in India. Similarly, other company armies also fought in the wars. The narrative, above indicates, how through different routes, the wealth, was transferred from the colonies, to the mother countries, in an unabashed manner and how these colonies became the captive markets of the goods, manufactured in the mother countries. A significant portion of the revenue, came to be transferred and added to the national treasuries, of the foreign governments, which were invested, in the mother countries, neglecting severely investments, in the colonies and their infrastructure. Education for the multitude, was totally neglected. Agricultural productivity, was never paid attention. Incumbent industries were discouraged, as they were competitors and no new industries were undertaken in the colonies. Banks were set up in the colonies, only to work for the foreign government and cater to small business interests of the urban Indian businessmen. A class of pro British English medium educated class, was pampered, to promote the British interests, acting as brand ambassadors, of the British rule in India. Similarly, in other colonies mother country language educated elite held sway, in the economy of those colonies, in favor of the foreign government. With national revenue of the colonies, shrunk and income of the workers way below the cost of living, made the people of the colonies, suffer in grinding poverty, for decades until the mother country, desired to rule these colonies. Vexed by poverty, when the peasants from the colonies rebelled, against the foreign rule, as the colonial government had millions of armies recruited cheaply from the colony itself, the army was used to quell the rebellions. A number of peasant uprisings took place in India in United Provinces, Central India and in Madras and they were quelled using the army, which consisted of people of Indian origin. As they were recruited by the British administration, they naturally exhibited loyalty, to the foreign rule, to quell the rebellions. Thus, uprisings were not in any way successful, to make the British treat the peasants better, in future, as with strong army, could be put to action, to quell the uprisings. Huge value deduction resulted, from divide and rule policy, where ethnicities and religions were factors to foment divides. Sometimes, at the time of granting independence, the nations got divided and on other occasions belligerences among diverse groups, within the independent nations, robbed the free colonies of their peace. The civil wars, became the order of the day, in some of the freed countries, especially in Africa. Most African countries, saw the civil wars, due to this exploitation of the mother countries, to foment and accentuate divides, among multiple ethnicities. Due to colonization, the cooperation among African countries, were very hard to come by. Lot of European countries, were on prowl in Africa, to colonize it, among dividing regions, among themselves. They imposed a foreign administrative system, a foreign culture and made their own language, as their official language and also medium of instruction, in the urban schools. After independence it was hard for even educated people of Mozambique, ruled by Italy to understand the intelligentsia of Senegal and Morocco and similarly Senegal intelligentsia found it hard, to communicate with Benin, Senegal or Morocco. Over and above, the intra country ethnic divides of these African countries, an overarching European culture and language, got superimposed that divided the countries even further. These negatives happened to countries, which the European countries only used for revenue and raw materials, for their own countries, their education, infrastructure, industries and agriculture were not promoted, by making investments. Except some trickles of expenditure, in urban areas, the rural areas were left soaked in poverty. Unlike India, where village system and local administration, in revenue, education had a lot of ancient heritage and there was semblance of infrastructure, on which value addition, could be effected. Even the British set up investments in urban India, significantly, nice schools, roads and drainage and sewage works, The British also took a number of memorials which stand beautifully to this day. Memorials, libraries, museums and the government buildings from the District to the National Capital were very pompous, probably because India, was regarded, as the jewel among the colonies, as said Mr. Churchill, the British Prime Minister.

French speaking Senegal or Morocco could find it odd, to be close to English ruled Ethiopia Kenya or Nigeria. Nigeria could never reconcile in its groups, as east north and south had different resources and different religious following, that landed them in bad civil wars, at one time.

With civil wars, in many countries in Africa, including some time or the other in Angola, Nigeria, Ethiopia, Eritrea, Libya, Syria and the like, with numerous tribal groups, as many sometimes as 30 in each country, with distinct subcultures, languages and food habits could never coalesce, with a national fervor and timely develop their country. With lack of development, the GDP remained small and so was the GDP per capita. A lot of money came to be spent in wars, though they were missing on civil wars, each group, mindlessly buying from America and the west, arms, at a heavy cost. All of these moves, many of which, were the outcomes of, the macho colonial colonization of the colonies, weekend the African countries financially. Governments being dysfunctional poverty visited these countries severely.

It is in the developed economies, where armaments industries, are located, by the private business owners, making a lot of profits. The countries, which are involved in frequent wars, happen to be their clients, at the expense of peace and trade in that region. Whenever nations have the schism and civil wars go on, the developed countries also side with one group or the other and nations globally are banded together, by the left or right ideologies, be it in the past, at the time of the cold war or even now. Finances for warring groups, within the nations, might come from a group of similarly thinking countries, in favor of the market or otherwise, believing in centralization. These groups would place orders, to buy arms, basing on their availability of funds and developed economy,. The US based armament industries, would supply them, the arms and enrich themselves, with rising bottom line and top line. The arms business owners, would also pay taxes, accelerating the job creation, in the developed countries. Some economies get dented, by more civil war violence and their economies get devastated, whereas the strong and well entrenched armament industry tends to benefit economically, both at the business level and also at the national budget level, at the expense of several countries, torn by either wars or civil wars. Here the activities that get heavily monetized, in the developed world, is not from an ethical purpose, but it is hard to close the industries, which have been in place, for several decades, especially when markets dominate in the economy and the government intervention in the economy, happens to be mild. If the arms industries, switch to other harm free economic activities, the government could be happy, though it usually does not happen, for those, who are financially so much rewarded, by their products, the arms, in which they had the monopoly globally.

Ideologues, on the left and the right, as well those nations that tend to like superiority and hegemony, tend to help warring groups, in nation that causes perennial poverty and lack of peace. Armament industry, located in the developed world, do not usually want to diversify, into civil products, researching on them, as they happen to be well entrenched, in the arms business and find this business, finally rewarding. Their profits depend on the demand, for the arms, from private and government clients abroad, if that is continued. It is an irony that most of the business of the armament industry, comes from the dictators, worldwide, mainly hailing mainly from 2 continents, the Africa and southern America. The arms industry located, in the developed world, tend to get more business from African dictators, who want to be militarily powerful, to quell rebellions of civilians. and if any. given to civil war, more in Africa, as national boundaries, were haphazardly made and countries given independence, by the British and other colonial masters. Some portions of the country, were populated by the people, from the neighboring countries, with which they have had ethnic conflicts. Hence, those regions in many countries, created trouble, for the central government and their rebellion needed additional arms, by the government. At the same time, the rebellious groups, though indulging in clandestine activities, against their state, could plan to procure arms, which arms makers, were to sell, as their finances were improved, by any business to sell arms. The businessmen, being businessmen, there is a possibility that the same armament business, may be supplying on indents, to both the warring groups of a civil war. Thus armament industry, moves and civil wars reinforce each other. Civil war turns more devastating, as they procure arms and when tempers fray, between warring groups, in the civil war, the demand for arms from both quarters heightens, for the armament industry, making it richer, on an annualized basis. More the wars in the world, it is a tragedy that the armament industry flourishes. Ideology does not preclude a centralized regime, not to supply arms, to civil wars. In a market economy, regulation on these industries, by way of market moves, is less compared to economies, ruled by centralized regimes. All of these civil wars and each warring group, enriching global armament industry, could be contained, if such nations catapult strong passionate and committed leaders, who morph the governance into democracy, reining in dictatorships, through public movement. Hence the lack of leadership, in Africa is the primary reason of poverty, more than the poverty trap, Africa has got into civil war trap and dictatorial regimes trap. Along with top down democracy, with a strong leader, bottom up movement, to free the nations from dictatorships, would go a long way, to improve living standards. Democracies, would bring the nations closer, to other democracies and developed country know how good will flows, along with aid. Though a lot of tragedy was inflicted, by the European countries, not many decades ago, the best course for the African counties, would be to forget history. Bad history, pulls back a nation, a race, a social group and to forget it is the best option, with a forgiving attitude, to the exploiters. Yesteryear's exploiters, with more education of their people, have come to realize that the colonies, were exploited and it was wrong. While developed nations feel guilty already, though covertly, this is the time for African countries, to forget the bad history and launch development initiatives, with some collaborations, wherever good. They have to be cautious though that an approach of benevolence outwardly, should not have some ulterior moves, to defraud the economy. Money glitters but nations need to be cautious, as there is an old adage, "all that glitters is not gold."

While leaving the nations free, the colonial governments, with a view to perpetuate divides, sometimes left overlapping boundaries. In other words, some portions of another country, which would not like to be with another new nation, were added. Such areas in many countries, were a thorn and rebellious, challenging the central government. Limited resources of the newly freed nations, were wasted to contain such divides, increasing national poverty. Some nations had a long history, of ethnic conflicts and differences, among numerous ethnicities, sometimes about 30.

During the cold war, some African countries followed, non-alignment, but most countries came, under the influence of the right or left ideologies, thus losing out on the help, which could have come from other superpower. Wherever, these conflicts exacerbated, the civil wars started and they continued for decades. Inter country differences increased, with cold war moves, of the 2 super powers and the African countries with skirmishes, lost out on economic development. For right oriented countries, financial help and even aid for defense, came from USA and for left oriented countries, aid for defense and finances, came from the erstwhile Soviet Union. Once used to buying arms with aid, the regimes also got used to allocating more budgets for defense and building up arms, neglecting economic development. The gainer was the global armament industry, which are mostly developed country based. At the expense of African countries, the people of developed countries got better emoluments, perks, who worked in armament industry and their government got taxes higher taxes, to spend on welfare of already developed countries.

Many African countries were ruled from time to time, by the dictators and they wanted to spend on arms, to rule over a long period. Rebellions needed to be quelled. Those interested in democracy, in the country, their voices had to be muzzled. In the scare that some group may overthrow, the regime and bring in a new regime, a lot of expenditure on building up army, building up intelligence systems and pampering police, became necessary and all of these moves required, lot of money, all at the expense, of economic development spurring increase of poverty. Wherever military dictators ruled, their first preference was to allocate huge budget, for the army and that accentuated poverty of those African nations. The worst affected, were those affected by civil wars, ideological civil wars, resource based civil wars, development neglect sensitized civil wars and religions civil wars. One thing that was common was that peace, was sacrificed and education, industries, agriculture all were devastated. Most people in such civil war torn nations, suffered misery, with unspeakable poverty and uncertainty, if they would be alive next month.

The countries, which promoted divides, during their colonization governance and did not attempt to deal squarely, with the ethnicities, to band them together, into nationhood, how could they be expected, after their colonies were free, to take a moral leadership, now, to genuinely help these nations, get over the civil wars. The lobbyists, working on behalf of the armament industry, caused the maximum damage, asking the US and European government authorities, simply to look the other way, when their African colonies were witnessing the civil wars..

The British colonialism in India, got reflected in widespread exploitation, of the small and marginal farmers, by the landlords. In addition, the development of some industries, purely due to private initiatives, also saw its demise, due to negative British policy moves. To replace the business of India's muslin and cloth of world renown, a high tariff was imposed on the Indian textiles, while importing Indian textiles, into Britain, free of tariff. These British moves, priced out the Indian textiles, relative to no such punishment meted out, to the local Manchester produced British textiles. While importing the Indian textiles, into Britain, which were hitherto a craze, among the British consumers, a very high tariff was slapped, on the Indian textiles. In the case of the import of the Indian textiles, the British followed a trade policy, just the opposite of what, Sir Adam Smith's free trade policy prescribed. It is not known, how the British and the Europeans, on the one hand, were touting the plusses of Sir Adam Smith's policy of free trade feverishly, and they suddenly for themselves, followed the opposite policy. The British government in India, gave no explanation to the international community, for violating fragrantly, Sir Adam Smith's popular trade policy, such a negative trade policy, against India. However, the Manchester, textiles, were allowed, to flood the Indian textile market. The availability of these textile goods occurred, to the detriment of the sale of the local textiles to the Indians. Hence the Indian textile industry died and the Manchester shone in financial performance. Other European countries were allowed, for export of Indian textiles. The laws were made not to export Indian textiles directly to foreign ports, but it had to go through the British ports and thereby the punishing tariff, on Indian textiles played out against India.

The colonies were hurt all the more in terms of more casualties and severe impact resulting from scramble for power. As Tagore rightly pointed out, "Today all the big nations, in their reckless career of political ambition and advances of greed. None of them has the natural privilege to day to stand for right when any great wrong is done to humanity." However, Indians also acquired the mobility of travel, to different parts of India, which had an incidental positive effect on India's economy also. The British used to pool up agricultural exports and about a million tons of agricultural exports, were permitted, to be exported to Britain, at the minimum. Grain dealers were indirectly encouraged, to export agricultural products, to Britain, even if it hurt the local consumption of the grains and created scarcity of food. No modernization of agriculture, was undertaken. Investments in irrigation systems, soil conservation measures and the like were frugally done. As a result, the agriculture remained for decades, at a level far lesser, than its potential.

Tagore was disenchanted to see the dirty poverty conditions in the rural areas. He stated, "the sight of the terrible poverty of Indian masses grew inescapable. I realized that perhaps in no other modern state, was there such a complete denial; of basic needs of living food clothing and health services. I knew at last was the emblem of a civilized nation' s contempt and callousness towards our vast masses." Tagore referred to the British rural India, in following manner. with a total anguish for being treated poorly, "This helpless country was denied the mastery, over machines, by means of which the British have strutted as a world power. India however bearing the immense deadweight of British rule, lies effortless and inert." Tagore visited and lectured, in many countries, such as China, Argentina, Hungary, Britain, USA. He felt that China was a great country, which was also not spared by the British, in their grandiose plan to thoroughly exploit. According to him, "I recall the tragic history of another great country.

China faced peril. The British doped the people of China with opium and followed up with territorial aggression. I have to tell this sad story of my gradual loss, of faith in the civilization of the west." Indian labor were known even at that time, as very methodical, hard working labor and they came up with textile products, which were immensely liked worldwide, especially the muslins of India. Internationally, the Indian peasants were known, to address, savings of grains, every year methodically, for next couple of seasons, in case the natural calamities occurred in future. But the Zamindars were given free hand, to collect land revenue, even during the times of severe natural calamities. Hence the trust, even in the government welfare schemes, plummeted and the schemes were viewed, with apprehensions. The extension of loans, for agriculture, at a far lesser rate of interest than was charged by the moneylenders, were surprisingly not availed, by the Indian peasants, as the grass root officials in British period, who were of the Indian origin, were known to be corrupt. With a view to consolidate the British rule strong, some constituencies, were strengthened though, the British administration knew that driven by the avarice of money, these constituencies were fleecing the grass root multitudinous peasants. In this category, primarily fell, the zamindars,the moneylenders. The third category, which the peasants found it hard to trust were the petty grassroots government officials, of the British government, whose honesty was in question. And they were known, to be corrupt, abetted by the British government. The British government looked the other way and allowed these petty officials, to indulge in petty corruption. For the peasants, it was difficult to avail pretty low interest loans, provided by the government, as they apprehended that the petty officers of the government, could delay loans and also may indulge in corruption. Thus with the active knowledge, of the British government corruption as a highly negative trade, was initiated in Indian administration in this manner. Already being harassed by the zamindars and moneylenders, the peasants had to face the agony of the corruption, of the these petty officials, of the Indian origin. It is such bizarre, attitude of the locals that again denied the peasants, even to avail the positive moves of the government offering loans at low interest rates. To keep the empire going, the government looked the other way. The advantage of the British was that by paying low salaries, to the officials and allowing them to fleece bribes, on petty issues, from the public at large. They saved money and sent the same to the British government, in London to be in the good books of the crown. In the process, how much poor India's masses, are turning poorer, appeared to be the least priority, to think and contain.

And making the Indian educated work, they were maintaining the British rule, which was a tool to transfer wealth, collected from agriculture to British government. British government in turn, invested the same amount, in British infrastructure. Further, the young British officers, who came from foreign land, to work at the top, were very lavishly paid and lot of perks were given to him and a lifetime pension was given to them even if they had worked there for few years.

Thus to keep the low paid Indian employees happy and also to keep them loyal, so that no opposition, to the British rule will come and also to take their help, to identify peasant revolt if any, it appears the government deliberately looked the other way, when these petty employees indulged, in petty corruption, in dealing with peasants. Hence although the government offered loan, at a very low rate of interest, the peasants, in the fear of being harassed, by the Indian employees, of the British administration, were not interested, in borrowing, from the government.

Further, borrowing from government, at a reasonable rate of interest, was accepted, in some cases and they faced the ire of the moneylenders, who was also in a hand and gloves, with the zamindars. Hence in many cases, peasants borrowed at usurious rates from the moneylenders, because going for government loans would have meant anger of the moneylender, again those peasants and harassment to them, in collusion of the zamindars. When the poor peasants, were facing such vicissitudes in life, it is strange that the lieutenant governors of the Presidencies, District Magistrate, the Superintendents of Police how were they looking the other way naturally with cover instructions from the viceroy who cane to have at the middle class and the rich with them so that the empire flourishes in getting more and more wealth transferred to Briton. in this manner the viceroy was busy impressing his British government in London to earn praise from the crown and aggrandize wealth and future wealth after returning to Britain for himself.

Very few British Viceroys were aware of laws, benefitting the poor, in their own country and they had an inherent dislike, for ameliorating the poverty of the poor people, in the slums of London. When the British viceroys were posted to Calcutta, how could they be expected to be kind to the poor that too, when India had a very large population of poor. Malthusian theory that more population and more poverty go along together, was also coming up, for discussion during this period, in the 18th and 19th centuries. The British had ire against the poor people, having a large family size and challenging the British India with higher incidences of poverty and in accompaniment higher incidence of diseases. The British officials had already encountered, how even in the city of London, the poor people lived in highly congested homes, with no piped water supply and not adequate toilet facilities, and people surviving on community living, with several members in the night sleeping in halls. At this time, there were the British men and women, who were working 16 hours a day. The women and children were exploited, in the factories, with payment of 20 % to 30% of what was paid to men. Even children were made to work, instead of allowing them to go to schools, in very unsafe factory conditions and many died. Many children lost their limbs, with no treatments. In a small country, with less population, they had seen how government could feel helpless, when poverty levels go up in quality and in misery. Hence, poverty due to shortage of money and food in rural areas, used to bother the British officials, but since they were not committed to address it, surely they allowed it to go, looking the other way. Moneylender, petty officials, and zamindars were three major categories of the British favorites, who contributed a lot of finances, for British Indian government. When they wanted to make money, from hapless people, the British officials simply looked the other way. Several oceans away, it is possible that the crown did not know, about the collusion between the two. The British people only received censored news, sent by the Lieutenant Governor to the British crown. The British people had the wrong impression that Indians had a contented life during the British rule.

In the middle of the 19th century, there was a progressive decline in the British rule in India, In the middle of 19the century, Macaulay praised India's development and went to the extent of appreciation that during his extensive tours of India, he did not find beggars. Similarly, Florence nightingale in her letters mentioned in the 1799s that she has not seen many beggars in India, in fact far less than the beggars, which are seen in Europe, as peasants in India are most hard working in the world and they have a great habit of saving the grains, for the rainy days.

She however mentioned, how the petty officials, the zamindars and the moneylenders fleeced the hard working saving centric, calm peasants, who had the self-esteem, to suffer but not to beg. Her quotes profusely condemn the British, for allowing such heinous exploitation of the Indian peasants. In the middle of 20th century many authors, have validated the neglect of the peasants, by the locals, by indifferent attitude of the frugal Viceroy and highly indifferent attitude of even the British Prime Minister. Towards the poverty and famine in India. Mr. Winston Churchill, inebriated with winning the second global war, against the axis powers, headed by Germany. Churchill's stance could be compared with that of Nero.

If the 'jewel in British crown' could be treated so indifferently, then one could understand how the abject poverty stricken, African countries.

For several hundred years. India and China had witnessed until the British came, their exports as a percent of GDP, the highest in the world, and even their GDP was pretty high. European countries that shot up with industrial revolution, were not producers of surplus either in industry or in agriculture, and these countries were at war for about 500 continuous years. The Balkan countries of central Europe, always saw divisiveness, and they never cooperated in trade, leading to their facing a lot of economic downsides. Italy and Germany did not even exist as a country, until the German unification under dynamic German leader Bismarck, occurred in 1870s and Italians also saw the unification of their country, around the same time. Belgian and Holland too had histories that were not very long. British had to face the Norman conquest and the Normans became the French rulers of Britain. These Normans united France and Britain, under one French jurisdiction. When French monarchy, did not have the child for succession, it became an issue and the British wanted to rule both France and Britain.. It is here that the war between the French royalty and the British reality started and inconclusively continued for 100 years.

The French and British thus fought, the famous 100 years' war. The Catholics and the Protestants fought a 30 years' war, for achieving supremacy of the Pope. In this war, not only the German King's armies fought, but the Pope's representatives also fought and this was a war, between Germany and Italy. The war ended with acceptance of the defeat of the German royalty and the German ruler paid obeisance, to the Pope, who thereafter came to the central point of obeisance, for all of the Catholics of the world. The Europeans fought wars in Europe, for 500 years. The France and Britain out of which fought the 100 years' war. A war was fought, for a Papal supremacy for 30 years and all of these disturbances of the long drawn wars, in Europe, created a lot of challenge, for the economies in Europe, to function normally and one could surmise, why only India and China, which never went to war and which were in peace, could dominate the global economy, until the 18th century, when the Moguls in India turned weaker.

The British chartered East India Company, which established its business, as early as in 1600, in India, paying obeisance to the Mogul Emperor Jahangir. It operated very gradually in politics, understanding the administration of the Princes. It ruled India in verticals, in different pockets of India and then harbored political ambitions, known nowhere in the world. A business turning into a sovereign political power, has no other parallel, other than East India Company's relations, with India. The company took the governmental role, of raising an army, waging wars, signing treaties and the like. Finally the East India Company established the rule in India and ruled a part of India, since 1757, after defeating Nabob Sirajuddoula of Bengal.

Gradually, the Eat India Company started even waging wars, against the local Princes, making one set of local Princes fight, against others and applying Doctrine of Lapse, to usurp local Prince's jurisdictions, who did not have a male heir, to sit on the throne. EIC also went to the South India and defeated Tipu Sultan, who was killed in the battle field. Nizam of Hyderabad, was the richest man of the world, and it became the company's ally. All of these gross violations of the international relations and business code went on in India presumably, with the covert support of the British Crown and later on, with ratifying their illegal actions. The British kept the Indian rich and the middle class, in good humor, and took up developments which would keep these two classes, happy. As these 2 classes in Africa, were near absent, no development was undertaken, in African continent. It was only carrying away the asset, from the slave labor, by capturing them free of cost, heinously making slaves work in the mines. The colonials took away a lot of raw materials for industrial use in the mother country. The raw materials were not paid for to the African nations and no welfare measures, no investments in agriculture, industry or infrastructure, was undertaken, in the African countries. With such abject neglect of these African economies by the British and thorough exploitation to procure raw materials, without paying its cost, such a poor scenario was created that much development could not take place immediately, after these countries were free. How could these countries be, in the second half of the 20h century, expected to make waves, in the realm of economic development? African poverty is the seminar subject of international meetings, over decades now and so are the debt defaults. The African countries are faulted, for fledgling development in their countries, and negative economic growth, and high level of poverty. In this context, Rabindranath Tagore the Indian Noble Prize Winner, in literature mentioned, "I have said it over and over again that the aggressive spirit of nationalism and imperialism religiously cultivated, by some of the nations, of the West, is a menace to the whole world. The demonization that it produce in European politics is sure to have disastrous effects especially upon the peoples of the East who are helpless to resist the Western methods of the exploitation."

In such circumstances, one really wonders, if any of the worlds' social groups, or racial groups, if they would have lived in that continent, with such highly obnoxious exploitation history, would have brought about economic surplus and prosperity, either at the national or corporate or individual levels, in decades after the grant of independence, by the foreign rule. Best way to judge a country's economic growth or deceleration, is to step into the shows of that country and then think pensively.

The follies of wrongly drawing maps of African countries, are still keeping them face rebellions. Religious conversions by 2 major religions, almost on an equal footing, created religious/cultural divides of two halves that also complicate the governance of many of such African countries. Too many small countries, which were economically not viable, are in place Many colonial powers, deliberately, divided bigger countries, into smaller countries, while granting them independence. Some of the colonial rulers, such as Britain, given to the practice of divide and rule, tried the same, with 20 to 30 ethnicities, in African countries. Thus, instead of leadership, in integration in those countries, ethnicities had serious edges by the time, the colonial rulers left. The cooperation among neighboring countries, also became tough, as they were ruled by people, with different official languages. Cooperation was very difficult between countries, speaking French, Portuguese, Italian, Danish and English, the reason being English, as an international language, as a whole took considerable decades to happen.

Chapter 2

Industrial Revolution and Increase of British/ European Poverty

When feudalism of the agrarian times, went to the back burner, there came, the knowledge of science and engineering, industries to make goods, on a mass scale came to be set up. The business owners through mass production of goods saw, big money, never seen before and came to be desirous of earning more money. Money greed of some sort was born in Britain, as never seen before. They became interested in higher profits. Since, during feudalism, some landed gentry were given to use their power, over large number of people as they employed them on farms, they felt that they could make instant gains from that power as people then were meek and less demanding of higher wages. They looked for economic opportunities, now to recruit workers in the factories, by paying them low wages, which were higher than farm wages but highly insufficient to live in London well due to high cost of living in London. London then was a place of limited infrastructure of housing roads, drains and the like, and too many people from villages had started coming to London for jobs, which were not yet plenty. Supply of labor having increased thus, the employers had a party with high bargaining power. They now recruited the labor in industry and industry work was tough work, with more boredom and monotony, in the closed factory premises that dented the good health of the factory workers, as breeze and openness of the farms were missing and flexibility of going to farm work were supplanted by a fixed timings on a daily basis. They had to rush to the factory and they had to continue to be in the factory premises, until the close of the factory sirens blared in the evening generally at 5 pm.. From 8 m to 5 pm, the industrial workers' were, in a kind of bondage. Safety standards being low, in the initial phases of industrial revolution, many workers were injured and lost some income and sometimes injured workers could not work after injury. Such conditions continued, till industrial democracy was brought about by labor meetings, among themselves and organizing protests. That was only after they faced poverty for decades. City housing being meager, they had to live in extremely congested conditions. Slums sprang up in large numbers in London and other industrial cities. With agrarian revolution in agriculture, a lot of surplus labor came about, in parishes and hamlets, which started moving to the cities, for jobs. When jobbers exceeded jobs, in industries, the unemployment arose and the unemployed started joining the congested one room slums houses of the industrial workers, who were related or distantly related. Water came to be, in short supply and which led to dirty conditions of human living. People skipped baths and wearing the clothes sometimes for weeks. Those who were given to drinking, they in frustrations, smelled alcohol, to make slum conditions worse. Modes of transportation, being unavailable, people moved around the unpaved streets, at many places, which further soiled the living conditions. Mass production of footwear was yet to be large enough, to make everyone in such industrial cities wear footwear. A lot of people especially workers and the unemployed went around bare foot and so sauntered the poor children. To make both ends meet, in the industrial cities, as the profiteering money greedy employers of industrial revolution, paid meager wages, compelled the family also to join the industrial workforce. Poverty compelled them, to leave rural homes and join factories. They worked odd hours and long hours. As many as 12 hours were spent even by the women and the children in the factories, with no benefactors, to question the rich employers. As per the whims and fancies of the rich industrialists, the wages that were meager, were paid to male workers and female workers and children workers, were paid a pittance for 12 hours of work. Such was the grinding poverty in Britain, even in the middle of 19th century. The children were not motivated to go the schools, as the factory owners wanted to exploit them, to make extra money making them to work long hours, for very low wages. Heinous practices of cleaning the chimney, by making the children, to climb up the chimneys, a horrible and inhumane practice, arose with little protests in Europe. A lot of children nervously got bruised and injured. In Europe, some children even died in the chimneys. Parents also did not protest, as the chimney cleaning children fetched extra money. Such was the lack of ethics arising from poverty of industrial revolution which many scholars, historians and technical people wrote. Even to this day, one hears in India remarks, like though India missed out on industrial revolution, but was not left out in the technological revolution and in fact it is in the center of action, in technological revolution. People have been so much dazzled by the life's plusses for the rich and upper middle class that they forget that prosperity of the few came, with lot of agony, exploitation and poverty, for the multitude The poor lived life, smeared with rarity of baths and cloth washing, in smoked polluted environments, of the industrial cities, suffering from lung diseases, due to pollution caused by factories. In cities of London, Manchester and Leeds people lived in slums, in small accommodations with little sanitation and physical hygiene.

During the industrial revolution in Britain and Europe during the Victorian times, for Britain while there started, some educational institutions, for the gentry, but the laity went without even learning the alphabets, working in factories and getting physically injured, handicapped their hands and legs mutilated, from long hours of the factory work.

During the Victorian times, the crimes were also high, due to the slum living and the hardships people faced. Those who famished, from hunger on London streets, were sent to their parishes, as parishes had the responsibility that parishioners, do not suffer from hunger. Adult as well children in small numbers, also were termed homeless, as they slept on the streets.

Such was the ignoble impact of the industrial revolution, which historians extol so much as generators of wealth, for some rich people, higher national wealth, and national income. development in cities, starting to take place with the taxes paid by the rich, to the city municipalities in a few cities. Inclusiveness on the part of the business owners, following the Hindu scriptural advice of moderation in life and also that of Greek philosopher's message, to be adherent of moderation in life, would have avoided, all of the inhuman treatment of the poor. Both rich and the poor could have gained, from the industrial revolution, bringing improvement in general quality of life. Mass usage of life's joys, hitherto concentrated with royalty, nobles and the rich, came to be broadbased and a life variant from farm life came into being. On the other end, as the goods enjoyed by the royalty, nobles and the rich had percolated, to the masses, in the new millennium, it would be prudent for the average people to exercise moderation, in consumption of goods, following India's ancient spiritual belief in moderation. In the US and most of the European countries, people at large in recent years, have started to acquire the goods and burden themselves, with huge debt. With indebtedness, comes unethical approach to deliberately default loans. Such practices are undesirable, socially and economically and also affects mental peace, causing mind to land in depression. Now is the need of the hour, for the people to spend, with restraint. Economic crisis that European Union and the US, is witnessing intensely since 2008, with slow recovery with far too low job creation, in the horizon. These negative occurrences in economies of the developed world, is the result of not taking industrial revolution, with moderation. Along with industrial revolution, the trade within the country and globally prospered and trade was undertaken, by those countries, who came to be experienced, in business and trade. Industrial revolution brought about prosperity in Britain and promotion and advertisement of goods were made, so that other nations could buy their products, which in turn would enrich those, who ran businesses in Britain. As flow of information was minimal, and tourism was very limited very little was known in regard to poverty in Britain. European powers excelled in naval warfare and continuously engaged in war among each other, in the process established hegemony, over other economies of the world. Study of economies generally take place, in the atmosphere of peace and tranquility, which eluded Europe, as it was engaged in war, for about 500 years. The boundaries of the nations kept changing. Central Europeans and in the Balkans, there occurred perennial wars, on petty issues. It is the ego of the European nations that turned them into feuding nations, to maintain supremacy over thousands of islands. They constantly fought, though those conquests, brought in very little, in terms of economics. The Balkan region was so much ravaged by perennial wars, fought in that region that the term 'balkanization' was coined to refer to any war zone or war skirmishes. Czarist Russia could never rest, in content and was always trying to expand its boundaries. As early as in the early 20th century, it was expanding towards Asia and when it came near India, Anglo afghan war took place and Russia was defeated. But India had to pay a huge cost. India's famine money was diverted, by the British and spent on the Afghan war. Millions of Indians died of famine in India, due to financial shortage, to buy grains and for lack of government relief, in time. Grains could not be transported, to the famine stricken Bengal. After allocating grains, for domestic consumption, the government proactively turned, to help business owners to form monopoly of trading companies, to help them export their goods to different parts of the world. To spur domestic consumption, the goods were made even cheaper and of better quality. Foreign business owners, were helped, by violating the free trade principles that Sir Adam Smith had theorized. Protectionism was resorted to, to give enormous affluence to the rich. Inequality between the haves and have-nots heightened, during this period.

With unionization of labor, inequality reduced, infrastructure improved. With more taxes the poverty within the economies of industrialized world got reduced.

Chapter 3

Wars and Poverty of Nations

Wars trigger national poverty of the victors and that of the vanquished. Europe and the US at their grassroots level, would have been far more educated, integrated in development, entrepreneurial with significant percentage of savings, if only their economies would have been not been affected by the serendipity of wars. Each American's balance sheet would have been honorable and job landing time, would have been far less, than it is today and living on government doles would have been far less, but for the expenditure on wars. All these would have been possible if only the countries would have abstained, from war mongering.. Abraham Lincoln would have left a far more prosperous scenario at the multitude level, had the civil war not bedeviled America, for five years on race issues.

Germany was militarily extremely aggressive, annexed several European countries but after facing severe defeat, had to pay severe reparations, face runaway inflation, currency devaluation, along with very high incidence of widespread poverty.

The cold war certainly bestowed a whole lot of obligations on the superpowers, especially financial duties, to keep their sphere of influence, expanding. But Soviet Union could not be sustained and disintegration became eminent. Even the shrunken Russia witnessed huge unemployment rates, high levels of corruption, high rates of inflation and poverty, leading to the Russian crisis. National debt of USA could have been under control, but for the expenses of the cold war that America was embroiled with Soviet Union, for decades. Global wars not only impoverished the common Europeans, on the axis side but also the allied powers. Debt went to stratospheric levels, as the wars are phenomenally expensive. The European countries had to depend, on each other, as they faced deficits in supplies of food and other goods. Due to devastations of wars, the industries suffered. The industries had to be closed with goods production, either reduced or stopped. Only industry that did well was the arms industry. As the industries were devastated in Europe, as a whole, the US economy boomed. US became the supplier of industrial goods, in the world. Profits of business owners skyrocketed, as it was afar from war scene, except for a brief period at the end. Britain was financially bleeding and had to borrow huge funds from USA and latter obliged. America's reluctance to enter the war, especially the debates against war participation by Congressmen, helped US prosper. President Roosevelt besides making business owners rich, by leaps and bounds, also raised his taxes. Accordingly, US could turn benevolent to Europe, after war, to pump funds under Marshall Plan, to reconstruct Europe. Timely assistance and relationship with NATO members, made America very close to Europe that naturally benefited the nation as well as its MNCs in making their businesses thrive globally. The lessons learnt by the MNCs, in conducting European business, helped them do business, in the rest of the world, including Asia, Africa and Latin America. Thus staying away, by and large, from the global wars made US the financial super power of the world with US dollar, as the world's premier currency, replacing sterling pound.

China, despite being a powerful communist power, never got entangled in wars, to create its own spheres of influence like Russia did, during the cold war period. China concentrated on economic development, within the country. It was also welcoming foreign businesses, to come and set up their shops in China. Gradually, it also gave the sops of free or cheap land, electricity at a lower tariff rates, to induce the European and the American big businesses, to come to China and set up manufacturing plants. Foreign businesses were mandated to allow the labor force to form labor unions, the labor were also guided to remain disciplined, with the employers, to bring prosperity in China. Its staying away from wars and paying attention to its industry, banking, finance and foreign direct investment promotion, yielded huge dividends to make China, the second largest economy in the world next only to USA in the new millennium. Russia and China were on the same footing as communist countries but while Russia's finances tobogganed and it got into financial crisis, China prospered, with an unusually close friendship with capitalist America. Occasional mild criticisms rent the air from the US government and the Congress, against China's business practices and human rights and similarly mild criticism rent the air against the USA, from Chinese government spokesperson. In reality, both countries cooperate in matters of mutual gratifications to the hilt. In economic and financial matters China could help US, in matters where America needed help. This has been possible as China though militarily powerful had not got embroiled in wars.

The historians stated that on 28 June 1919 the Weimar Republic signed the treaty of Versailles, under threat of continued advance of the allied powers. While discussing the entire war blame, Germany was blamed for the entire war, by the signatories of the treaty of Versailles. A lot of Germans felt humiliated, for forcing the treaty and imposing very harsh conditions, on Germany. Germany was required to pay as imposed by the victors, 132 billion marks, about $31.5 billion, in reparations, which the Germans felt was way ahead of their ability. to pay to the allied powers.

The close of the First World War led to inflation, going through the roof in Germany. It was termed hyperinflation that occurred from 1921 to 1923. In this period, the value of Paper marks, with respect to the earlier commodity Gold marks, plummeted to one trillionth of its value. German currency lost all of its purchasing power and literally bags of this currency could only buy a palm worth of grains.

The runway reparations, inflicted more on Germany, at the instance of France, was deemed too high by Germany, relative to its capacity to pay the victors. Though it goes beyond question that the tragic global war, was started by Germany. Germany was already devastated by the war, vanquished by the joint efforts of a number of countries, which battered its economy. The casualties included the German infrastructure, its factories and war hollowed out its employment market. Impregnated with infliction of runaway reparations, was a sense of despair, among the German people. The German people felt gross injustice had been meted out to them, that Germany was singled out for all of the losses of the first global war, when other major powers, also fought the war. With hyperinflation and the value of currency, having gone deep south, Germany, lost it's purchasing power in 1921 and it appeared that the German government would default on payments of its reparations. The poverty conditions accrued from the war, got further exacerbated with punitive actions, brought in by the allies due to its inability, to pay the reparations. Germany was declared a defaulter, by the Reparations Commission, in December 1922. It led to the Belgian and French armies, occupying Ruhr in January 1923. Ruhr continued to be in occupation, of the French and Belgian troops until 1925.

As per the Versailles Treaty of 1919 conditions, German government restricted its army size to 100,000. It also destroyed its armaments, such as u-boats, ships and tanks. It destroyed its air force too, as per the Versailles Treaty of 1919. In addition to all of these material losses, people in Germany, it is needless to state, felt utterly humiliated in Europe.

Germany returned the conquered areas, in the war, to the original powers such as France Czechoslovakia, Denmark Belgium and Poland. Germany also had some colonies which were taken over by the allies and distributed among themselves. The British took over German colonies, in African continent. According to scholars, what hurt Germany the most were cessation of city of Danzig to Poland and the separation of East Prussia from the rest of Germany.

The wars, besides inflicting impoverishment in the country and spread of poverty diverts funds from welfare budget to fight wars, as a result country suffered a decline in economic growth. As a fall out of wars, the redrawing of borders of countries take place and sometimes even new countries are formed. In such a situation whole lot of people get separated from their near and dear ones, sometimes they never meet in their life times. Sometimes, after the war the ethnic minorities could become a part of another country, where that ethnic group could be a majority. It also leads to the poverty, from the neglect of the minorities. Thus the wars bring about multi-dimensional poverty, especially among the vanquished. In a global war, too many nations, suffer deprivation, poverty conditions for years due to refugee problems, hunger and starvation from families, due to new borders being drawn for many countries.

The wars devour millions of people. Even civil wars are equally devastating. At the time of armistice, in regard to the first global war, Russia witnessed civil war, in which about 7 million people died and the country was severely devastated. Russia saw economic disaster. As to her border territories, Lithuania, Latvia and Estonia gained brief independence, until occupied again by the Soviet Union in 1940. Finland got independence and also Latvia Estonia and Lithuania. Soviet Union made Armenia Georgia and Azerbaijan, as republics in 1922, making them a part of the Soviet Union.

In the 1930s, the German Chancellor, Hitler, harbored the desire to be the European conqueror and subsequently brought so much of disaster to Europe, with his dictatorial policies. Germany's highly pungent military aggressions, towards its European neighbors. coupled with the aggrieved feelings, among the German people, who had felt bruised by huge reparations, that caused poverty to many Germans, resulted in annexation of Austria, Poland and even France. Paris fell to the Germans in 1940 and continued to be in the German occupation, for over 4 years, which heavily bruised the French pride. The British under Sir Winston Churchill, the war time Prime Minister, gave a tough fight and finally Germany was defeated. A treaty was signed to close the war.

The Second Global War, ravaged the European economies. European industrial infrastructure, got destroyed and so was its regional economy. The war left millions homeless. A lot of people suffered immeasurably, when annexations of Germany and Italy were rolled back, as many turned refugees due to frustrated relocations. The estimates indicate that about 50 million people died in the global wars and the countries did not reach their pre-war level of population in 4 decades.

The aggregate demand for the goods, required by European countries, had to be met, with supplies from USA, until its industrial infrastructure got fully repaired, as a part of the European Reconstruction Program. This gave a lot of fillip to the business success, of America and helped business owners, to earn runaway profits. Tax earnings of the US government boomed and prosperity became all time high. Sterling pound was replaced by the US dollar, as the global reserve currency, which made America, all the more prosperous. As reconstruction of Europe reached its completion, its businesses also gradually improved. The rich in Europe and elsewhere in the world, got interested in investing in short term and long term investments in USA, which further consolidated the prosperity in the USA.

After devastation in Europe, after the global war, USA, though an ally of the victorious block felt it necessary, to take up quick European reconstruction work. It was an unique and fine gesture, from the then President Roosevelt who is known to be a great visionary. He got an advice from his Secretary of State, George Marshall, to help European countries, under an economic plan. President came up with a Program in 1947, called "European Recovery Program",. This program came to be popular, as Marshall Plan globally. Under this plan, the USA allotted $13 billion, for the reconstruction of Western Europe. Later on, President Roosevelt, with a gesture of reprieve to Germany and Japan also gave small portions of fund, to Germany and Japan's reconstruction.

The Soviet Union initially was, reluctant to receive US Marshall plan funds and borrowed some money from Britain and Sweden, as its economy was in disarray, after the Second Global War. Soviet Union's causalities ran into millions of soldiers of red army.

The wars mostly, prove to be detrimental, to the economy. No useful purpose seems to accrue, from the wars. Wars often take place among divisive social groups. As divisive social groups have lack of understanding of each others in terms of language, religion and other social practices that raise a lot of apprehensions in their minds. It's this misunderstanding and lack of communication, which prohibits them, to come to an armistice. In ancient times, the wars were fought on religious lines. However, the two Global Wars in Europe, which were fought, in the first half of the

20th century, were neither based on racial differences nor on the religious differences. The difference in skin color has also not been a factor in these two wars. Yet these two wars were fought and fought virulently, devastating several countries, people and economies. Quintessentially, both the wars were fought for years and on both occasions, Germany was trounced by Britain and France and its other allies. So much poverty and death of millions of people were inflicted by these wars. Millions of the bread earners died and their families saw woes. Wars destroyed factories and that had hit production of goods real hard. and also caused joblessness and enormous poverty. Even agriculture was heavily affected, which caused scarcity of food. Food for the army often went in short supply. Army's rations were given top priority and only after dispensing food to the army, food went to the civilians. Hence, the civilians often faced hunger, in many European pockets. The Germany knew that paying such heavy reparations imposed by the treaty of Versailles, would have meant, at the cost of poverty and hunger for multitude in Germany. Such a huge reparations was avoidable and probably if reparations had not been so large, then Germany would have never returned Hitler, to come to power, through the democratic process. But French obdurate attitude came in the way, to reduce reparations. US intervened and insisted not to inflict such huge reparations, but French were assertive and their voice prevailed as Britain went along. Later the French had to bear the consequences of their decision. They were humiliated, when their capital city, Paris was occupied, for over 4 years, by the German troops. Hitler had dictatorial propensities, but Germans as a people would have appreciated, a much lesser reparations Hitler probably would have been less vindictive, in the years to come.

Britain, though victorious in war, against the axis powers, was deeply in debt. It won the world war 2, along with other allied powers and inflicted huge punishments on Germany, to compel Germany, to return all of its conquests, to the respective countries and kept allied forces, on the west Germany.

A lesson, is to be learnt for those, who do not take into account, the devastating consequences that leads to the aftermath of all wars and look at victories, as a feather on their caps, which would massage their egos. Mr. Winston Churchill, as the British war Prime Minister, was very proud and excited, about forfeiting Germany, vanquishing it and inflicting huge reparations but the British people suffered, so much due the prolonged engagement in war, that there was little excitement for them. Numerous families lost their children, as soldiers fighting in the war. Many young children were heavily wounded. Many lost their jobs, as factories and farms closed their operations. A lot of buildings and factories devastated, which had to be rebuilt again. Mr. Churchill though won the war the British people felt that probably their Prime Minister, could have shortened the duration of the war. Some might have felt that Mr. Churchill could have closed the war, much earlier saved a lot of expenditure. Probably, such public opinion resulted in Mr. Churchill's defeat in Parliament elections and Mr. Clement Attlee, from the Labor Party replaced him in 1945.

After the close of the war Mr. Churchill pleaded with the US government, for huge loans and he succeeded in convincing President Roosevelt of USA, to help Britain, in that hour of financial crisis. In response to repeated pleadings for the loans, submitted by Mr. Churchill, finally, Mr. Roosevelt agreed to grant the request, for a big loan in August 1945.

The war debt was so huge that the Britain's war debt, was described by some in the American administration, as a "millstone round the neck of the British economy". After receiving the Anglo-American loan, from the United States, in 15 July 1946 Britain showed signs of some economic stability. This loan was meant to meet the British overseas expenditure, in the immediate aftermath of the Second Global War and to implement the domestic welfare reforms, of the British labor government. The key industries were nationalized, by the British labor government, after the war.

As a result of the war, the Soviet economy had also been ruined. Industrial and agricultural production, at the end of the war, drastically plummeted, even lower than the pre-World War II levels. The Soviet Union faced a huge financial crisis. Though challenged financially, the Soviets did not seek the financial assistance offered by the United States under the Marshall Plan. The Soviets were so much devastated by the war that they took lot many years to rebuild the Soviet economy. The wars appear to be a typical recipe, to invite national economic challenges and increase in poverty of the citizens. In these two Global Wars, it did not seem, to matter, where the perpetrators and who the vanquished, so far as rise in poverty is concerned. Both the victors and the vanquished, seem to be financially hurt, though as a result of unfair treaty, sometimes the vanquished tend, to financially suffer a lot more than the victors. The Soviet Union obtained loans from Sweden and Britain, to rebuild the economy. The Soviet reconstruction program, could also receive finances, from the reparations payments from Germany.

Factories and farms in Soviet Union suffered, due to wars. With challenged finances, the country could encourage only some industries, more than the others. It paid attention to the steel production, which saw marked increase, in production in the coming years. However, the consumer goods received least priority, as it was a communist economy.

Unfortunately, the production of food commodities, was also much less than it was in 1920s.

The Soviets also lost in the war, lot of men in the war against Germany.. The population of Soviet Union, decreased during the World War II, so much that it took three decades to achieve the pre-war level population. After the war the population of Soviet Union, decreased by forty million and of these 8.7 million died fighting the war with Germany. Many died of starvation due to food embargo, imposed by the Germans, when they put a siege, at Leningrad. Many Soviets died, as a result of famine and other diseases. German took several prisoners of wars, who were made to do forced labour, in the factories, some were also kept in prisons and concentration camps. It is estimated that about 19 million Soviets died, under these categories. Thus an idea can be conjured, as to how even those who win the war, suffer ignominiously. How many counts of human capital are lost that cannot be replenished in a nation, even for those who are victorious, in the global war. Under the light it is easy to understand, India's pacifist stand. India and its 10,000 years of cultural heritage has never waged a single war against any other country. China's history as far as waging war is concerned, is not very different from India. Buddha the apostle of peace and his teachings had profoundly influenced both India and China, since time immemorial. India's Hindu religion and culture preach unity of mankind and inclusiveness and the message of pacifism had a strong hold in the minds of Indians.

Germans were driven out by the Russians, from the Central and eastern Europe in the post war era. East Germany was formed from a part of Germany and was retained by the Soviet Union. Poland, Bulgaria, Hungary, Czechoslovakia, Romania, Albania. West Germany came into being in 1949 by the American, British, and French zones in 1949. Saar was formed in 1957.

Immediately after the war in 1945 the US remained indifferent to the vanquished powers, such as Germany and Italy. But in a couple of years President Roosevelt felt that the victors need to dilute the harshness on Germany. To this end, the US took positive measures, so that in decades to come, Europe could see peace with Germany and Italy and carry them along as partners of the development of Europe. US gave government aid to Germany during the middle of 1946, through the GARIOA program. Under the Marshal Plan some capital flows also started. However the fact remains that Germany as a result of the defeat in war had weakened financially, as a nation which have increased financial challenges and poverty for a lot of people around the region. U.S. policy from April 1945 to July 1947 stated that no help need be given to the Germans, in rebuilding their nation, save for the minimum required to mitigate starvation.

In cessation of future conflicts and timely action to ensure that people in European nations do not have to further suffer severe financial challenges and poverty that they had already been through in the two Global Wars, the US initiatives to the vanquished nations need to be appreciated. Especially the prudent and fine leadership in foreign affairs shown by the then US President Truman. After the defeat of Germany in World War II, there came a directive, that had ordered the U.S. occupation forces to "take no steps looking toward the economic rehabilitation of Germany."

The allies collected reparations from Japan. A lot of relocations were ordered of the Japanese to move to the mainland and that caused a lot of suffering. A permanent US base came about in Okinawa. Japan was made to return all of the war annexations such as declaring independence to Manchuria and Korea. The Philippines came to the control of USA. The Dutch got back from Japan the Dutch East Indies. Burma, Malaya and Singapore were returned to Britain. Hundreds of thousands of Japanese were forced, to relocate to the Japanese main islands. Okinawa became a main U.S. staging point. The U.S. covered large areas of it with military bases and continued to occupy it until 1972, years after the end of the occupation of the main islands. United State's military bases still remain in the region.

It was strange that after being a part of two global wars the allies still wanted to latch on to their colonies in Asia, inflicting on them the negatives of a colonized rule. The annexed,nations, were fighting for their independence, but the allies kept their stranglehold on them to exploit. After the close of the second global war, when Japan was defeated and accepted a lot of the treaty conditions, the British, France and the Dutch conscripted some Japanese forces and used them to quell rebellions of freedom in their colonies. UK, France, and the Netherlands conscripted some Japanese troops to fight colonial resistances elsewhere, in Asia. As long as these allies could rule the countries in Asia, they could transfer wealth from those countries, to elsewhere, by keeping the people from these colonies impoverished. Similarly after the defeat of Japan, they did not follow the principles of natural justice and converted the prisoner of wars as forced labor by classifying them as surrendered people to skirt the Geneva Convention and used them to build industries. Alexander from Europe wherever conquered nations collected slaves and engaged them in forced labor similar moves were strangely was seen even during the second global war too when the allies instead of taking prisoner of wars in Japan and treat them as per the Geneva Convention agreement took them as salves for rebuilding their economies and also to fight on their behalf to suppress freedom movements in other colonies. General McArthur appointed a Far Eastern Military Commission in Asia. According to the Far Eastern Commission with a view to remove Japan as a threat from another war, it was decided by the allies to de-industrialize Japan and the process of de-industrialization began to reduce the standard of living to what existed in between 1930 to 1934. War experts viewed that the de-industrialization program in Japan was lesser in degree, compared to the one imposed on Germany. Japan, also like Germany, was the recipient of the benevolence of the US President Truman's Administration. Japan received emergency aid from GARIOA, as did Germany. In early 1946, the Licensed Agencies for Relief in Asia were formed and permitted to supply Japanese with food and clothes. In April 1948 the Johnston Committee Report recommended that the economy of Japan should be reconstructed due to the high cost to U.S. taxpayers on continuous emergency aid to Japan.

The 1947 Treaty of Peace with Italy spelled the end of the Italian colonial empire, along with other border revisions. The 1947 Paris Peace Treaties compelled Italy to pay $360,000,000 (US dollars at 1938 prices) in war reparations to Yugoslavia, Greece, the Soviet Union, Ethiopia and Albania. In the 1946 Italian constitutional referendum the Italian monarchy was abolished, having been associated with the deprivations of the war and the Fascist rule in Italy.

Chapter 4

Inward Orientation Phase of the Indian Economy and Perceived Poverty

India did not want to relax as some countries wanted to relax and address nothing but invest capital and multiply wealth, when the securities market boomed. So they could play the market prudently and invest money in offices and banks earn interest and then interest over interest, without addressing themselves to be the manufacturers of goods, be it trucks cars, shaving blades, bikes, motor cycles, ice creams, dairy products, furniture, three wheelers, carpets, blankets, textiles, cooking pans, radios, electric items such as bulbs, table lamps, switches, wires, electric fans, air conditioners, washing machines, cars, machinery for power generation, machinery for sugar factories, railroad coaches, steel to be used in all industries two wheelers. India did not only want to develop financing of organizations, and did not want to be only promoters of the entrepreneurs. India did not want, to outsource all of these important national activities to foreign businesses, to set up the plants in India and rely on foreigners making decisions, about making goods for India and to determine how much to export and how much to retain in the Indian economy, for Indian consumers. India simply did not want to relax, from being in the industrial field.

Similarly, in the hotel industry, India did not want to relax with no domestic hotels, which is nationally built and run and did not want to open, the field to developed world foreigners, to come and set up hotels in India, to build and run hotels in India.

A lot of nations import food, as they do not want to work hard, in the scorching sun, to do agriculture and do not specialize in non automated agriculture, of multi millenniums heritage. India does not import food from America, Europe or other countries and developed its own agriculture. It invested in agriculture, in a big way. India specialized in vegetables fruits, floriculture, sericulture rice millets, pulses and wheat. It is the second largest producer of silk in the world after China. It took the initiatives, having 500 district organizations, to promote solar energy, bio energy, wind energy and the like. In numerous villages the government introduced solar cookers as early as in early 1980s. In many villages and especially villages at higher altitudes, for street lighting, solar energy was attempted, with fair advantage. Much, of course, remains to be done in this area of non conventional enrgy.

Hence India was not so much in the good books, of the market economy world, the developed world, which have through industrial revolutions, had already created competencies, in different industries and they could meet the demands of their own economies and hence wanted to target big markets, like China and India, to make more money, revenue and also more profits. For them, India's reluctance, not to be relaxing and making goods without importing the same from the developed world, created an ire, as they could not get the market share, which they had lot of appetite for. Hence, they, particularly the economists, of the developed world, at that time were head over heels on markets, in the 1950s, 1970s and 1980s and in their disappointment, for not getting access to the huge market of India's middle class, called the economic model of India, autarkic economy, which meant that India was an inward oriented economy. The developed countries felt that India missed out, leveraging the play of the market forces, in enrichment of its economy. India knew the economic theory of the nascent industries. British exploitation of 200 years had unfortunately left India, in a stage where industries even in the middle of 1960s, were still in the nascent stage, the formative stage of businesses, trying to understand the market to serve, properly trying, to convince the bankers that they need additional funds.

India did not hesitate, to collaborate, with different economies, as it followed the Non Alignment Policy. It could liaison with both the groups of the cold war and leverage their knowledge. Its massive steel plants got technical knowhow, in some cases, from the erstwhile Soviet Union and some steel plants got technical knowhow, from Germany and Britain. It set up its premier engineering institutions, such as the Indian Institute of Technologies, receiving technical knowhow and collaboration from USA. Similarly, its premier management institutions received, collaboration and technical knowhow from American universities, India addressed its Green Revolution in the late 1970s, with the scientific advice and assistance of the eminent American agricultural scientist, Dr Borlaug and made great strides, with huge cooperation and hard work of the Indian farmers. The green revolution moves of India made it, self sufficient in food. It was not a small feat to be able to feed, a nation of 1.3 billion population and in fact it was a marvelous feat, with bottom up and top down efforts sync. India's civil service had its training exposures, to Britain as well as to America, on a regular basis, enabling them to learn the latest management techniques, developed in the developed world and apply the same to India, sometimes with a time lag. While India remained aloof, from partnering with any block, during the entire cold war period and it could develop itself, according to the Five Year Plans, which was quintessentially a Soviet Way of Planning. It helped India, focus on particular areas of development, with a limited budget. Anti-poverty programs of Lyndon B Jonson and Mrs. India Gandhi had approaches, in common and both felt the need for special attention, to the poor, due to burden of history. In Indian rural landscape, there was no slavery and rich and poor coexisted, in the village republics, administered by a democratic village head. However, the village, as characterized by Durkheim's Theory of the Division of Labor, the brunt of labor for agricultural work, fell on the labor castes, who were paid wages. They had the freedom to work, with any employer. However, due to self-sufficient nature of the villages, the wage could not rise, with competition, from different areas. Hence the Prime Minister Indira Gandhi felt that India has to be self-sufficient in food and the poor need a lot of attention. She developed welfare schemes, from minimum wages, to food at a subsidized price, from the public distribution system; free education for their children,; hostel for the poor children, where their food and lodging would be met, by the government. Her slogan was remove poverty. Lyndon B Johnson felt that the blacks had a lot of agony, for being enslaved by the white farmers, of the south of USA, particularly and therefore they needed, specialized government attention. He called anti-poverty programs, as war on poverty. Thus in poverty reduction approach, which started in the 60s, in USA as well as India, there have been some aspects in common. It can thus be seen that India was always open to the ideas, flowing from outside the country and internalized, whatever good it found, in both the blocks of the cold war, without specifically partnering with any block. It opened its economy for FDI in 1993. Until then, it was an inward oriented economy, stressing on self sufficiency. Having seen, what the trading companies could do, to damage foreign countries, from India's experience with East India Company, a monopoly company chartered by the British government and having arrived in India in 1600. The East India Company, transferred the reins of Indian government in 1857 to the British Queen. East India Company coming to India to trade and then its moves to rule the country, raising the army, attacking the local small monarchies, annexing their territories, collecting revenue from the peasants through middlemen such as the zamindars and allowing the money lenders to charge usurious interest rates, were enough material, for India to be highly apprehensive of the incumbent regimes of the developed world and the multilateral institutions such as the World Bank and the IMF, as to motives of the foreign companies, in asking India, to open its borders for investments.

Once India developed its competencies, such as managerial competencies, financial competencies, legal competencies, medical and engineering competencies, scientific research competencies and industrial and business competences and the like and when it felt comfortable, to open the economy, it opened not in a hurry, but with prudence and introspection. It kept India in great stead, as these competencies, could keep India pretty much Indian, in its economic moves, despite the developed world interface, wherever felt necessary. The very fact that India today, receives huge appreciations, in the developed world, is also invited, to even G 20 meetings and is perceived, as the leading country in information technology, all of these encomiums validate that building competencies, by following inward oriented economic policies, after attaining independence from the British rule was the appropriate step for India..

Indian doctors, serve in city hospitals and even rural hospitals in USA. Indian doctors serve the National Health Service in Britain, with one third doctors, hailing from India in the NHS. The doctors in both America and Britain enjoy lot of popularity, with the patients, due to their dedication, to the duties. Engineers are tapped, by the developed world, as and when necessary and enjoy good reputation. Universities in the departments of sciences, engineering, management and economics have significant representation from India. It has been an area, which has been led by India, by solving the y2k problem in USA, very efficiently and since then, the US based firms and other firms, have come to depend on the IT talent of India, in a big way.

A number of countries, in Africa, listening to the Washington consensus, approach of sudden liberalization of economies, privatization of enterprises, convertibility of currencies and invitation of FDI and FII and the like immediately, after few years of independence, got into serious dependence on the developed world. The need for borrowing increased. Very few of such economies, have seen the sunshine, as once big MNCs started operating and once foreign developed world academics, ran the universities, the local talent development, was heavily eclipsed. This dependence did not address the base of the economic pyramid. That explains, why the Washington consensus gradually, came to have fewer takers, among the African countries. Soviet Union, which lived with communism for 7 decades, \with many east European countries, disintegrated in 1991, granting independence to east European satellite countries and break away nations of Soviet Union, under President Yeltsin. The economic reforms were taken up too fast. Russia seems to have gone too many extra hundreds of miles, to be receptive to the west and it almost accepted Washington Consensus. The speed at which, Russia opened its economy, was too fast and acclimating to the market economy, created a huge shock for the Russian economy, with a lot of negative effects. This all the more, validates the prudent economic management of India's economy, which cautiously build the professional management financial and economic competencies and then only, with a caution, took up the opening of the economy in steps.

The countries like Russia, which as per the western advice, went global, instantly, opened economic boundaries, suffered a crisis, known as the Russian Economic Crisis. Corruption mounted high at a place, where corruption was at least unknown. Earlier, property ownership was unknown and people had had limited choice of goods and services. They had to be on the breadline, mutton line, milk line every other day. They also had no association, with the rest of the world, as there was iron curtain. They neither had the passport nor had the permission, to go abroad. No films from Hollywood wee exhibited, in Soviet Union and only Indian Hindi films were allowed to be shown. International actors that the Soviets knew were Raj Kapur and Nargis. Once divestment and privatization of state owned enterprises, was hastened, those close to the government, bought the assets, at a very low prices, thus denying the government, a lot of revenue. They could not run the enterprises, as they lacked professional business experience. Foreigners in a haphazard manner, bought properties in bulk. New find freedom of the press and expression was created. Russian people started losing pride of Russia and the Soviet Union and the countries in the west, started taking Russia easy. The result was a chaos and a corrupt economy. This is typically the opposite of the caution, with which India opened the economy gradually only in 1993.

Jeffrey Sachs, the economist from Harvard University, advised Russia's transition to market economy, during 1993 and 1994. Some economists commented that the shock therapy advised by Jeffrey Sachs, did not succeed well, in Russia. To this comment, Prof Sachs stated in details what he meant by shock therapy, had nothing to do with Russia's privatization moves. According to Prof Jeffrey Sachs, "Shock therapy refers to the rapid end of price controls, in order to re-establish supply-demand equilibrium, in a context of pervasive rationing and blocked trade. One important element of such a rapid liberalization may be, the trade in foreign exchange, to allow for free convertibility of the currency, for purposes of international trade in goods and services." He further said, "In its second meaning, shock therapy refers to the dismantling of all government intervention in the economy in order to establish a "free-market" economy."

Thus it can be seen that Prof Sachs was not supportive of shock therapy, in its neoliberal context, as he regarded free market economy as a textbook fiction, not a practical or desirable reality. It's common knowledge that Prof Sachs was "beginning to advise Russian government in November 1991 on macroeconomic reforms, not on privatization,

It always pays a nation, to open the economy, with gradualism, no matter what free market ideologues, have to say or proponents of free market governments, have to say. Its question of the morphing the structure of the economy and a lot of constituencies and people need to adjust and they need to be given time, while economic liberalization is implemented. In fact Dr Sachs opposed to the idea of allowing the oligarchs, to be created in Russia as it would be a "costly mistake." Tens of billions of dollars of natural resource assets, were given away, and hundreds of millions were collected in return as campaign contributions.

Researchers in this area, observed that the hyper-corruption, surrounding the massive giveaways of the oil and gas sectors, may have been was linked to the campaign financing for President Yeltsin's re-election.

Another theory was that the communists were still not converted to free market and many in the liberalized government of Russia in the 1990s, were apprehensive of the return of communists, unless the government assets, were very quickly privatized. Towards this, end when haste was done, to the process of privatization, probably the due diligence, went to the back burner, hundreds of miles away and this aspect the oligarchs profited from, to the hilt.

Chapter 5

Poverty and Mistrust, Emanating From Media Demoralizing Officials and Politicians

We hear a lot of middle class criticism, of the Indian politicians. Politicians pursue multi party politics and at the end of elections, no clear majority is held, by any of the 2 political parties. Both parties try to get allies, from caste based parties and from the parties, which have very little membership and are state centric parties. The kind of general conversation is audible, in the drawing rooms of the middle class intelligentsia, about the quality of our politicians. Citizens get the government they deserve. If citizens do not know the variances of ideologies, then they would make dictators to form government or form a military dictatorship, as they are not given to agitations. Most people while discussing politicians forget that majority have no exposure of political science, majority of people do not care for definition of capitalism and democracy and they are not aware, when constituent assembly met and Indian constitution was adopted. Politicians who were trained as politicians, in gram panchayats, panchayat samiitis and Zila Parishads at the district levels, contest for assembly and parliamentary concession.

The District politicians run, for assembly elections and run in parliamentary elections. They are not raw in politics, picked up as candidates. Very few highly educated brilliant, with lot of exposure to international community show there interest to join politics.

Neither do the middle class of urban India, motivate their children to turn politicians, nor are the children remotely interested, in getting elected to the legislatures and the parliament. If people do not send their children, to law making bodies, probably they have no business, to comment on politicians. Why is it that that the middle class and the rich class from urban India, are seen, not sending their children, to become politicians. It is pretty obvious that they want to avoid the challenges, associated with becoming a law maker, representing whole lot of rural people, some of whom are very poor. They know that the comforts of the urban middle class, will evaporate. They will have to tour on the dusty roads, smeared by village dust, will have to rub shoulders, with poor people and receive sweat soiled petitions to address grievances, written there on. The life is extremely difficult, to move about in villages. The MLAs and MPs between sessions, most of the time interact, with the people of 30 to 35 villages, in each of their constituencies They maintain constant social communication with them, trying to identify with the villagers and know about the issues, such as fodder scarcity, some teacher not showing up, engineers delaying construction of community hall in a particular village, landlord, misbehaving with the poor people, in another village. These problems need resolution, for which the politician conducts informal enquiries, visiting the villages, a few times, calling the concerned parties and giving them a patient hearing. He attempts to bring down the frayed tempers, on both sides and to bring peace. Visiting these villages in tough climatic conditions, when the roads are very narrow, with all the bumps is challenging. Only a couple of decades ago, the roads could not carry cars, but only rough jeeps. The MLAs and MPs were habituated to visit on such rough roads, to suffer from backaches later. Interacting at the village level affably, with different demographics in poverty conditions, in India's countryside, is no small feat. There would be in the village demographics, the carpenters, butchers, agricultural laborers, blacksmiths, many of them will have low physical hygiene. One need to appreciate that the Indian politicians, happily melt into such a crowd, while visiting villages and all of these inclusive behavior of the politicians, toward their constituents, keep Indian democracy alive. They heighten the self confidence of the rural India and particularly the poor, stating repeatedly that they are not alone and the government is their benefactor. The government would stand by them, in their weal and woes. Interacting with brethren voters, whose physical hygiene is poor, who are not very articulate, many of them may not be well behaved, but politicians cannot lose their temper. They have to maintain their cool, in all of these interfaces. At the minimum, such is the law maker's life, at least for 10 days, in a month His family cannot be moved, to the state capitals or the national capital. He has to maintain 3 homes, at three places. To be able to hire these homes, maintaining the semblance of a home and hire a person, to look after the home, one can imagine, what type of money, we are looking into. Family will not get his company. It is kind of intoxication for him, to be with massive humanity. He will be deprived of his family's proximity. Thus for 5 years he is literally cut off, from his family, which could indicate that somewhere in his life, he misses out a lot and at the same time, his family also misses out a lot. White dress is politician's dress in India. He attunes his mind, to wear very simple dress, all along, every day. He can go around in a multi colored top and jeans, like his classmates of from his college, who work in private companies. Politicians have to maintain sobriety, in their 30s, to wear a white dress. This is not an easy discipline. If he wears multi colored dresses, he will not be acceptable to his voters, who wear white relaxed dresses. It is a kind of indirect compulsion that few people understand. He needs to show his emotions, when some grief dawns, on the voter's family. He has also to participate, in the joys of his voters. In a country, like India, where the incidence of poverty is high, courtesy neglect of the rural India, by the colonizing government for centuries, and funds turn out, to be in deficit for development, it is a herculean task to keep the constituents happy.. The number of people, who are taxed is not high. Further, a lot of people suffer from some caste and class exploitation, and the law makers feel it their duty, to strive to give encouragement, to the poor.

A lot of development requirements, in the rural India, remain unmet, for want of adequate government revenue, as the tax base is not very large. Those in the tax bracket, in the unorganized sectors of the Indian economy, tend to transact quite a lot of business, in cash and do not pay the tax adequately. Some are seeing some economic betterment, in the current generation, due to the hard earned income having risen, without their knowledge. Thus category has also have come to the tax bracket. but they have no idea about it. Culturally, they live such a simple life. with very simple clothes that even tax authorities sometimes are not aware that a particular constituency, now have to be tapped for taxes. One such category is that of the hawkers selling vegetables and fruits and the like. Thus in matters of increasing revenue, through revamping of the Indian tax system, is the need of the hour, to be able, to meet the genuine development needs of the villages. But its inadequacy and Government consciously having excluded many constituencies from the taxpaying responsibility, also keeps the gaps in development needs, unmet, in the villages. For the gullible and illiterate villager, criticizing the politicians, is the first thought in their minds and this thought in a democracy, gets egged on, by the opposition parties and also the media. The media in India, has tuned pretty yellow, in the new millennium. Thus the media criticism of the political class, has also skyrocketed, in recent years and so has the informal criticism, in the drawing rooms of the urban middle class.

The hawkers make between Rs 25,000 to Rs 30,000 of the Indian currency, in the urban India.. They are so simple, in their demeanor and as they are uneducated, sometimes illiterate, the tax authorities tend to look the other way. Many of them lead a very simple life, in the urban slums, but their children go to college. Tax authorities may not have come to know that they make taxable money. They also do not pay any taxes. Tax authorities also look the other way. These combination of factors, do not make collection of taxes very high. State being a modern state, it has to invest in research, technology, education and also the state has to give financial aid, to the countries such as Bangladesh, Mauritius, Burma and the like. In the nutshell, when the budget is not high, even small demands of the people appears high. Those demands remaining unmet, in a lawmakers constituency, in which, on average there are 30 villages, there is likelihood of some frustration.

These semi educated and many illiterate masses, do not have comprehension that why their small demands remain unmet. Such people come to the conclusion fast that the ruling party may have pocketed their eligible money, as the opposition parties, make the canards. The Media and the opposition parties, practically never try, to explain the reasons of the unmet development needs, in the villages. They would not give a clear picture, to the rural masses, that demands remained partially met in the villages, because the tax collections have been limited. They are also not enlightened that the tax inflicted could not be very high, to meet the development needs, of villages fast enough, because of the heavy exploitation of the peasantry, during 200 years of the British rule. The opposition party takes advantage of criticizing, the incumbent government alone and like to talk about corruption. Any event of corruption that happened 25 years ago, also, would not be forgotten unlike in the developed world and the public would be reminded again and again, to gain political mileage, instead of giving confidence to the masses. Propaganda of corruption, will be unleashed, with the opposition and the media in hand in gloves, with each other. Once howling about corruption begins, in the media, the national atmosphere gets polluted. Most people do not know, how much amount annually a village can get and most people do not know, the estimated cost of a bridge on a river for 1 mile or estimated cost of laying a one mile of road, and how many roads, bridges and building, the state is taking up, during the year besides the details, of \taking up big works. That,explains, while villages get money, for development, but there would be unmet needs, for many years to come. Farmers remain content, with the price at which procurement of agricultural produce, is done by the government. Food Corporation of India procures food grains and makes it available, to the consumers, through the outlets of the. the Public Distribution System, which in some states are more spruced than others. The poor tend to get food grains, at a higher quantity and that too at a lower price. If the market price of say rice is 6 Indian Rupees, a kg, then the Andhra Pradesh Government started the scheme of giving 5 kg of rice, per person, per month, at Rs 2, a Kg. The Chief Minister continued to give rice, to the poor, at 2 Indian Rupees a Kg even after several years, despite hike in the market price., knowing fully well that the differential price, had to be paid, by the government. This was a kind of food subsidy, which was a part of the state budget in mid 1980s. Quite a number of officers argued before the Chief Minister of Andhra Pradesh, a province, that a large number of engineering works will suffer for want of funds. The then Chief Minister said emphatically that first the poor people, will have to be taken care of, and their nutrition levels also had to be increased. He said that whatever funds remain, after implementing this scheme, engineering works will be paid attention and not before addressing this duty of feeding the poor, at the state's expense, if their earnings were insufficient to feed themselves. A family of five was given 25 Kg of rice a, month. When the state supported the poor, the poor could feel better. Procurement of wheat, bajra, sugar and the like is done and a support price is fixed, by the government, taking into consideration inflation, prices of other goods and services and the cost of living of the farmer. Though the farmer, wanted higher price sometimes which was examined and if the demands were reasonable, the price asked by the farmers were given.

The credit to feeding a nation of 1.2 billion people, goes to the farmers, who lead simple lives, are content with the incumbent life and remain happy to work hard manually, with some automation of using tractors, on a community basis. No country in the world, can boast of such responsible and hardworking farmers, with whom politicians keep, in constant touch and praise them for dedication of duty and for feeding, such a huge population. Paying from the foreign exchange- reserves, out of 190 countries in the world, most countries would be importing food annually. India is self-sufficient in food. US is also self-sufficient in food. India is not only self-sufficient in food grains, but also produces numerous categories of food, ranging from bananas, apples, peaches, plums, grapes, man. Indians rely on vegetables a lot, because predominantly the Indians are vegetarians and they do not eat non vegetarian food. Those, who occasionally take non vegetarian food, also consume non vegetarian food, only on average, once a week. Indians have remained highly disciplined in food too, because they are hardworking and make their fresh hot meals, every day each time. Workers in construction carry simple food, such as rice and curry with them, to eat at the lunch time and prefer homemade food, to food sold in the market. Even officials, carry their own food packets and so, do the students in the school. Food courts in schools, workplaces and on general streets are conspicuous by their absence, in most of India. While lifting heavy weight items, fetching vegetables and groceries from the market, getting electric appliances repaired, if those go awry and the like, are basically perceived as duties of men, taken up happily, making hot meals is perceived, to be the duties of women, which is taken up happily. Going for outdoor activities, require walking in the scorching sun, carrying heavy weight and walking and getting into a speeding bus quickly, which is sometimes heavily loaded, with passengers and stand through the journey or stake a seat, if seats are available after sparing them to all of the women travelling, are rough parts of daily schedule, which women realize about men. Similarly, women preparing varieties of food items at home, is appreciated by men. There is no gender divide, on this account, as to who should prepare the meals and on which days. Even as per the norms, families, in India, being one income and 2 parents families, the employers pay enough, to pay food bills and utility bills, to lead a simple living. Most jobs in India, are outdoor supervising and guiding agriculture, irrigation construction of irrigation, water supply, and tank excavation, construction of roads and bridges, construction of homes survey of lands and identifying encroachments of government lands, and the like.

Poverty due to human capital neglect and indifference and too much automation

Prosperity of a nation, is found to be directly proportional, to the care one takes, to promote and develop the human capital. A lot of economies, do not realize that even a few elite members, in the cities want their prosperity, to be consolidated. The consolidation of prosperity of elite, comes easily, when the rest of the population, is treated inclusively and affably, finding out their needs and meeting them. Nations that develop their human capital nicely, develop fast and prosperity is widespread, as well as the GDP of the nation gees up. There are other set of nations that are hinged too much on GDP and though they achieve GDP centric development and appear to the world, as rich nations, but a critical analysis of goings on, within the nation, bring out that the rich poor divide and high and rising inequality is occurring, despite GDP figures, looking attractive. However, the world economic development literatures, pay a lot of emphasis of GDP, to measure development. GDP is one of the measures, undoubtedly of how the nations, are prospering, but it is only one of the measures, which a lot of economists and development scholars, fail to appreciate.

Human capital development implies a few aspects, such as promoting education across the board uniformly, spending uniform per capita funding, both in the rural and urban areas, building their academic competencies that would continue to refine, economic development in the nation, keeping the academic development rigouts that would have the potential to distance entertainment centric development products, being out of bounds of those, who are students. For example, some films are rated in a manner that it can only be seen by the adults and not the minors, on whose mind, it could leave a bad impact. Similarly, be it video games industry and audio visual entrainment or so called social networking sites, are huge diversions that could disturb academic development, among the children and even adolescents making them, to pay more attention, to multi-screen products to the detriment of knowledge, education, and development of cognitive aspects of mind, even if as a routine they go the schools. Conducting final exams, every year and indicating, how nicely or how poorly the student fared in different courses, need to be a necessity and to underline with red ink the marks and the subjects, where they have failed, to achieve the passing marks, to remind them that in the next class, they have to pay attention, to areas of study, to improve their academic performance, even if no one is detained, in the earlier class. Detention promotion, despite faring poorly, in few subjects and passing with no blemish, have been the pattern, for a few years now, which kept the students to fetter their diversion to play and pay attention to studies. Removal of these distinctions, has harmed the children's future, keeping them green all through the school life, until then fare very average, in the high school and fail in interviews for employment. Then blaming the employees that they are profit greedy and recruiting foreigners may not be right.

As it is known, to the masses that middle income jobs and high income jobs, tend to come only to those, who have an exposure to university/college education. While state universities charge less tuition, even they charge pretty high tuition, compared to Higher education in the private universities, which are too high and mostly out of bounds. Thus keeping education in the private sector, some nations have kept them out of bounds, for hundreds of millions of people. Thus starts a kind of despair that when human capital investment by government, is low enough to exclude people, out of the ambit of higher education, Average Americans get pessimistic about their economic future and their career. They turn aware that they could only be able to live, at the base of the economic pyramid. Automatically they tend to lose interest even in passing high school. It sounds strange that while Olympics and big sports events, are organized massive sports stadiums in cities and universities and even high schools are built and expensive games are organized, are nicely developed and new buildings for commercial places come up, with huge private investment and also government support the government fails to subsidize higher education, which could improve human capital across the board by leaps and bounds.

Though the taxes and through the primary and secondary equity and bond markets are supported, by none other than average Americans, the multitudes of hundreds of millions of Americans, who play the markets, offering enormous investments, in the capital markets and paying taxes. Could these 2 institutions cannot eliminate the debts, from the balance sheets of the individual Americans and keep them relieved of the ceaseless burden of loan installments relieve them of the infliction of these loan burdens, in an unjust manner not learning from other countries like Germany, India and Scandinavia. The corporations seem to have totally forgotten that they are not created and perpetuated by the CEO and the top managers financially, but by the American individual's funds and that of the institutions. The least that the corporations need to address, is not make the US economy, a laughing stock by denying workers living wages, long term benefits, health care benefits and paying fixed monthly salaries and certainly not hourly wages. Further, the least the corporations need to address, is not to burgeon the hordes of the part time workers and be called fortune companies. In any economy, the part time workers, are a microscopic minority of 5 to 10% and most of the jobs, are nice well-paying jobs, in a nice firm, recruiting well paying full time jobs to the extent of 90 to 95%. If a country of the GDP per capita of 1/16 th of the GDP of USA, Indian economy could treat its employees honorably, by allowing labor unions to bring issues to the table of the management, on a regular basis and could pay bonus and annual raise on a regular basis and if government could provide state funded health care or a very inexpensive private health care, through a network of boutique clinics of doctors/ general physicians in the private sector, dotting small villages, towns and metropolises and prescriptions given by the doctors, with a consulting fee of only $4 to$5 dollars per consultation, why would the health care in USA for the poor and the lower middle class remain unaffordable, to a tune of 50 million Americans? Why should an average American, to seek a prescription, to buy prescription drugs for stomach flu, fever, backache, and the like need to by go to a private doctor, as an uninsured American and pay the doctor $80 to $ 100 for a prescription? Is there any justification in a globalized health care scenario? If an Indian doctor, who after his degree in medicine, can address 3 years of residency and then the Indian educated doctor is allowed to do medical practice, why should US health care not examine the Indian model of boutique medical clinics, to be located in USA, where the doctor do not fleece the patients. As against $100, to be paid for consultation in US, a doctor in India, charges only $ 2 for consultation. If so many trades go on line, why should consultation of American patients with doctors based in India, paying $5, do not go online so that the consumers can consult the doctor, take prescriptions and go to an American pharmacy to pay for medicines, which again has been kept too expensive, courtesy pampering the pharmaceutical industry and health insurance firms. If US based hospitals be allowed and they could get medical transcriptions analyzed and received in 24 hours, from the back office operations that are addressed by Indians, working in the IT, allowing the hospitals to save on costs, denying the jobs to the local Americans and paying way less to the similar Indian employees and save on costs, why should the ailing Americans, not consult Indian doctors online and take a prescription at 5% of the American cost. If the corporations can leverage the online facilities and make profits and savings on costs, why should the ailing Americans from the poor and middle classes, who are unable to approach a doctor, because they are unable to pay $100 worth of consultation, per patient, be permitted to approach the Indian doctors online and consult them and get prescriptions and buy medicines in America. The private doctor's fee in America would then dwindle to affordable limits, once such online consultation practices, are allowed by the regulatory authorities. Two children in the same family, studying in similar schools, one going to the medical steam later and another going to non-medical say engineering stream later, need to be consistently treated, by the economic system, in such a level playing field manner. The doctor brother, with his income and wealth, way ahead of other educate siblings, stays in mansions, million dollar homes drives a BMW sedan and the non-medical siblings live in ordinary homes and drive around in a Honda or a Toyota sedan. Why on the face of it, such inequities are permitted, by the economic system, by the government and the corporations. Non-medical sibling would on average earn $80,000 a year and a new recruit medical sibling would get about $180,000 a year. How does the system in America, justify such inequity in the two professions? This is bizarre, compared to European and Indian practices.

It is these inequities boisterously perpetrated, for decades and sometimes, centuries and the imbalance in financial advantages, accruing from the government, though a positive favorable stance or visible and hidden subsidies, between different constituencies have feudalized the economy, in recent decades, some making runaway money and others slogging with multiple part time hourly jobs and commutes, latter category exceeding, the advantaged constituencies, by a very wide margin. That explains the evaporated savings and mountain of debt, load and a big population of very average educated, high school educated population, with small islands of related debt, free investment comforted islands of prosperity. That need not be the financial and economic configuration of US economy, ruled by a democracy. That capitalism brings prosperity and happiness, to the largest number of people, appears being proved, in such an economic and financial American scenario.

Indian poor have been sending their children to educate their chidden in large numbers and even sending them for higher education, taking care of the monthly bills, either with one income based on simple life or with a part time job, of the woman and a full time job for the man. Consumption loans, to celebrate birthdays or celebrate marriages, or going on vacations, or buying clothes' few times, in a year, and also buying cars and buying homes has been out of bounds in India. Borrowing is considered, to be a habit, not very afar from drinking heavily, not looking after family finances and the like. People tend to shun borrowing. Friends maintain distance, who are used to more borrowing. Parents dislike adult children, given to borrowing habits. In the nutshell, in India society abhors the idea of not living with simplicity and particularly, depends on borrowing, to show off in life and living beyond means. Synchronized with societal thinking in this realm of millenniums, the government and lending institutions tend to lend, with lot of due diligence, only for investments that give returns. Lending consumption loans, have been unknown in India, until solving of the y2k problem, which endeared India's IT professions to America and not so prudent, American financial and lending practices scampered into India's banks. I see a lot of slavishness, among India's banks, suddenly not only lending consumption, but also to buy cars and homes but putting up ads, in ubiquity in metros cities and even villages suddenly forgetting their half a century of very conservative prudent leading for businesses. This is a temp situation, would soon correct itself, as in the past also spikes of western slavishness get corrected.

Average Americans have been drowned in debt, as consumption loans, have been a pattern, to give short term happiness, to average Americans. It has been going on, since probably more than half a century. In recent decades, the volume of debt deployed, in the economy went up, by leaps and bounds. Credit card companies went so irresponsible that they kept on, issuing credit cards to the young university students, whose money making potential, was hardly 20 hours of temp university campus jobs. They were insisting on higher debt repayments on cards and suddenly made their borrowers more irresponsible, by only asking them to be current, on repayment of interest portion, of the credit limit. Further for no valid reasons, to enchain the young with ore debt and for debt to act as intoxication credit limits came to be raised by positive surprise communications, while lenders received no positive information of enhanced ability to repay higher loans from any quarters, about the borrower. As much as on weekends, in a bar respond to increased request for more drinking from friends or fellow drinkers, the young student borrowers responded similarly to these higher credit limits, by mindlessly accepting these credit limits. A further step poverty generations were with a future goal to make them permanent clients of credit cards high credit limits and higher rise in credit limits and little interest only recipients for all of these borrowings. Credit score was most oft repeated word heard in America among the young. It mattered so much that this was enquired before dating and certainly before saying yes to matrimony.

A lot of young debtoholics could not find, a date and were late to someone, ready to marry as their debt burdens, were too heavy, to deem them as a responsible spouse. Thus American lending on credit cards, before the young landed a proper job, already made them similar to a poor person globally, with runaway debt hanging on the personal finances, with little or no savings, whatsoever and a balance sheet that would be too ugly, to peruse or show anyone. If not real poverty, in terms of living like a poor, all of the poor person's features came to be in place, for tens of millions of the young, with multiple credit cards. Another poverty generating institution, has been the auto lenders, who lent capital for buying new cars, even more expensive cars. Almost everyone with debt centric credit scores are termed eligible, with slightly varying interest rates, both for buying cars and buying homes. Banks take the excuse of being liberals on consumption loans, for cars and homes knowing well that though the collaterals make the lending safe, as mortgaged properties could be attached by the banks, auctioned and proceeds realized deposited in the debtors' loan account. However, they deliberately ignore the fact that the value of collaterals, could plummet considerably even inn normal times leave aside during recessions economic and financial meltdowns and of course during economic depression and stagflation. The housing crisis

Chapter 6

Poor, the Politicians and Indian Democracy

We hear a lot of middle class criticism of the Indian politicians. In the recent years, the politicians pursue multi-party politics and at the end of elections, no clear majority is likely to be held, by any of the 2 political parties. Then both national big parties try to get allies from caste based parties and from the parties, which have very little membership and are state centric parties. The kind of general conversations, that one comes across, in the drawing rooms of the urban middle class, is about the quality of our politicians. Citizens get the government, they deserve. If citizens do not know the variances of ideologies, then they would not be so interested in the challenges of a democracy. Most people, while discussing politicians, forget that majority who criticize the politicians have no exposure of political science and majority of people, though educated, in their respective fields, do not know even know, the definition of capitalism and democracy. In India, these urban middle class critics may not be aware, when the constituent assembly met and when was the Indian constitution adopted. Politicians who were trained, as politicians in the village councils, development blocks, and the district politics, run for Assembly elections and in Parliamentary elections. They are not raw in politics, picked up as candidates. Very few highly educated brilliant persons, with lot of exposure to international community, show their interest, to join politics.

In India, the English speaking gentry, especially fashionable category of the urban middle class, are the beneficiaries big time, of the public policies that politicians have brought about, along with the officials, for the long term benefits for the economy. Heavy subsidization of higher education have turned higher education, accessible to the masses. However, the day to day life for them, once settled, with nice higher education, is not dependent on the politician's help. Hence the members of the urban middle class need not have to visit, a politician in the conduct of their life. While in the day to day life of the rural India, people remain in constant contact, with the politicians and they have a very positive remarks, to make about the Indian politicians, when objectively asked about their impression about politicians.

If industries that produce essential goods, in an economy, when those goods are not the need of the few but for all, then the market for such goods is huge, due to the very nature of the goods. These businesses deeply entrenched, in these areas of businesses, do not want to leave their economic power and engage lobbyists to influence, the government, not to interfere with these industrial activities. All said and done, government has its own regulation of industries, in different realms and it is not precluded to interfere with industries, where demand is an absolute necessity. It is here that a good and benevolent government need to be inclusive. Whichever government proffers these industries, dealing with goods of non utilitarian nature for the public, and leaves them fairly autonomous, it brings a lot of poverty in the lives of its citizens in general, as they cannot escape consuming them, as human beings. While price fixing among businesses, in an industry, is a crime under US laws, but what price a firm is going to fix for its goods, is the business privilege. For example, in the house construction industry of America, the US Government, decades ago, could have asked the representatives of the housing industry, to come up with homes that are fragmented, based on the fragmented income levels of the Americans. Those with high school qualifications, those who go to college, and those who are researchers, in major academic fields, land jobs that fetch naturally, different levels of income generally. House construction industry, with a rational and kind heart, could have come up, with housing prices, affordable to the different categories of the Americans, instead of coming up with construction of homes that are, way too spacious and way too fancy, for different categories uniformly and without regard to their affordability. Even the monopoly of such firms, could have been broken, asking banks to promote local level home construction small firms. Such a move of decentralization of the housing industry in USA could save on transportation of materials, could use the local materials and could have built homes, customized as per home buyer's tastes, as it happens in India. Profits then would have been distributed, to about 50 state premier housing firms and also to the county firm builders, in each of the 50 states, as it obtains in India. Government's decision, to look the other way, about the home construction industry structure, has triggered a lot of poverty, in terms of evisceration of savings, heavy debt liability, ugly balance sheets and tension load, in their minds, to pay high mortgages every month, for decades to come. Instead of home buying transactions being simple and straight, a thriving real estate industry that makes a lot of business owners rich, challenges the home buyers, because the overhead charges of the realtor firms, also get added. Real estate industry, to thrive in business and for furtherance of their affluence, try to make the industry highly liquid, unlike in India. These American realtors tend to \manipulate the minds of the home buyers, to change homes, by buying new homes that perpetually make American short of liquidity and increases heavy reliance on their debt. Government could have contained Americans, sliding into poverty, from over consumption of the homes, could have set a moderation limit, of the velocity and intensity, with which the real estate businesses function.

US Government has looked the other way, in regard to other major necessity of public transportation. Auto makers, set the price of vehicles, too high, for a number of varieties of cars that they proactively advertise, to the consumers. Then they constantly egg on the car owners/vehicle owners, to go for new models of cars,. These new cars every few years would have no additional important operational features, but only additional cosmetic features.

In India, the paradigm of home construction industry, is highly decentralized with distribution of profits, to numerous locations and containing the concentration of wealth. Indians value same ownership of houses emotionally, as it carried the memory of the children, having grown up there, parents having lived there for years, the marriages of children, with their spouses having been celebrated, from there and the like. In India the homes are constructed, when the chief earner reaches, the middle age of about 45 to 50 years, to be lived there and not to rent the home out. There has not been any practice of speculation, in the Indian home market, unlike in USA and hence people getting into sudden poverty, has been unknown.

Those in the middle class, buy simple 2 wheelers, which are inexpensive and require no loans or use public transportation, the network of which, the government saw, it to cover most city dwellers. Economy of scale in travelling, within the city and intercity kept the bus fare costs pretty low and the journey is comfortable, with no stress to drive oneself, every day, while commuting to the office. Government's role to make people fetter their temptation to borrow heavily and toboggan into poverty, to buy cars and change cars has been praiseworthy. Similarly, India for decades, have limited the models, churned out to hardly 3 or 4 cars and most of the purchases have been for the institutions. The middle class could barely buy cars, unless they saved enough, as consumer loans until the 1990s were disallowed, preventing indirectly people getting into poverty with loads of debt to repay. Firms are restricted by regulators, not to incessantly badger the consumers, to change the cars, by spending on ads. In USA huge expenditures are incurred on the ads to go for creation for wants of car.

While viewers crib about the TV ads, but yet psychologists are aware that ad message, fills up the mind to go, for new expenditures and make new borrowings to buy a new version of goods, like vehicles and homes, which have little utilitarian value, as the incumbent goods are nice, at the time of making new borrowings. In the past, there went a saying that friendship with an insurance agent, was costly as he sold a number of insurance policies, without the buyer, even realizing it. With ads all the time on TV and TV, hollering 24 hours in a day, the badgering to buy homes and autos, to say the least, hundreds of millions of the average Americans. It can be gauged that corporations see their top line and bottom line look gorgeous, while the balance sheets of hundreds of millions of car buying Americans are damaged. The government is stated to be in the good books, of the affluent business owners and align with them, as they accept campaign contributions, from the businesses. The system thus in the US, tend to look the other way, when the debts rise for average Americans, which with time could cause them poverty. Visually they look comfortable but mentally in their thinking they feel the poverty of the debt and no savings, all the time..

6.1 Denying Election Opportunities, to Politicians Who Have Criminal Case Pending Against Them

There has been a virulence of discussions, in the electronic and print media, that the politicians, who have been facing, either criminal complaints or criminal charges, in the Court of Law, should not be allocated election opportunities, by the political parties. This need to apply according to the discussants for both the State Legislatures and the National Parliament. A number of TV channels, in Hindi, English and Regional Languages, have found this theme, quite interesting and they have been taking up talk shows, for months on end. All these discussions, are polluting the minds of the people, especially the urban middle class and their young adult children. Many of these youth, are waiting for jobs and they are already frustrated. Frustrating them with too much statistics of which law makers are into criminal charges, have the potential of, raising their frustration levels. In a poor economy like India, these frustrations could easily take the form violence and agitations. Law and order, could be a serious causality. All of these consequences of these talk shows, where venoms are spewed against the politicians, are not seriously comprehended. TV channels remain busy, upping their channel popularity, to make more money from the advertisers, without thinking of what happens, to the brand equity of the nation and to the peace of the nations, when violence and agitations rear their ugly heads. The judicial core value in Indian judiciary is that an accused, until the charges are proved, has to be deemed innocent, appears to be totally, alien, to the opposition parties, as well the media persons. A complaint by anyone, against a politician is enough, for the media, to use even rough language and calling him criminal. It has become a strange recent practice to glorify the complainant and condemn the person against whom the complainant brings complaints. Indian practice, especially, in the electronic media, to gain higher approval rating of the viewers, in the new millennium, one of naiveté to conclude that whoever complains is truthful and right and whoever is complained against is the devil. They forget how some children growing up, in their own families, would be expert in hurling accusations, against other siblings, who are reticent and latter find it hard to lie, to criticize other siblings, unnecessarily. No parent should jump to the conclusion that the complaining child is right and start scolding the other children. They would talk to both, read between the lines from their conversations and then they would advise them accordingly. When media persons would probably understand their children and would not be gullible enough, to conclude that the child who complains is the angel and those who are complained against, are simply devils, how do they in the talk shows, discuss too much about the complaint and the complained against is faulted, without verifying the truth. Jumping to conclusions, on the basis of complaints with the police, has done more harm than good, to Indian society, in the new millennium.

Most members of the urban middle class and their young children are simply unaware about the politicians, most of whom come from the rural areas. English speaking makes the urban rural divide, a reality. The urbanites in India have limited interface with villages. Further, since they earn higher than others and maintain a nice economic and social status their interface with politicians is simply, few and far between. As the interface is missing the understanding and the perception of politicians is based more on how he looks how he is surrounded by very ordinary Indian people, and how their children have to wait for jobs and not based on objectivity.

There have come to existence, courtesy lack of due diligence and lack of consultation with the legal and social experts, before passing the laws that could impinge on Indian society, though being sensational they could be very dear to the yellow journalism centric media. These laws are draconian for one constituency and is a tool of harassment by another constituency. Any person interested in harassing another person, could easily evoke some draconian laws that could embarrass the victim immeasurably, for a life time. Even evidence at the time of filing FIR, is not brought and expectation is that the complainants complained need to be looked into immediately and arrests made against the person complained. Such is the huge expectation of immediacy of arrest, of the person complained against. It is bizarre that the same cops, who are just with both sides, until investigations prove one side to be wrong, also have morphed to meet the complainant's expectations, before any investigations are taken up.

The cops need to hear both parties patiently, finalize enquiries objectively and then take legal action to file cases, if necessary It is common knowledge in the last decade that. numerous complaint cases were brought against their husbands but the metro educated, English medium educated women, which ended up with acquittals. Wherever the cases were brought with mischievous intention, to harass the victim of the case, Then the drumming in the media, of each and every case, of sensational nature, need to be fettered by the media regulators. The media also need to have, self restraint rather than spewing venom against the victim of compliant, trashing his dignity to the garbage. Such unnecessary embarrassments are fraught, with dignity risk, not only of a few government employees, it could hit senior administrators, doctors, engineers advocates, even judges, business men, accountants and stock investors. It needs to be kept in mind that any disgruntled person could start a criminal case, against the victim of a complaint be it a student friend or acquaintance. Protection of Civil Rights in India, is known to have, been misused, in some for the cases, where false cases have been filed. Some laws tend to make some constituencies, very vulnerable to court case embarrassments. Out of sudden anger sometimes, complainants come up with lies, to extort money, promising to withdraw the cases or not to pursue the cases, in the court of law, if a given sum of money is paid to the false complainant. In the light of this falsity of cases again, a lot of committed to development politicians, who have been in politics for decades, could be ignominiously denied tickets, as per the oft repeated media criticisms. A number of ministers, legislators, senior bureaucrats, senior police officers, even judges, doctors businessmen and the like have already, in India turned victims of many marital false complaints, by daughter in laws or the wife for no fault of theirs. A lot of agony passes their mind and they face their lifetime duties blemished, with such false cases. This has become a trigger for poverty for many families. Families of the bridegroom have to shell down enormous sums of money to save their faces, many a times, though they are innocent, because they do not want their social image to be blemished, by false cases that could take years to conclude. Many are complaining that they are not only paying to the false complainant, the daughter in law but also spending a lot of money to pay the advocates, who would represent their cases in the court of law, to prove their innocence. Some cases may be correct but in 98% cases it is alleged that cases have not been proved, in the court of law. Some bizarre laws could convert an innocent decent educated person, into a criminal in the eyes of society overnight and media in 2000s appear to be waiting for such busting of a family, to trash the image of an educated professionals image by putting the news on the first page. Such news in the developed world, would ordinarily be a small column in the 5th page, rightly so, probably because falsehoods and misuse of such cases are well known to the mature media acts in a mature manner.

Women on the Indian TV media in the TV serials and ads are depicted, to wear western dresses that reveal more and cover less of the body, in the theme, before marriage and after marriage, in sharp contrast to the dresses that Indian women actually wear that covers and not reveals the anatomy. An attempt is made by the TV serials and TV ads, to convey the message to women, to shun serious aspects of life and be clotheshorses, wearing revealing dresses, in conflict with Indian values and culture. Westernization of Indian society is attempted to popularize, its MNCs, to promote to the hilt, the sales of their products and also debt, on the lines of the countries of the west, in the developed world. Even the media in the west could be prudent and rational to depict, their own way of life and not ever mention the plusses of Indian way of life, on their TV ads and their serials. They punctiliously deal with their social themes.

In contrast, how could Indian media be so mindlessly slavish, to promote western way of life, to reach out to the viewers in Indian society, which is following a multi millennium stable societal values, where economy of scale of the joint family, is appreciated, where young adults care for children and the aged, where marriages are for lifetime and spouses are viewed with same permanency of relationship, like siblings, children and parents, where a spouse is not discriminated, criticized, faulted and parted while misdemeanors of the siblings, children and parents are tolerated, for a life time, as it happens in the US and the West.

In this kind of scenario, when nothing has been proved, against the person in custody, national political parties disengaging proposed candidates, from giving tickets, to contest for MLA elections and MP elections, probably may not be just. We have to wait and see how political parties would react to it.

Harassment while participating in politics could take place by filing false complaints because some political leader belonging, to a particular party could be fastidious supporters of certain public policies, which some constituencies, do not want to come about, for implementation. Such constituencies for all one knows, could band together to come up with a false police complaint.

6.2 Media and Politicians

For example, lot of people, do not want the subsidies, to be granted to the poor and different schemes of poverty reductions, to be taken up, to improve conditions of the poor. Lot of people do not want the labor's voice in factories and industrial democracy, to be in place. Sometimes international community of the developed world, could be interested in removing industrial democracy, from Indian labor scene. The flexibility of labor market, as and when introduced could make a lot of savings for the foreign MNCs and they could earn much higher profits, from the plants transferred to India. It is a common knowledge that the business owners have acquired enormous bargaining power, through labor union bashing and denial of industrial democracy, gradually since the 1980s, both in the USA and in the UK. Numerous interests from within the boundaries of the nations and abroad, may not like the inclusiveness and constant interface of public representatives, and it may be true of the pro rich pro business political parties. False cases from such constituencies could overnight turn a reasonably dedicated politician, to be termed a criminal.

These constituencies may like to morph, the configuration of the parliament, from simple white Khadi clad farming community, to suave sophisticated urbane members, as it obtains in the developed world and in a lot of emerging and developing economies also. Though the law making body may be urbane and sophisticated to articulate fine debates, but it could happen that in those economies, the poor remain isolated and alienated from the goings on, in politics and little funds could have been allocated, in the national budget, for the poor. In India, where ratio of allocation of national budget funds to the rural areas, right from the beginning of the First Five Year Plan and in successive Five Year Plans, have been substantial, there could be some radical urban pockets, who would envy. There is a lot of talk that these not so educated politicians, should not sit in the Indian parliament and those who are educated, need to be a part of the parliament. Some critics have gone to the extent of saying that those, who are from the IIM and IIT, should be adorning the parliament and not rural people of limited educational qualifications. When the economy is in flux and the poor hold the voting power and are so well engaged in democracy, the middle class and the rich are urbanites, given to more living comforts and are also partially influenced by the Hollywood and the western media, could want their taxes reduced even at the expense of the lack of development of the poor in India. That would probably result in the poor remaining an underclass forever. Such constituencies could engineer false complaints, against pro poor against the pro poor rural politicians, to countenance their financial interests. This contingency also cannot be ruled out, where poor hold the sovereign democratic voting power and the affluent hold the financial power.

With multiple dimensions of the falsehoods, of the complaints filed in FIR, a lot of caution will have to probably be exercised, before disallowing citizens, from participation in elections, who have criminal cases against them. However, a conviction would be a better measure probably, to disallow participating in elections.

With so much negative energy, being spread, condemning the government, the law and order could be a serious casualty, and media need to realize that once law and order becomes a casualty in a nation, a poor nation of low per capita income, violence and crime could be the order. Do the media not realize that it is easy with canards of its type, to confuse hundreds of millions of people, who happen to be illiterates and who have never gone to a school to learn? In such a situation, either the government would give up, to the anarchy or anarchists would rear its head, with covert support of those confused, among the masses, by incessant negative news broadcasting repeatedly broadcasted on a 24/7 basis. It is simply incomprehensible why in a poor country, like India where nation has to be built over decades, with professional hard work, so much of 24.7 entertainment and negative venom spewing by the media, was granted by the Information Ministry and why did the media pitched for 23/7 time, knowing well that broadcasting in all of the 24 hours programs could lose quality of the programs to the trenches. Media has weakened Indian democracy, by creating a chaotic disrespect of the authorities that it is supposed to govern. One can see how, each one for himself paradigm, has weekend the economic condition, of the multitude and have taken the income and wealth of few, to the stratosphere, creating huge inequality in some of the countries. This is happening in the developed world. Blind and mindless slavishness of the developed world, from where the media seems to be taking its inspiration and lionizing it in India, is fraught with lot of negative consequences, for Indian democracy. Freedom of expression in democracy, does not seem to imply 24/7 criticisms and abuse of some constituencies and polluting the minds of people and professionals, who make tangible contribution to India's economy.

Many a times, false complaints are known to have been filed, in the villages out of jealousy and ill will and to save one's official promotional avenues astonishingly, the police officials also have been known not to take chances, in recent years and start investigations. Some meek police officials, are known to be extra cautious, not to be termed as siding, with the affluent and therefore even file charge sheets, even if the evidence is found to be highly inadequate, basically passing the buck kind of attitude. This is a dangerous trend and is seen to happen in Indian policing in current times. Political parties have had this dilemma, for several decades, as to how to deal with false criminal cases. Numerous people in the villages, below poverty line, vexed with their life, could be feeling jealous of the financial success of the landed rich and they could sign on a false complaint, either because of jealousy or induced by monetary gains. On the false complaints, filed by a political opponent, to give hard time to the accused, his political followers, would probably be ready to sign, on a complaint, particularly in factious villages, which are known to the district administration. Thus, one would not be surprised, if numerous poor people, who are followers of the political opponent of the incumbent legislator, come up to sign or give, thumb impressions, on a complaint against the incumbent MLA. Caste based social stratification, also plays a role in filing of the false complaints. Many villages would have still two dominant castes, who have been landlords for centuries and the loyalties of the labor castes, were divided between them. Even in such cases, using the tool of filing false complaints, with the police, to humiliate the other group, has not been unknown.

In the western countries, it is only the rich and poor divide and sometimes the racial divide, which create societal division. In India, the caste could be a major factor of societal negative groupings. In many villages, despite a lot of inclusiveness, to grab political powers, despite caste rivalries, rich and poor rivalries, family rivalries, sub cultural rivalries in certain regions are not uncommon, in the Indian villages and to grab political power false complaints are not unknown in several villages, where in a jiffy a false complaint could get filed, in the form an FIR, and a cautious police officer investigating the same and filing charge sheet, though not in a haste. For the middle class, which is vocal in India, who have barely seen a visit and could have seen villages, except only through the windows of the railroad coaches, are oblivious of the village issues, hardly known any of its complexities or socio political conditions, a criminal case against a politician, appears too scandalous. The judicial view that unless the charge is held proved, against an accused he/she is being treated as innocent, has not percolated, to most educated people in India and for whom, the word criminal case almost always, drives them to think that those complained against are criminals. This could be true in big towns and metros, where divisive social groups are near absent and such schisms rarely happen, driving people to file false complaints and signing by a lot of people, on a group basis, on a false complaint, would very rarely happen. If media is keen to see that its outreach expands, to the rural areas, which has already happened in India, in the new millennium, they need to make serious studies, about rural life, rural plusses and rural social divides, especially in the context of grabbing political power. With little exposure to the rural areas, like the urbanites thinking that a complaint, implies the complainant is truthful and the complained against is a criminal, would be common and unjust too.

Those tried by trial courts, have the opportunity to go to the High Court and to the Supreme Court. There is likelihood to go on appeal to the bench of the Supreme Court, merely because of the conviction, by a lower court, when they have access to his/her Appellate Court and conviction, is not finalized, disallowing them to contest for MLA and MP and disallowing grant of tickets, for contesting by individual candidates may not be fair. As they may have done decades of political service sincerely. Ultimately the judicial decision, would prevail and that would be binding on the political parties. The media has been asking, for disallowing even candidates, who are in police custody or judicial custody. It is not known how the political parties react to this and view it. When nothing is proved and no evidence has been marshaled, by the complainant and no charge sheet has also been filed and the case could be just to create some sensation, and trial could finally lead to, the court throwing away the case, for want of adequate proof, one would argue that punishing a candidate, by disallowing him/her to contest legislative or parliamentary elections could be unfair. The respondent may have been in custody, on a request by the police, to prevent him from manipulating evidence.

In this kind of scenario, when nothing has been proved against the person in custody, national political parties disengaging proposed candidates, from giving tickets, to contest for MLA elections and MP elections, probably may not be just.

Further there could be false cases, to indirectly reduce a politician's political approach, which he may be advancing, in favor of the poor. Lot of people do not want the subsidies, to be granted to the poor and different schemes of poverty reductions, being taken up, to improve conditions of the poor. Lot of people do not want the labor's voice, in factories and industrial democracy, to be in place. Sometimes, international community of the developed world, could be interested, in removing industrial democracy from Indian labor scene and also inflexibility of labor market, because their MNC s then could make, a lot of savings and earn much higher profits, from plants transferred to India. Such anti industrial democracy approach centric constituencies among the developed countries may sprout, from experience with lab our, in their own economies, where over the decades, they have acquired enormous bargaining power, through labor union bashing and denial of industrial democracy gradually, since the 1980s both in USA and in UK.

Numerous interests, including within the boundaries of the nation and abroad may dislike the inclusiveness and constant interface of India's public representatives with the poor in many constituencies, among all political parties. These constituencies may like to morph the configuration of the parliament, from simple Indian white home handloom cloth (khadi) clad farming community to suave, sophisticated, urbane members, as it obtains in the developed world. In a lot of emerging and developing economies, also the poor remain isolated and alienated, from the goings on in politics. In these nations, where interface with the poor, is limited, little is allocated in their national budget for the poor, unlike in India, where ratio of allocation of national budget funds, to the rural areas, right from the beginning of the First Five Year Plan and in successive five year plans have been substantial, with envy of people of urban pockets, industries and service sectors of the economies. There is a lot of talk that these not so educated rural based politicians, should not sit in the parliament and those, who are urban and educated need to be a part of the parliament. Some members of the middle class community, have gone to the extent of saying that those, who are from the IIMs and IITs, should be legislating, in the parliament and not rural people of limited educational qualifications.

Chapter 7

Corruption and Poverty in India and West

Corruption, like poverty could be visible, as well as non-visible. In countries, characterized by high and rising inequality, where the government and corporation top managers both hold a lot of punishing powers and the labor unions are not strong, the corruption could exist at the top and it could be denied, at the middle and lower rungs of the administrative /management ladder. Where the government is only moderately strong and top managers of the corporations are only modestly strong, with punishing powers fettered by strong labor unions, then the top layer of the officials cannot keep corruption centralized. Then it is observed that the corruption to expedite decision mostly and reducing delay, in decision making, gets democratized becoming a reality, at the middle management level and base management level, also, along with the top management. One could term this corruption, as a democratic corruption. In a democratic corruption scenario, most officials remain afar from corrupt practices but few officials with authority and too much driven by consumerism of goods are participants of corruption, at middle and base levels of management. India could be an example of few officials corrupt in all of the three managerial levels..

In countries of EU and USA, where corruption and financial irregularities, at the top management level, is voluminous and could be termed, autocratic corruption. In such economies, the corruption phenomenon cannot be democratic, as the punishments for corruption at middle and lower levels could be severe.

As the labour unions are getting weaker with talks of flexibility of labor markets, in the developed world, the level of corruption though very high, confines itself to the CEOs of corporations, Governors of the States and Senior City Officials and the like, but never the middle management and base level. Occasionally, financial irregularities, in USA, could occur, at lower levels too, but is very rare. With low compensation low of average Americans, but for the highly punitive management system, the corruption could breed. US economy, awash with debt availability and too many temp jobs, to rely on to pay extra debt acts as a deterrent for the base level,. not to indulge in corrupt practices at the grassroots level.

7.1 Low Compensation, Coupled With Globalization and Availability of Venues of Spending, Triggers Corruption

,Government with its tax collection competencies, law and order control competencies and with authority to regulation and opportunities to bring economic development in the country is an institution, from which people and particularly the young expect a lot of service and not hurling of criticisms, at each other. The educated citizens expect that the Parliament in India and Congress in the US, to calmly and seriously discuss national issues and take up sachems to develop the nation. The least that they expect is noise in the august body, on a regular basis and paralysis of decision making.

Public meetings need to be organized to address educated people, about national achievements and the positive steps, being taken for the public welfare. Opposition parties need to address in public meetings, telling people how supportive they were to the incumbent government, to pass development schemes for the nation. Public platforms, need to be used, for not fomenting ill will, in a poor country of such a low per capita income like India. Blaming the incumbent government and incumbent government blaming the major opposition, are likely to sap the energy, to develop a large nation, where the poverty still is large and needs to be addressed, with suave and calm bilateral approach.

Each political party, need to respectfully refer to other party and its leaders, rather than making undue criticism, merely to evoke public laughter, at the expense of law enforcing body. In a nation, populated by 1.3 billion people, once the government is taken easy, as a result of the manner, the media and opposition collaborate sometimes, to denigrate institutions, the law abiding discipline of the masses, could see a drastic southern movement, leading to anarchy. In a weak government scenario, corruption at different levels are likely to emerge and also increase. Hence to fetter corruption the government both the ruling and opposition parties need to conduct seriously, giving no scope to people, to comment in the government in a derogatory manner.

7.2 Americanization of Indian Middle Class Youth and Family Pressure on Wage Earner to be Corrupt

Americanization of the Indian middle classes, has taught them young urban middle class, who in a slavish manner, take up issues, organizing meetings with candles, in their hands protesting, against corruption. These public demonstrators are not the poorest of the poor and neither do they belong to the traditional poor families, either of the villages or of the towns. These appear to the young men and women, who might be getting hand expenses of the order of 25000 rupees per month, well dressed and all dressed in western clothes, with little Indiana exuded from their group.

They appear to be the children who influenced by the TV ads pursue, their parents to buy new big screen TVs, a new house or a new car and might be knowing that pressured by the family, the main income earner, the father would be compelled, to be corrupt to meet their demands. The candle holding children appear to be those, who demand and quarrel, vitiating the peace of their home atmosphere and know pretty well that these consumer goods, are out of the bounds of their parental income who might be already deluged with consumer loans. They also might be knowing that current request/ pressure to buy new goods, would mean for the principal earner to make money though corruption. and hence now would be possible to be met only through the petty corruption. Several researches indicate that the corruption indulged by singles, is negligible and so is the corruption indulged by the families, which are childless. Even the joint families value simple living and individual constituents, working parents elders are not so much, under pressure from adult children, to be corrupt and buy consumer goods that come to the market, as number of adults in the family are not small. An old car serves their purpose; a black and white TV serves their purpose; a simple small screen color TV serves their purpose, a set of 4 chairs in the drawing space serve their purpose and they almost never eat out.

Hence the role of the young, in the middle class, in the urban areas, is in no less degree, responsible for the nefarious practice of corruption by their parent. As long as they would not stick to the Indian cultural writs of simplicity and austerity, and in a slavish manner go after western way of life and culture and imitate the west in consumerism, the corruption will not go, merely by some people assembling at maidan and holding candle meetings against corruption. As soon as these young adult urban middle class Indianise the pressure on the principal earner in the home who is usually the father would evaporate and corruption would be gone. As an ancient society, India holds a surfeit multi millennium great human values that has sustained this civilization for 10,000 years.

In fact the urban young belonging to the middle class and the rich are answerable, to hundreds of millions of corruption indulgence free poor people, who slog, under the sun, who supply vegetables fruits and milk, to these urban middle class and the urban rich at a reasonable price, to improve their health. In modern times, influenced by the west and turning slavish to the west, in materialism, and consumerism and individualism, the young children pester their parents to buy latest goods or at least latest brands of the goods. After turning adult, they constantly pester their parents, to buy at least a car, an ordinary car, at least an air conditioner, at least a nice TV with big screen and pay them monthly hand expenses, to frequent fast food eatery place, twice a week that too with friends. Consumerism touted by incessant advertisements, by corporations, abet large scale multitudinous consumerism, to consume goods and services

Corporate India's expenditure, on ads, is in no small measure, responsible, for increasing corruption. Too many billboards have come up. Too many ads are in magazines and newspapers. Too many electronic ads are shown on the TV. So many electronics adds. for goods and services, are shown on the DVDs that are available on hire. While the multitude cannot resist the desire, to be enslaved by corporations, in so far as buying their products, are concerned, this leads to corruption and in many instances, thefts in the big retailing shops. The white caller workers, is seen, indulging in sophisticated white collar crimes, of insider trading etc., while dealing with the stock market. Craving for latest goods and latest version of goods, constantly whipped up by the ads, have made enormous wealth, for the firms and their shareholders. Those in the top management also, make huge money, through ad triggered sales of goods and services, but concomitantly, it has been destroying, the balance sheets of a lot of citizens, of the developed world, leading to economic catastrophes, seen in Europe and economic meltdown seen in USA. Courtesy slavish attitude of the former colonies of Europe, including India, a lot of the MNCs and their business activities that are not so good, are allowed through the route of economic liberalization. Political leaders welcoming MNCs, are usually termed good public policy makers, by the developed world and they are not bothered, how much harm, in multiple directions tend to happen, even in India, due to the manipulation of consumers, by the MNCs and big Indian companies. The advertisement at the door of the house, in the living room in the bed room TV and movement on the hand held equipments and the like have been turning the minds of especially the young, crazy, about buying newer and newel versions of gizmos, laptops TVs and even new and new even homes. Families are unable to live in peace, until their desires, are met, to the extent of at least 50%. Tax avoidance in India, creates a scenario, where right from parliamentarians, legislators, ministers, civil servants, technocrats, professions such as doctors, in the government hospitals and at the base of the economic period the assistants and officers, even the police officers, all of whom have a long range of duties are paid barely, enough to lead a simple life and not a life, meeting the TV ad driven buying inflating desires. The government is aware that the compensations are barely enough, to pay the bills and encourage higher education, among children,

It is here that the desire of democratic corruption, in a democracy has its origin. India is a rare country, where corruption, unlike even in the developed world, is, democratic. It is a common knowledge that in the totalitarian States such as civil and military dictatorships, but that does not imply hat total volume of corruption or rent seeking in a developed county of high GDP is less. There occurs big corruption and big nepotism, but so much at the high level that except a few a lots get scot free, with what they call in America, a slap on the wrist. Some even escape with big connections at high places slap on the risk too. In Dictatorships, the corruption is s very big and centralized. even in China where communism is the political ideology, and fear of the central government is intense the corruptions is canalized. Once foreign companies get a nod in Beijing, in the local areas, the question of any impediment to implementation of their business is conspicuous by its absence. Even in the developed world, both in EU countries and in countries of North America, while corruption is known at the highest levels, both in the private and government sectors, of the economy middle managers and at the base of the official pyramid, the question of petty corruption, is near absent. To get a seat in a coach or a railroad, for a long journey, one does not have to pay, any petty bribe to a petty official. Not centralized as it is in totalitarian dictatorship, such as China and developed world democracies such as USA and EU.

As important matter as a legislation is stated to have been prepared by the industry that is supposed to regulate according to policed opposition every now and then. This semblance of regulation, the legislation put forth by the big players, can escape regulation, though its legal loopholes.

Any unjust usurping of monetary gains is viewed, as corruption. The CEOs and the top managers of the US based corporations, driven by their runway money greed, are drawing stratospheric compensation, which is 550 times that of those, who are located at the base of the economic pyramid. Similarly speculators through excessive speculation, are artificially booming the stock market, to make capital gains and then making, whole lot of people impoverished, as the market would crash, due to excessive speculation, practiced by the money greed of the speculators. Those CEOs maintaining corporate jets and claiming 550 times compensation compared to the small compensation, which he pays to the slogging workmen, is a result of his nefarious financial practices, which they as a group have been perpetuating. to support such nefarious financial practices seem think tanks have been funded in America by giant corporations, recruiting economies another scholars from better universities to come up with research work that such wayward money gouging of the mangers is very good for the economy and its future. These think tanks do not openly, declare as right thinking. Sometimes they prepare report that appears pro poor, or pro base of the org pyramid. The think tanks influence the public thinking and that explains why a lot of people, who annually earn only 20,000 dollars a year are inclined, to call themselves right ideology oriented, who speak against welfare measures. Such are the effects of the think tanks that corruption could be supported, by ordinary people too, at the expense of living standard of the poor, once they are impressed by the ideology of the right.

All of these nefarious financial practices that take little cognizance of the value addition of numerous employees, in the organization and giving them, non living, hourly wages and every quarter converting more number of employees, into part time employees hurt the employees in America. The employees are made to feel shamelessly servile to the supervisors, who condescendingly allocate, hours every week afresh favoring, some of his favorites, for reasons best known to him and even deciding, what time to what time, the temp has to work each day. An arrangement with. dignity of employees, would have been, the employee, knowing about his /her work schedule, from the time it begins, to the time the work ends and keeping it reasonably the same for 6 months and allotting fixed number of hours The allocation of work schedule on a daily basis and also each day the timings for each temp employee, by the supervisors judgment, making numerous the temps, in different locations, make them feel uncertain about the start time and end time of work each day. In addition, the attitude of the supervisors, to make employees chaperon around, for few extra hours, tantamount to almost treating them shabbily is bizarre. Such HR practices appearing in firms which have multi country outreach and which make billions of dollars of revenue, is unbelievable.

Corruption in America and EU is invisible and not visible to the public, because corruption is highly centralized, as high standard of living, travelling around in corporate jets, and drawing huge compensations are.

While in the west, the corruption at the bottom few layers of organizational architecture, is directly controlled by its flexible labour market and instances noticed, lead to immediate discharge from work, without appeal. Such draconian measures, without even making proper enquiries, can be possible only in economies, where the writ of the flexible labour market prevails, with no labor unions in place. But in places, like India, where even companies, have to follow the principle of natural justice and enquire and prove corruption, at the bottom level and the employee will have appellate right, to higher authorities, it becomes a very expensive and cumbersome task to deal with it. Like the amount of compensation, in general in India that supports one car, for life, one 2 wheeler for life, one refrigerator for life, subsidized education until higher education, and state aided medial health care system, Network of medical boutique clinics that charge very small amount of money, help these employees. To buy consumer goods and to improve their life style, with much TV ad exposures, pressured by the family, some principal income earners may indulge, in petty corruption of a very small amount. Those who are in great hurry, to get goods in rationed goods, do not necessarily mind, paying bribe, because the bribe amount is easily affordable to them, often egregiously pursue the goods provider to seek rent. Influenced by media, family's pressure to buy consumer goods and sprucing the home, in recent years, is unnecessarily leading to the nefarious practice of corruption. Family pressure to buy a home, buy a new nice car, over a new big screen TV driven by incessant TV ads in the west, is also ruining the personal finances of many American/western families. The ubiquity of availability of debt, is helping the principal money earner to get ready to borrow and buy goods under family pressure, though individually he /she may not be inclined to borrow.

In Indian scenario, the TV ads, are creating similar pressure, to buy expensive goods, beyond means putting pressure on the principal economy earner,. This is happening in an economy, where unlike America, debt is not easily available and therefore the principal income earner might stoop, to the rent seeking. This is not to justify rent seeking by an Indian or debt consuming by the American but mindless role of the media to show incessant ads to buy goods and services. The media ads create a divide in the family creating different intensities of magnetism for the goods, which would add little value addition. Hence the main culprit for goods buying driven corruption is the 24/7 media through, which corporations manipulate the mind of the viewers to buy goods even if it means to be unethical to be corrupt in India. One good aspect of Indian way of life is simplicity and a desire to be content with buying TV, once buying car once, buying home once in a lifetime, which makes the personal fiancés of Indians far superior to the personal finances of the average Americans.

The rent seeker at the petty official level covertly thinks that it doesn't hurt the common man but it enlivens the families of ordinary employees. It is undoubtedly unethical, to seek rents and buy family pressured TV and several other ad influenced, goods and services, but when the practice, takes a voluminous proportion, the shame and concept of ethics, tends to evaporate. It is like a criminal living in a neighborhood, after release from prison, is at comfort, where whole lot of ex criminals tend to stay. There goes a saying that a bad human attribute, needs to be nipped in the bud. Once it expands like Californian fire the fact that corruption is unethical evaporates, from the minds of the people.

The CEOs in America are looked down upon for drawing high and rising salaries and perks, even when company is tanking, its shareholders are suffering from huge losses, in paper money since the early 1980s. Even after 30 years, their reputation in money greed, has not improved. Instead, the money greed has increased, their reputations have fallen south, beyond comprehensions and there are few takers for this position. CEOs have not changed, to change the business image of America and their own image, because this money greed of CEOs is ubiquitous among most of the CEOs. So they in their own world of comfort,

In India, talk about corruption is far more than corruption. Corruption is criticized not because it really bites but purely on ethical grounds. Strangely a lot of those people who visibly criticize corruption and make loud talks against the politicians stating they are responsible for corruption in the country are strangely themselves not above corruption. Pointing figures to others, in vituperative language by the media, in the new millennium is a reality. Owning properties disproportionate to the known sources of income, is under radar watch of the investigating agencies, in so far of officials are concerned, no matter how low or high placed the officer may be. If the radars are placed to watch, the private sector in this area a lot of skeletons in the cupboards could be visible. A lot of people, from the private sector, with very meager fixed income, from their employers, have quadrupled the sizes of their homes, adding 3 more floors in the last 2 years naturally, with ill-gotten wealth. This is true in many cases of the media representatives, and of extortions and blackmail, by some of the media representatives at the grassroots are coming to the fore. Some media persons are known to have turned overnight quire rich, with inability to explain the wealth acquisition in short time.

But since the radar is not usually directed to the private sector, it is emboldened to keep the criticism of the government sector, alive year through year damaging its brand equity. The conduct rules, restrict the employees and the officers to go to the press, as it is in violation of their conduct rules and this restriction, gives more opportunity, to the media, to blacken the government employees, as a pastime. They have twin disadvantages. The employees do not give rejoinder. The public gets a skewed view which include a lot of the demographic dividend the young, who have finished education and are waiting to land a job. Their frustration of remaining unemployment is prone to believe any negative media news about the establishment. The developed world media, though not always objective, does not rant negative news ad infinitum. Such negative news, make the young unnecessarily frustrated with misinformation and the middle aged employees, get highly demoralized and vexed with ceaseless ranting of a lot of misinformation. The practice of ratings of the channels through yellow journalism, in the new millennium, and due to 24/7 government permission to exhibit media, have dome huge harm than good for the future of the country.

Too quick an expansion of professional colleges, has increased corruption in India, in recent times. Bottom up desire, for quantum socio- economic mobility, through education and a general attitude of inclusiveness, by those, who are well off, towards the poor, have led to charging fees by the colleges, much higher fees that government charges, for meritorious government quota students. The colleges are also charging variable capitation fees, to improve college infrastructure from students, who have not competed through entrance examinations but are inclined to study. Among this category, from the not so good, students the college charges more, for admission, who have scored far lesser marks and less, from those, who have secured higher marks. To be able to get their wards, admitted in non-meritorious, non-government quotas seats, based on the intelligence level of their wards, are aware from information floating, how much money, at the time of admission and how much annual fees, the parents have to pay for each of the growing children. Even if this planning is to be done in about 5 years time. It is not easy for a private small business owner to make this amount or for a private executive, to change and land jobs that would give that type of savings and also for government executive to find that kind of money even selling gem assets of the family. It is at this point of time, the family pressure makes the chief economic provider, to suddenly move to corruption levels which may have not been the case earlier. If the corrupt employee is caught by the law enforcing authorities, he would read to jail sentence and children in next years would strive hard to compete and study with low government quote miller fees. If one is not caught the corruption and study in engineering would go on. thus the desire to see the younger generation tuen professional, the staring of too many professional private colleges and founders with an eye of money from varying nature of capitation fees and societal desire being the government not to regulate too effectively the tuition fee structure are some of the factored that combine the emergence of corruption. Those wrong in inventory management or accounting in private sector are not far behind, to make clandestine extra money to admit their children to professional colleges.

The visibility of too big a house, too expensive and highly branded cars and the like are reasons, for few, for whom, ultra materialism could be the goal that drives their corruption levels up. Such humans take huge risks but are also caught to be sent to prison. Investigative authorities and the police need to be paid well. Otherwise they tend to make money, from a wrong path of diluting investigations and for diluting regulative action against the corrupt, which fails to act, as a deterrent to other police officials.

Intra family and inter family income differential, by a wide margin between private local /private foreign corporation employed and the rest of the economy, both private and government, where compensation is way behind, leads to a competition to lead a better life and visibility of wealth by way of a modern westernized culture, who earn more have increased the desire of people to be corrupt for some people. High debt availability for consumer loans, which is rising, will make corruption among multitude difficult to arrest, as they would like to be current on loan repayment.

The sedentary habit begets laziness and desire for a life of comfort. That drives people to buy air conditioners, sofas, cars and makes them desirous of flying by air and staying in hotels in comfort. All of these require a lot of money. Hence an opportunity for using the discretion to help the rich comes and there they go making a lot of money expediting decisions and helping business owners out of the way.

Corruption through public policy making favoring some industries and some firms in particular industries happen, due to absence of state funded electoral campaigns. People need to be educated to contribute to political parties on a regular basis, to keep democracy alive

Loose talk from heights, calling politicians and professions as corrupt, has a huge demoralizing effect in India. Even honest people being unduly criticized and their brand equity driven, to trenches causes huge ire in the honest minds, about the futility of honesty and at least affluence through corruption because in any way such loose talks will go on and prevention remaining flat about corruption.

7.3 Once Economy Becomes Globalized, the Corruption Tends to Increase

When economy of India, liberalized since 1991, a number of foreign firms, started operating some small, some medium and some large firms. These firms, to obtain better terms for doing business, naturally approached the authorities, be it for supplying power at fixed tariff for, or for requesting to buy certain qualities of goods, at the minimum for a given number of years at affixed price or giving supplies of some intermediate goods at a low price, to improve the FDI. In turn the MNCs may assure for the creation of employment and economic opportunities, for downstream industries. For example Enron, has been known to have greased the palm, to get Indian government concessions, which private firms objected. Enron, through its rent seeking techniques, could keep government, by two major opposition parties, in series in good humor. This would be true of similar placed foreign firms. Whichever political and executive accepts, favors from foreign firms, by way of corruption, foreign firm's capacity, to pay bribes in, could be manifold higher than the capacity of domestic firms, in different industries, to keep government happy. Hence once corruption starts, playing out in a liberalized economy, then there is no competition, between an MNC giant and a small domestic firm. Thus even in the eyes of one's own government, the domestic firms, could get a cold shoulder. Further, the middle class market of India and China, being very big, who are relied upon by, foreign based companies, they start operating in advance, in other areas of business. Interface in other areas, foreign firms start, basically to leverage huge middle class market, to sell their goods. As a first mover, into host economy, these MNCs not only tend to only influence the governance to grant them the permission to set up the plant but also by rent seeking techniques. In addition, due to their giant nature, and global outreach, they could decide to could set the cap of the price of their goods artificially. very low say in India. They could also raise the prices of the same goods, in high GDP economies such as Singapore, Taiwan Hong Kong, where they may be operating for long and know the consumers are affluent to absorb the rise in prices of goods comfortably. Such low price moves artificially done by the MNCs, could kill the domestic firms, who due to smaller market, no global business may have to compulsorily charge much higher prices and certainly above the cost of making the goods. MNCs could play these tricks of business, as they could get compensated, by slightly hiking, in some emerging economies and some developed economies. These moves of the MNCs explain why their operations abroad, have cannibalized many local firms. Several local firms get closed or bought out by them, and gradually entrepreneurial expertise, start to turn south, in the next few decades, unless the emerging economy government remains firm to prop up and protect the local industries too. All of these MNCs have accentuated poverty in different economies.

In India one used to hear about the cereals made by domestic Mohan Makin's firm and now in the recent decade consumers always go for Kellogg cereals which is a US based business presumably the Mohan Makin cereals are gone into oblivion and closed. Thumps up used to be a well know nonalcoholic brand in India in 60s70s 80s but now with Coke and Pepsi ruling the roost in India whether Thumps up has been bought up by the MNCs or have been closed. If this can happen to a huge sized GDP of India then one can imagine how corrupt moves of the MNCs could influence the African economies.

Foreign business expansion, through bribing of the local government, were banned in 1977, by a law in the US. This law also make one infer that there was no formal ban for the US based firms, before 1977, to bribe the host country authorities, though US was a free economy, since 1776. It implies that there was no ban to bribe foreign governments, by the US based MNC s, even in developed economy like USA, for 201 years. Could it be that developed country based MNCs possess tremendous power to promote rent seeking activities in host authorities and they could kill domestic firms by sheer size of their firms and their cash availability on a global scale.

Even today, there are many European countries, where US type of 1977 ban on bribing by the MNCs have not come about and no legislation is under contemplation also. In those countries their MNC s bribing foreign governments would be deemed absolutely legal even now.

Rich countries and their MNCs, earning huge profits, from their worldwide operations, possess very high financial power and find it easy, to magnetize host governments, through inducements, to get runaway favors. The fact remains that the MNCs got runaway favors, in many countries in Africa, South America and to certain extent in Asia. India however remained conservative and India didn't mind, being referred, in the international conferences, as an autarchic economy, which protects its industries effectively. So as long as the foreign firms continue to bribe the powers that be, to stay afloat the local companies too would have to keep the local government in good humor.

The tall talks on the TV, castigating corruption in India may have to be accompanied by how level playing field Indian economy will get, if foreign firms continue to indulge in corruption, to influence the local governance. Repeated references in the media only whittle down positive energy. Instead these issues of financial defalcation, corruption, with faith, needs to be left to the law enforcing authorities and then on the learned judiciary, which is globally known to be a highly respected independent institution, instead of vitiating minds of the young, which is country's democratic dividend, free from such spread of negative energy.

Law should be allowed to take its own course, rather than attempting to indirectly influence the system, by continuing with media trials. Ministry of information and broadcasting and Ministry of Law need to prevail upon the media, not to indulge in ramblings, repeating the same news, since morning to evening and then against giving some twist starting the news i all over again next day.

In the new millennium, the media when it receives, some news of financial irregularity/ corruption, it needs to be content, keeping the viewer informed and then allow the investigating, agencies to investigate in the cool of their minds, in a calm manner undisturbed by the talk shows, designed on such suspected crimes. Law needs to be allowed to take its course, as objectivity of the Indian judiciary is well known globally and is also respected. Calling a few so called experts and seeking their views, in the matter, days on end, in a shouting manner, tantamount to media trial, which is harmful for those suspected and creates mistrust in other agencies such as law enforcing agencies. Judiciary is independent and its independence needs to be complied with by the media. Negative news spewed by the channel disturbs the minds of tens of millions of young minds, who are a demographic dividend and need to be encouraged by all constituencies, with positive energy including the media.

7. 4 Corruption Works not Infrequently Through the Route of Nepotism and Divisiveness

Societies that are sparred, by too much of divisiveness, are likely to have more incidences of corruption. In a particular African economy, on an average, there could be 25 to 30 tribes, which have distinct identities, with some differences in customs, in food habits, folklores and even social and religious practices. Each tribe, also tend to speak a different language, though official language is English. In many countries, which were formerly the British colonies, since the British times, the best that they could do for each other, is to confer favors, when one of them go up in political and administrative hierarchy. Though an African country is free from imperialism of a European power, but it is still shackled by divisiveness, of as many as say 30 tribes, in some countries.. They speak different languages, though there are no distinct scripts of those spoken languages. It is the sheer existence of these divisive characters that create centrifugal tendencies and each tribe is happy to serve his tribe group or his tribe people. Thus in contracts for works, many a times, favors are conferred and for conferring undue favors, informally corruption goes on, within the tribes if a member of a tribe, holds a concession dispensing position..

Even in US, the economy is sparred by multiple divisions. In addition to divisions, there is also burden of history, in which the blacks have a lot of sad memories, of how white American southerners, had treated their ancestors, who were slaves and worked on their farms. These African slaves were captured, from West Africa and then sold in America. American southern whites also traded these slaves, putting the slaves in auction. All of these weird memories, naturally would ache their minds and some of them could be indifferent to other enslaving groups. Despite living together for 400 years in America, the whites and the blacks, still live in segmented neighborhoods in USA, probably go to different markets to shop and their children go to different schools. Similarly, whole lot of illegal Latinos that have come from Mexico, at a very high rate of about 1 million a year, for the last almost 15 years, are generally confined in their own ghettoes. Whites also want to stay afar, from neighborhoods, where the Latinos reside. In some states, they are treated all right, while in other states, the compartmentalization is intense. With such divisions, it is quite understandable that nepotism would go on, when recruitments have to be done, or a work contract has to be entrusted. The race of the officials could matter and favors in some cases are likely to occur and corruption would be a reality. However, in the USA, those who are at the bottom of the economic pyramid, like all lucrative benefits such as a good pay, severance package, long term benefits are all denied to them. In the similar vein, flow of bribes too, are strictly regulated, for those lying in the base of the pyramid. Corruption thus in America, is autocratic and highly centralized and is mostly in big financial deals. One notices this from prosecution and conviction of mostly, top officials and politicians, who are in the news, but very rarely, a person at the middle or lower level, would be caught indulging, in corruption. The department, where public interface is high, regulation is very strict and question of someone favoring ordinary citizens, taking small bribes is not found to be seen. Thus the corruption in the developed world, is neither visible nor does it affect, the member of general public. It is not democratic. While the top officials could indulge in financial accounting reporting irregularities that may impact life time savings of ordinary Americans, but such people usually belong to very high echelon of society and are often pampered. Only when the volume of corruption becomes too high, with systemic impact on the economy, they lose their jobs and civil cases are initiated against them for heavy financial fines. In some cases, prosecution also comes about, with conviction of a jail sentence running in decades. In America, the convictions in large financial irregularities result in very long sentences, unlike in other developed world economies. But numbers are not high, for a country of 50 states.

A lot of the favor conferring activities, in the developed world, is camouflaged by institutionalizing pursuance with the government and the law makers, either for an executive decision or legislative decision. Special interests freely operate, through their lobbying firms, that pay taxes and openly charge the firms heavily, to liaison with the law makers and government. Lobbyists as an institution, is as old in America as 1920s and there are very rich lobbyists firms that have a lot of clout, in the Capitol Hill, in Washington.

Chapter 8

Poverty Caused by the Divides

Poverty results from a kind of discrimination, by those who are endowed with tangible and intangible assets. Tangible assets could be the farm lands, the factories and the like, where as the intangible assets could include knowledge, educational qualifications, professional experience and the like. Poverty also emanates from the lack of confidence, in one's life, to organize matters related to life. Weight of wealth of some people, who go very wealthy, with the leverage of their assets, are so high, over the poor that it denies the poor, to come up in life. It has been documented in the global research that when the inclusiveness to the poor goes up, poverty in the economy goes down. Similarly, when the divisiveness, in an economy, goes up, poverty and inequality, also go up. Hence those, interested in abolition or reduction in poverty, need to increase the inclusiveness, by ensuring that the dimensions and levels of divisiveness are reduced or abolished.

8.1 Neglect of Human Capital and Poverty :Caste Based Poverty

The concept of caste system in India, is associated with poverty. Caste system though has its own utilitarian values, to make the Indian village like a republic, not dependent, for its existence, on other geographical areas. Society, having been categorized into castes, makes the artisan/ professional talents, to flow from generation to generation, with artisan skills, getting refined over generations. With geographical mobility, among villages and towns, remaining static over time, the Indian villages have had always the advantages, of being self-sufficient, in so far as leading life is concerned. A village would normally have, the presence of a washer man, fisherman, potter, blacksmith, goldsmith, carpenter and those given to sheep rearing, livestock rearing, poultry, and agricultural labor. India's self-sufficient village model, has been unique in the world, in possessing such wide varieties, of professional / artisan talents.

In the midst of these phases of quintessential Indian villages, where about 60% of India lives, there remains the hardship especially for those, belonging to labor castes. The labor castes, in this caste system, lacks the economic mobility, people practicing one profession did not move to another profession. The wage levels among different trade / artisan / professional groups that coincide with particular castes get decided, from an age old tradition, of how importantly, a particular trade / artisan / professional has been viewed, in the perception of the village society. In the absence of geographical mobility, there has also been near absence of the wage competition. Hence the wage cannot be determined, by the intersection of supply and demand, occurring for particular trade / artisan / profession. This economic arrangement could lead to monopolistic configuration. When people belonging to one profession, cannot move to another profession, where the wages could be higher, within the village, one cannot raise the wage level simply by changing profession. Further, the society supports, people to remain in the same village.. The village custom for an artisan, to serve people, in one's own village, as artisan comes in the way of the operation of the market conditions. This relative economic hierarchy, might have unfortunately continued for centuries. In other words, the relative poverty of a family, is difficult to remove, in this otherwise self-sufficient, socially utilitarian economic structure, in India's village economy. Though with flux of time, the absolute wages of different professions/trades tend to move up.

Those in higher socio-economic positions, in the village caste structure, carry some concomitant petty advantages of village influence To this category belong the social groups, such as the learned, the businessman or the farmer. In terms of prosperity, they would be very marginally better off, nothing to rave about. The discriminatory features of the caste system, have been abolished, with adoption of the constitution in 1950. The segregation of the labor castes neighborhood, in a village has been legally abolished.

In the context of ideas, regarding the abolition of discriminatory features of the caste system, a clarion call was given by Mahatma Gandhi. He appealed to people, to be nice and kind to the poor and not to discriminate against the labor castes. Mr. Gandhi's move, carried the potential of egalitarianism in future India. It could release the economic opportunities, for all Indians, irrespective of one's caste affiliation, in society. It was a recipe for development of human capital, in a big way. Since the 1990s, the millennium development goals for the nations came about. Mahatma Gandhi's overarching influence on country's governance, came about, purely out of reverence, for him, in his life time and later. All the political parties respected Mahatma Gandhi's ideas

Young officers / professionals took upon themselves, as a raging fashion, to take up the cause of the poor. Not in frequently, the affluent social groups were chided, on complaints from the labor castes, if they had ill-treated the poor, driven by their ego / arrogance. Law being, on the side of the poor and the young administration, imbued with the spirit of poverty reduction and welfare of the poor, the upper castes, especially, in socially conservative villages, were heavily challenged. The affluent, if faulted, could go to jail, being humiliated in public by authorities. The pro poor moves, by the Government authorities, became a norm in India.

In effervescent, democratic environment of India, the poor not only vote, but they are pampered, all through the elected Government's tenure. They are also protected, from being wronged by the rich. The Media, in India, in the last decade, has got into the habit of picking up 6 negative cases, where people may have been unhappy with the government, and discuss it, add infinitum, though remaining 6 million families, would be happy with the government. Thus incessant criticism of the government, goes on, based on such statistically insignificant number of incidents.

Misinformation about the welfare schemes of India, could do a lot of harm, to running a democratic governance. Towards this end, the current private media in India, has not been responsible. Self-restraint by the media, is at its lowest ebb, in the new millennium. Self-regulating body, is mostly in slumber. Lack of knowledge of how self-regulation by media, is exercised, in the developed world, the governmental authorities in India, strangely looks the other way, even when the media gives a blurred Indian picture for the viewers. The negativism of the media, irresponsibly, has been causing huge bottleneck, to poverty reduction programs. Media's negative stories, are depicted, with lot of slight, for the professionals. Those, who professionally work, with the base of the economic pyramid, to make them move up in life, could get heavily demoralized, with such media irresponsibility. Denting the image of many of the country's institutions and slighting the government, as a pastime, often the media organizes the talk shows. In these shows, the participant specialists are used, to pass sweeping judgments on the country. Many of these delegates, to the talk show, may be knowledgeable, in general, but unfortunately could be wanting in the interface experience, with the poor These talk show delegates, more often than not, carry little exposure to the rural scenario and they are mostly arm chair, tearjerkers, for the poor. They might have not visited villages and they might not have interacted, with the poor people. They seem to be knowing little, about the transition, in the quality of life and heightening confidence levels, of the base of the economic pyramid. Most of those running, the talk shows, probably went to school, in non-motorized transport, had probably one electric fan for several family members, like anybody else of that generation. They do not seem to realize the progress they have themselves made, in their quality of life, courtesy progress of the nation. They probably move in air conditioned cars, live in homes, with multiple air conditioners, multiple Plasma TVs, multiple computers (desk tops / lap tops), wear fashionable clothes and probably party on weekends. They seem to take credit themselves for all of these plusses in the lives, which is far from the truth and appear very stingy to give credit to exogenous environment, in the nation and to its governance by the politicians. They erroneously take the credits, for themselves. They forget that it is the political / economic / social / administrative / corporate environments, which have coalesced, to make all of this economic progress in India. Many of such arrogant people, with such swollen heads, keep incessantly talking, through their falsehoods and heavily jaundiced opinions. They tend to confuse the young, the demographic dividend, who are yet to land jobs, after acquiring high qualifications, relative to the critics of the talk shows. Such a negative trend of the media, is highly unfortunate and it is fraught with negative consequences, for the national economy.

If the media in India, is not regulated, at least, in moderation, the media, could toboggan the economy, to doldrums. The media needs to be appropriately guided, to play a positive role, and not to play a supercilious role, treading territories of other democratic institutions.

To give 24/7 time to the electronic media, has been erroneous. In a country, of a low per capita income, like India. Each development player has to fastidiously address responsibilities and duties, to make events happen, to accentuate economic growth with emphasis on poor. Diverting a busy nation to entertainment and criticisms of the media, on a 24/7 basis, is a folly, which is now hard, to rectify. It is too much of a responsibility, for the media, to fill up time, with its programs. Redundancy repetitions, frivolities are bound to arise, when an institution functions ceaselessly. A rich nation probably could afford to watch more media. But for a poor nation., like, India media, exposure of 3 to 4 hours a day, should more than suffice, for the adults. The media in India need to remain objective, but not celebrate and magnify negative country events, as it has been doing for years now, in the new millennium..

Mahatma Gandhi's quote in "Gandhi CE" by Mr. Alan Axelrod, is worth reflection "Two brothers quarrel, one of them repents and reawakens the love that was lying dormant in him, The two again begin to live in peace: Nobody takes any note of this. However, if the two instead, fall to shooting at one another, their doings would be immediately noticed in the press."

Mahatma Gandhi also said, "Hundreds of Nations live in peace. History does not and cannot take note of this fact." "Truth force social-force was responsible, for dissolving the little quarrels of millions of families, in their daily lives" as well as the peaceful existence of

Mahatma Gandhi knew that preaching to abolish the caste system, which was practiced for centuries, would not overnight make caste system, wither away. India being an ancient system, of multiple millenniums, understandably, takes time to change, unlike economies that may have been in existence ranging from 150 years to 1000 years. To introduce a dynamic, in the thinking in the villages, about the negatives of the caste system, instead of out rightly rejecting it, probably Mr. Gandhi thought it prudent, to attack effectively the segregation part of the caste system only. Mr. Gandhi asked people to only, view caste system as four Varnas, instead of myriads of castes, in which even each caste groups, had come to be divided, over a long period of time. Mahatma Gandhi's thoughts brought about positive change' in regard to caste system reducing its divisiveness substantially. In Andhra Pradesh, a province of India, 2 social groups of scheduled castes Malas and Madigas are socially distinctly divided. Among the tribes similarly Lambadas, Koyas, Kondadoras, Jaataapus and Savaraas are socially distinctly divided. It is in this light, Mr. Gandhi's acceptance Chaturvarna system of caste may have to be, viewed, as an alternative, a harmless alternative, with no overt hierarchical ideas, major areas of life's responsibilities were ensconced in 4 major castes. The quote of Mr. Gandhi in this regard is as follows.

"The most effective, quickest and the most unobtrusive way to destroy caste, is for reformers to begin the practice with themselves and where necessary, take the consequences of social boycott. The reform will not come by reviling the orthodox." "Caste has to go"

Harijan, November, 16, 1935.

Mahatma Gandhi was opposed to the idea of segregating the labor castes. In the Sabarmati Ashram, Mr. Gandhi had given employment, to a person of labor caste, who had important duties. Mr. Nehru India's first Prime Minister, who served India, as Prime Minster fro 17 years, with a pro poor policies He is known to very inclusive to people of all castes. In his paternal house, a mansion in Allahabad, known as Amanda Bhawan, where a lot of meetings during the freedom movement form the British were held and attended by the national leaders hailing from different parts of the country had many domestic help from the labor castes including those who addressed home management responsibilities such as laundry, cleaning, gardening and even worked as cook. Mr. Nehru's personal and favorite attendant was a person name Hari from labour caste, who accompanied Nehru on his travels throughout India.

Under the leadership, of those, who led the national movement, the antiquated the segregation and nepotism part of the caste system, came to be removed and that is one of the reasons, why India could come up so fast, when it shed the social distinctions and punished those, who wanted to perpetuate them, by way of mandatory punishment, under the Protection of Civil Rights Act. Constitution contained abolition of any expression of segregation of the labor castes, as soon as India, became independent. Strangely the US constitution, kept the slavery intact, without interfering with it, in the provisions of its constitution and only after about 90 years, of America's independence, my Abraham Lincoln, the humane and kind President of US, abolished slavery in 1863.

But for Mahatma Gandhi's proactive, pro-poor stance and repeated pronouncements, against the negative aspects, of the caste system and bringing about this revolutionary change, giving a simple Chaturvarna, alternative caste system, probably poverty would have continued, to be imprisoned, in certain labor castes, more virulently, for many more decades, to come, In that case, the democracy of India, would have probably remained far less engaged and effervescent. Today, with effective participation of the poor, in India's democracy, democracy is highly engaged and effervescent, unlike the scenario, obtaining in many developed countries, despite their democracies, being older, compared to India, by few centuries. Mahatma Gandhi's avoidance of criticism of obscurantist forces, which would have incited to perpetrate caste system, deserves appreciation. Mahatma Gandhi has taken steps, to accelerate the growth of human capital, by fighting against racism in South Africa, as early as in 1894. The democratic freedom of the blacks came exactly, in 100 years ending the white apartheid rule in South Africa. The year 1994 witnessed the first democratic elections in South Africa and the democratic race blind Government was installed in an inclusive manner, with Mr. Nelson Mandela, as the President of South Africa.

Self-confidence of those, belonging to labor castes, exacerbated and gradually increased, over time,. Thus arose increased economic interaction, in the Indian Society. Top down measures were successful. Social / Economic, distinctions among castes, decreased over the decades. Significant number of people, from labor castes, transcended socio-economic boundaries, to reach heights, in politics, education, profession. The National Parliament, came to be highly sensitized and aware, about the need to be increasingly inclusive, of the labor castes. Some laws were stringent, providing mandatory punishments, for exploiting poverty of people from labor castes. The public policy formulation, came to be pro poor and anti-caste, not without subsidies to people from labor castes. The bureaucracy addressed poverty reduction programs, with dedication and inclusiveness towards labor castes, closely working with politicians, sensitizing the latter, the advantages of an economically integrated social system, in the rural areas. Working with poor, working to reduce negative aspects of socially divisive caste system, became a fashion in India, with administration and politics, priding in humane aspects, of multi-millennium Indian culture.

All the above pro poor, anti-caste moves came from constant appeals by Mr. Gandhi at numerous forums, asking people, to move away from hierarchical social system that inhibits economic growth and impedes, a whole lot of people, for no fault of theirs, to move up in socio-economic leader. Mr. Gandhi, popular with the peasantry and the masses, made masses feel self-confident. They came to realize that in the years to come, they would see ever expanding economic opportunities, for those, who would like to move away from their traditional professions. Suppression of those, belonging to labor castes, in whichever provinces, if existed came, to get whittled down. The poor from labor castes, encouraged by Mr. Gandhi's attitude to caste system, came to question the economic discrimination, and it reared its heads. Those in upper echelons, did not find the change, very challenging. with the respect, Mr. Gandhi commanded among all cross sections of Indian Society, be it landlords in rural India, industrialists in urban India, professionals, and the approach that Mahatma Gandhi, had with British Government, with his representative style of National Movement, for self-rule of India by the Indians, people belonging to relatively affluent castes including asset owners, accepted the social change, of gradually demolishing, inter caste economic barriers.

Some of the quotes of Mahatma Gandhi are worth mentioning here:. "One does not become a Brahmin by calling Brahmin. Not until a man reveals in his life the attributes of a Brahmin can he deserve that name." "Harijan Bandhu, September 23, 1934.

"All honor, credibility and authority flow from the words and deeds one produce one day after another." Alan Axelrod in his book, Gandhi, CEO.

8.2 Acceptance of Caste Dynamic in Villages and Towns

Wide varieties of occupations, came to be opened to labor caste members, since the 1940s, such as electricians, plumbers, auto mechanics, factory workers, construction workers, floor tile workers, brick layers, roof layers, window grill makers, carpenters, blacksmiths auto drivers, vegetable vendors, fruit vendors, mobile eatery owners, security personnel in shops, establishments, factories, bus drivers, track drivers, in addition to traditional occupations. Executives in Corporations, banks, Insurance Companies, Government came to be drawn from labor castes. Lawyers, taking up cases of injustice constituted another profession, which members of labor castes, took up to represent the cases of the poor.

Those who continued their arrogance, in the treatment of the poor, from labor castes, in some villages, in some provinces of India, due to the feudal social environment, faced boycott by labor, in agricultural operations. Some faced rebellious attitude of the labor, including filing of complaints about discrimination against them, capable of attracting mandatory jail sentence, if the offence was proved. In these villages, there were 2 way regulation, one formal regulation by the Government and another informal regulation on the arrogance of the rich, by bottom up rebellious attitude, towards exploiting landlords. The result was gradual disappearance of the arrogance of the landed gentry and dilution of the walls, between castes. There emerged, in the last few decades, more inclusive village environment, unleashing fine development of human capital. If India is making waves and is viewed by international community, to be one of the top economic players, in the world, it would be, in no small measure, would be due to the rise of poor. They came on board, in the mainstream of development, including a lot of self employment and small time entrepreneurships. The credit to spur this enormous enthusiasm, among the poor, goes to the sage, who with an open heart strived hard, to ameliorate the conditions of the poor, not only in India, but in his 20s, in South Africa also, where he said woes of the poor arose because they were, perpetrated, by the racism of the unjust, discriminatory ultra selfish white regime of South Africa. While majority self rule started in India in 1947, majority self rule started in South Africa, in 1994. That was the heightened level of indifference, to the cause of justice and the poor in South Africa, as against effervescent role of the poor, since the 1910s when Mahatma Gandhi, led the movement for self rule and in 1947 India achieved self rule.

Education, Entrepreneurship, Engagement in democracy, Egalitarianism by the Government and Equality in Law, made happiness of the poor happen, with reduction of poverty in India, in the first 60 years of modern self rule in India, after the British left India granting India, political independence.

Discrimination against the labor castes was feared and to provide protection against discrimination, Government at each level of administrative hierarchy, reserved certain posts for scheduled castes and scheduled tribes and promotion in accordance with the rules were reviewed by legislative and parliamentary committees. Forward castes executives paid a price, for the discriminatory practices practiced, by their ancestors, in the past.

8.3 Why Blacks in America are Poor?

Blacks are unfortunately excluded, from the suburbs, where a lot of economic activities take place. Unlike in Asia, in America each suburb is a hub of entrepreneurial activities that generate employment. Further a lot of retailing chains, have numerous franchises and branches in the suburbs. A lot of universities and research centers are also located in the suburbs. The density of commercial banks, mortgage lenders, realtors, insurance firms have their branches that dot the US suburbs. From all of these economic activities, the blacks are excluded, by conditions of lack of public transportation facilities. A lot of the blacks do not own personalized vehicles and those, who own find commuting to other suburbs costly.

Their living in inner cities, excludes them, from the jobs that arise in other suburbs. They only have access to the jobs, available in the downtown, mostly retailing jobs, for which there is competition, from other minorities and also from the whites. The inner city suburbs, over the decades, have been hollowed out of economic activities, creating a drought of jobs, for the blacks. The blacks were given to working in manufacturing jobs and with the exodus of manufacturing, to foreign locations, millions of blacks lost jobs. Offshoring of jobs, hurt a whole lot of Americans and the blacks suffered more. All of the employment of the main industry and all of the allied industries, evaporated overnight in the 1980s, with readiness of the Chinese, to work in these manufacturing plants. The Chinese labor was found to be disciplined, being in centralized rule in China and their learning curve was also high. The cost of living in China, being low and their paradigm being, simplicity of life, they were prepared to work, for relatively low wages and the US based business owners, driven by more money greed, preferred to relocate, the manufacturing plants. The US government obsessed with the ideology of globalization, looked the other way. Frustration of joblessness, usually carries the potential of getting converted into higher incidence of crimes, in the medium term. However, the US Government probably did not think about it, because of the euphoria of interfacing, with a foreign country. In a big way, the MNCs, seeing the prospects, of earning quick higher profits and consequent prospects of raising share prices, went ahead to relocate the American plants to the

Chinese locations. An atmosphere of gloom and despair descended, on the American manufacturing locations. In the past, it used to buzz with life, when the goods were made. The American pride and prosperity, both were lost to the Americans, of these manufacturing cities. Since the American democracy, did not have the characteristics of European demonstrations and to be sensitized, on national issues, taking out demonstrations, there was little noise. Each one for himself paradigm also did not make other States and pockets to think about this issue, as national and in their perception as only in few cities such jobs were gone. They were unaware that for the rich, desire for money begets more avarice for money. Business owners once, they would get the taste of more worker discipline, their high learning curve and their readiness to work for far less wages, relocation of businesses could expand, in areas, other than manufacturing, in decades to come. The whites also were benign, in their reactions, as moving the manufacturing jobs, overwhelmingly hurt the blacks economically more.

In black families, the rate of divorces, appears high and that leaves children, growing in homes today, which are single mother homes. Single mothers work odd jobs and too many jobs a day and black children grow up more forlorn, neglected, and with much less discipline for studies. That leaves a lot of black children, drop out young, from the public schools.

As public school system, is funded by the local resources, the quality of public schools, in black neighborhoods, unfortunately is inferior, leading to schools being not great centers of learning. Even those, who do not drop out of schools and complete high schools, find life challenging, when it comes to securing jobs, in terms of their inferior education. Higher education is out of bounds, for most black young and it is very expensive. Lack of role models; stem the ambition of the black young, to rise in life, unlike the white young.

The stereotyping of blacks to be tough basketball players and singers confine their focus for the future, to becoming either singers or sports persons that excludes them from many other high paying serious professions. Michael Jordan and Michael Jackson are their national icons that plummets their emphasis, to pay attention to other nice careers. The burden of history and even today media talking, about some blacks, as children whose ancestors were slaves in America, creates in them, a lack of self-confidence and with decimated self-confidence, for a population of tens of millions, to see sunshine, becomes challenging.

Social discrimination continues, though to a much smaller decade than the 1950s, 1960s, making them feel alienated and suffering from another bout of the lack of confidence, in their landing good jobs. A lot of talk also goes on that the blacks could be more serious in profession and studies and that their laziness, comes in the way of their progress. Such talks mostly come from conservatives and ultra conservative whites in America. Such negative talks about them also dents their confidence levels.

Lot of drug related crimes and petty crimes, involvement of the young blacks, get them incarcerated, which becomes a life time stigma, to improve their lives. A lot of safety net schemes, such as project housing and child allowances are drivers of decline, in moral hygiene that comes in the way of neat economic and social progress and mobility. Black continent's blighted poverty and its discussions, in the international forums about their poverty, hunger, malnutrition and corruption, probably make the blacks feel sad that it is this backward continent, from where originally they came to USA. It certainly makes one feel not nice that one belongs originally to a place which is a backward continent in terms of economic development, with little chance of an immediate sunshine, even in the medium term.

Negative talks by the realtors, against crime infested and lack of safety of the black neighborhoods, particularly have taken away the opportunities of making profits, on sale of properties, by the blacks, who own more than one house. A general impression has come to prevail, about the black neighborhoods that the blacks cannot be trusted. A lot of rich whites, would prefer Latinos, to address their home management responsibilities, such as home cleaning, laundry garage etc and even cooking, rather than recruiting the blacks, as personal attendants. Thus personal attendants job, is also one area of money making, from where the blacks unfortunately, in modern times, have been excluded.

In restaurants also, some of the jobs for the blacks, have been taken away, by the Latino illegal immigrants, as they do not mind, being paid a song. In big commercial places, food courts etc., the janitor jobs have been taken away, whenever there have been influx of immigration from either Latin American or Eastern Europe, after 1991. Dissolution of marriages have turned most black families, into single mother homes and that has challenged the blacks financially, more than, the communities, where the divorce rates has been lower.

Poverty over time, among the blacks have consolidated and lack of self-employment, entrepreneurship and education among the blacks, are making them, perennially face challenges, thought their ancestors have been living in America, in some cases, for over 400 years.

It is also an irony that those blacks, who rise economically, maintain a distance with the average blacks, out of selfishness, to be in the good books of the majority and may even identify a white spouse to marry. That further dilutes them, to be role models for the upcoming blacks. Mr. Gandhi maintained a few times that if the British are to be blamed, to maintain

India as a colony, the Indians are also are to be blamed, for accepting the British rule. If the Indians would have refused, to accept the British rule, then the British rule would have ended long back.

The same can probably be said, about big drug cartel businesses, making the poor young blacks, selling drugs in their neighborhoods, at the retail level. If a Gandhian philosophy driven movement, could be started, to cover large number of black neighborhoods, to motivate the young, to pay attention to the studies instead of effusing the request of the big drug cartel businesses, to sell retail drugs, then this exploitation of the young blacks, by the big drug business cartels, if the allegation is true, can be substantially contained and there could start, an emulation of such good deeds of the black young. They could be motivated to shun selling of drugs. The memory of Gandhi, whom Dr Luther king adored, in the black neighborhoods, could make a world of difference. Even installation of the a bust of Gandhi statues, in the black neighborhoods, could remind the young of his message," if you do not accept exploitation by others, with a sense of self-respect then no person can exploit you to see you fall into woes. Then you will see sunshine in your life."

The denial of freedom from slavery and the concomitant harassments, besides making the blacks work, so severely on the farms in south of USA have probably scarred their minds, as a community. The stories of those harassments have been unfortunately kept alive, as story telling has gone on in the black community. With the older generations, telling the young, how beastly the exploiters could be. Then came the freedom from slavery, allowing the blacks to move northwards, to see some sunshine. But the life was not without challenges economically, as they had to be trained to get jobs, in the factories and they had to slog in factory tough conditions, at a time when environmental and safety standards of industries, were far from being as good, as it is today. However the fact, that they were not slaves, made a nice beginning for them. However, no appeal existed for any wrongs done to them, as they were still to get voting rights and in many parts, there still existed several dimensions of racial discrimination, from denial of admission to schools for education, denial of travelling by school buses, denial of travelling by public city buses, to give way to the white moving away from his passage on the side walk and denial of using rest rooms that were exclusively meant for the whites and also denial of drinking water from drinking water taps that were only meant for the whites. Density of restrooms meant for the blacks and drinking water fountains were very limited, making them indirectly to suffer, even with thirst of water and lack of places, to respond to the nature's calls. Having faced such discriminations, even until the 1960s, when even the

European colonial governments, were liberating their colonies, by granting them political independence, expecting them, in large numbers to take up higher education, self-employment and compete to join big corporations, as technocrats and managers, appears too farfetched. It makes a world of difference to feel despair and agony, when a population is given denial of so many of these normal public goods and even a right to go to a public representative for grievances. All of these sufferings happened, despite their ancestors, having slogged in the country, for centuries and for indirectly helping, in the high GDP formation, through professional, hard work, at very low wages. In 1965, came the voting rights, for the blacks, after a prolonged fight for political freedom, for the blacks waged by Dr Martin Luther King. All of these stories and their negative impact, at the family level is transmitted at the kitchen tables, by the elders, which has the potential of societal divisiveness, thought at the employment place. The inclusiveness has arrived, with government's efforts on a regular basis and due to their affirmative action. All of these layers of negative experiences, that the blacks faced in their own country, where they have been living for centuries and where their ancestors were born and lived, where they helped the nation, add to the GDP of the nation, for years on end, hurt them. A lot of their self-confidence, plummeted besides diluting their trust in the institutions and organizations, because they expected fair treatment, in admissions and employment. Strangely, even in multi racially populated universities, one finds even in classrooms and cafeterias, the black students, clustering together, with an air of indifference, by the mainstream population. Even some restaurants in big cities, like Chicago have informally allocated among themselves dining time for the backs and the whites, descending there on racial basis, in two distinct windows of time, the blacks earlier and then he whites.

8.4 Fragmentation of Public Schools and Black Poverty

US educational landscape, at the primary level, suffers from a significant fragmentation.. Some public schools could have, excellent infrastructure and others could suffer, from want of it. Some schools could have excellent lab facilities and others may have no labs. Some may be maintained, with annual repairs and in others repairs may be an exception once in 6 years. In some public schools, the teacher posts are all filled up and in others, there may be 30 to 40 percent teacher vacancies. In many schools, the teacher quality may be of a high order, as the school can afford to pay high compensation of the order of 80,000 to 90,000 dollars a year, whereas there would be public schools, where the teachers would not be up to the mark, as the schools can afford to pay low compensation varying from 25,000 to 40,0000 dollars. Especially in science and math education, there is wide difference between the rich neighborhood schools and the poor neighborhood schools, in the quality of teachers.

It's one thing to have standard deviation, in the quality of school infrastructure, and another thing to have standard deviation in teacher's standards, different in different schools, in the country. Further, the students hailing from the rich families, enjoy the advantage of living in high end neighborhoods and going to far better academically endowed public schools, than the poor, from the inner city neighborhood, going to separate inner city schools with low teaching standards.

US public school rules provide that only neighborhood children, could go to neighborhood school, which is exclusively funded, by the city administration, with local funds. Hence as better taxes are collected, from the rich residents in high end neighborhoods, their children tend to go to the best schools. Whereas poor people stay and pay less taxes, their children go to the poor infrastructure ridden, funds starved public schools, where education imparted is a way is inferior, to the standard of education, in the schools of the rich neighborhoods.

Despite being democracy, it is a huge divide that is perpetrated, generation after generation, for several decades, wherever rich children right from childhood have a huge edge of better learning, compared to the challenges of learning, in the inferior schools, with poor teaching standards. It is an anomaly, raising a big question, how would the rich and the poor learning gap reduce or bridge. How would there be social economic mobility, in American democracy? How would the future generations, do economically better than the previous generations? Answer to all of these questions, naturally would be in the negative, because this inequality appears to be artificially perpetrated.

Another unfortunate dimension, to the outcome of this arrangement of the public schools is that a lot of the minority neighborhoods, happen to be poor and they lose the economic opportunities, to be equal citizens, to the majority whites, as a result of this primary school education dichotomy.

The solution to this problem, lies in paying the compensation, to the teachers, recruiting those teachers, for all the public schools, with high educational qualifications and the talent and paying them similar compensation, from the state budget funds, asking the city administrations, to credit the maintenance of the infrastructure. In that case, the quality infrastructure might suffer, but all schools will have similar learning opportunities. This step will probably bring about reduction in poverty, in a big way in America, if the President assumes the responsibility, to introduce these reforms in public school education, as a lot of inclusive schemes for the poor is being implemented by President Obama. India does not suffer from this fragmentation of public schools. In villages, ranging from a population of about 2,000 to 20,000 or even more, all the children hailing from rich landed gentry, small landholders and agricultural laborers, who are landless to go to the same public school and they are taught by the same teachers. They are all a part of the same infrastructure, which is no way fancy and are just utilitarian. About a decade back, in the 1990s, the infrastructure was poor and only in the last 5 to 6 years, infrastructure in Indian schools, have been spruced up. Here a semblance of democracy is writ large, with no hierarchy. The children, hailing from government high schools, are found everywhere and also hailing from all categories of economic groups, the ' rich, the middle class and the poor, to the engineering colleges to the medical schools to law colleges to liberal arts colleges to science colleges. Thereafter, they even enter high paying professions, by Indian standards.

Children hailing from some of the poor families in India today are found to top the competitive examinations, for the bank officers or even civil service officers. People from poor families, adorn the positions of Judges of even High Courts and the Supreme Court of India. Chief of the civil service or police are usually likely to be from the rich or very poor families, as it depends on the higher education pursued, which is within the bounds, equally of the rich and the poor. In filling up such high paying and responsible positions of even CEOs of the Indian firms or Indian commercial banks, neighborhood hardly matters. If there are 28 banks, at a given point of time, the CEOs would come from poor neighborhoods as well as rich neighborhoods. They are also a mosaic, coming from different states, some come from the south, some from east, some from central India and some from the west. From the last names, it is interesting to know the region that they hail from. It only reflects the ubiquity of democracy, in India and the poverty reduction that democracy brings, about, because one member of the family, holding high position, means a lot for the rest as they get moral support and tremendous inspiration to rise in life, through the permit of higher education, as American President Mr. Barak Obama calls.

Another unique labor practice in India, is for the employers to train their employees and try to retain the talent for long. The government and public sector employers, who populate India's national economy, as government plays an important role, in regard to job creation in the economy, provide to the employees a security of tenure for the entire work period and most retire after about 3 decades of working, in the organization. Taking a cue from this ennobling practice, even private firms follow this practice and attempt to keep the employees for long, giving them reasonably long, secure of tenure. The firms like Godrej, Kirloskers, Tata Consultancy Company, Larsen and Toubro, Dabar India, Bombay Dyeing, Raymond's, Shopper's Stop, Hindustan Motors, Raunak Enterprises, Oberoi Group of Hotels and the like offer jobs, with almost a lifetime tenure, though not, formally but in practice. The world of layoffs furloughs and pink slips are unknown, practiced in an inebriated manner in bizarre., in the lexicography of Indian, as well as unknown expressions even for those, who know excellent English, as these practices are unknown and would be abhorred when discussed. It should be appreciated that India's economic players generally have conducted moderation in profit making, except some exceptions in the new millennium. It is common, for a private hotel employee, say at the management level to be, in the hotel and getting promoted, from time to time, to join as a chef and gradually becoming the general manager, of the hotel, thus staying in the organization for over 2 to 3 decades. I have known the door man of the 5 star hotels, in my causal enquiries, in Hyderabad, India to have completed 16 to 18 years, a few coming from other states. Those include a Hindu doorman as well as a Muslim and a Christian doormen, in enjoying the same long security of tenure.

Those from the developed world, may look askance that even the MNCs, follow the ennobling Indian labor practices, of the Indian government, of keeping the jobs secure, for lifetime employment. Japan has this lifetime job practice, as it is in India. One would see ABB in India, keeping its manager for a lifetime and the IBM executives working in IBM, in India, for a couple of decades. I have known executives, working for a lifetime, in Unilever and ICI, which are British MNCs. Industrial democracy of India is infectious and all organizations follow it happily. It entwines the labor and management, into a fine family, like relationship to buttress and improve the organization. Trust level between these two groups, is very high, in India, unlike in USA today, where the employers enjoy stratospheric bargaining power, to be able to inflict pay cuts and furloughs, even in normal times, when there is no recession or depression.

In the Indian organizations, the labor enjoys the right' to form unions and sit on the negotiating table, while compensations of the employees, are revised upward, every 3 years. Annual raises are a routine. Bonuses are received first, by the labor and then by the managers and at same percentage level of the compensation, as a routine, whenever the firms makes a profit. Management also gives limited bonus, as an incentive to improve business also in a year, when firm has failed to make profit, despite sincere efforts. Labor involvement in decision making in India get their cooperation, when the firm faces challenges. The labor union leaders also help, when the labors unions try to disrupt work giving notice for the firm. Globalization firm mergers and acquisitions are such major decisions, where the management consults the labor.

In some of the firms, when the US practice of labor flexibility, was introduced recently in 2000s, there was near violence by the labor, though any type of violence is reprehensible. There was however immediate rollback, to treating the labor with sympathy and affability. Concern for the poor and the deprived, is indicated as a virtue, in scriptures and holy books of all religions and the best way probably, to follow religion, is to serve the humanity, with concern care and sympathy. it then envelops humans, to help each other and not be at each other's throats spreading violence. Those who are rich and super rich in America earning from their jobs, as well as from the effervescent Wall Street, they need to be far more inclusive, to prevent people from turning poor and reduce poverty. They need to offer by offering nice levels of compensation, with care, concern and sympathy. It would be possible, when like the niceties of political democracy, corporate America, would embrace industrial democracy also, with open mind, learning from the corporate experience of India, with industrial democracy. Corporate America need to remember that if India is producing numerous engineers, far more than any other country in the world, every year is able to send numerous doctors, to work in developed world hospitals, with a lot of popularity, with patients in USA, UK and other countries could follow suit which is enveloping.

If the software personnel from India, are managing the IT firms, ranging from fortune 100 companies, to fortune 500 companies, for firms of large medium and small sizes, besides city administrations and also state governments, all of these plusses are happening with security of tenure in jobs, in general as well as allowing labor unions to exist, even participate in strikes, when necessary, annual raises and bonus as routine,. India's middle class is bigger, than the total population of USA,. Probably, India's model of industrial democracy, the US private firms could experiment with and if it succeeds, then they could adopt it and consolidate it.

8.5 Poverty from Communal /Religious Divide

The divides have ruined the societies and economies, be it racial divide, educational divide, class divide, wealth divide, or income divide. The western societies, in the last centuries since they got the supremacy in the navy and in the firearms, did a lot of colonization of the countries, all over the world, by annexing them, by firearm force and then befriending the rich people in the economies/conquered territories, to collectively exploit the poor. The native industries, were not promoted. A native languages and culture were never encouraged. The superiority of the Western culture, was talked about incessantly, to make an impact, in the conquered economies, asking their people to relinquish their way of leading life and get converted to Christianity. Towards this end, even incentives for the jobs and the education were offered. Many Churches were constructed and so were the Christian schools. People were asked to abhor their own cultural practices, stating them as savage, primitive, backward and brain washing them. They were told that the western civilization was an index of advancement, in culture and values. In some colonized economies, people en-masse got this message and adopted it. In numerous countries, about 50% of people adopted western way of life, leaving the other 50% to the proselytization by other religions. Thus in a number of countries, religious divides were artificially imposed, through the process of spreading Christianity.

Such artificially divided economies have witnessed more violence, more civil wars and lack of proper governance, even dictatorships to at least keep some order, among equally divided people, based on religion and with numerous ethnicities. Most of these economies are a part of Africa and each country could have as many as 30 ethnicities, with distinct identities, ethnic pride, and distinct language though with no literature and script. While criticizing Africa for lack of education, lack of industries, lack of development, lack of prosperity, lack of professional work ethics and ubiquity of poverty, such divides, based on religion cannot be ignored, though in seminars this topic is ignored, as though ethnic/religious divides, do not create bottlenecks, to economic development.

In India too, such attempts to create divides, were made by the British, but the stolidity of ancient Hindu civilization, came in the way to maintain inclusiveness and dilute divisiveness, on the basis of religion. In the early 1940s, calling of round table conference requesting Mr. Jinnah, the leader of the Muslims, Mr. Ambedkar, leader of the labour castes, along with Mahatma Gandhi were requested to attend the round table conference was an attempt by The British government in London to balkanize India. A Communal Award was granted by the British deliberately, to balkanize India and divide the people, to weaken the freedom struggle. Since India's independence from the British rule the Christians and Muslims along with the Hindus live happily, pursuing their religion, though a minority, with their chin up, thinking themselves as much a part of the economy, as the majority Hindus feel. Secular polity and constitution keep their privileges equal, no matter which ethnicity /religion one belongs. Before the divide was created artificially by the British rule moves, since Queen

Victoria became the empress in India, India never saw any divides, based on community or religion. Indian Poet Laureate Rabindranath Tagore mentioned in this connection, "The Pathans came to India and the Mughals and they perpetrated misdeeds in their heedlessness. Gradually, they were growing one with us and just as the Normans and Saxons combined into one people. Our Mohammadan invaders would ultimately have lost their line of separateness and contributed in the richness and strength of Indian civilization."

8.6 Gender Unity Always Existed and poverty From Gender Divide, is a New 21 Century Phenomenon in India

Thus any attempt to divide people, into social segments, is reprehensible. While there have been leaders, to state that castes, do not matter and Brahmins and those belonging to labor castes are equal, in the eyes of society constitution and government and whoever tries to create schism is dealt, with as a criminal.

No leader has yet emerged, who states that there has to be no gender divide and none of the two genders, have to be pampered or deprecated, with special rights or denial of rights. Therefore one gender appears to harass the other gender, by dithering noble institution of marriage that has the negative potential, to make children suffer agony and live in utter neglect, socially interacting with gangs and drugs, neglecting their education and again repeating their parents profanity, in the next generation. As much as the technology, science and engineering could be learnt in the last several decades by Asia, from Europe and America, there appears no reason, why America and Europe cannot be modest and with humility learn noble life time marital practices of India, to gain socially and economically, to care for ther progenies and their elders, instead of sending them to day care centers and old age homes, to suffer and lead a life sandwiched by two such severe neglects, one in the beginning of life and another the finale of it.

It is not enough, to grant funds for research, to elongate life expectancy, but it is also necessary to treat old people, with care and respect, rather that forgetting them, while they stay in the old age homes. In USA a lot of loneliness they suffer from, because whole lot of the old people turn single, due to the divorce in the midstream of life that they undergo only for trifles, triggered by either of the two genders. These divorces happen so frequently and voluminously in the American and European society, that has turned in the last few decades, too tolerant of such social divisiveness, at the expense of the life of loneliness that men and women, in the western world, have to suffer, in the old age, when sharing and companionship is so important.

One need to see how in Asian marriages, old man and woman, after having lived a fine, lifetime continue to live happily, caring for each other, for eternity, until death set them apart. Even after death, the spouse, who is alive spends days, with the nice memories of her husband, appreciating her spouse, or his spouse, to acquaintances, to the grand children and to the adult children, how nice the life had been, when the spouse was alive.

A man goes asunder emotionally, when he loses his wife, by death in India and so does a woman, who loses her husband by death. Widows and widowers, living alone remembering the spouse for 60 years, are not unknown in India, living single. This is rarity, which western world can never match in today's scenario. Most people lead lives afar emotionally, though some exceptions in India cannot be ruled out.

Once divides are promoted or tolerated, a lot of injustice and agony society sees and falsehood spreads. Then the false complaints abound and more so, in a money greedy society, where money making, is considered and touted as a virtue, as in America and EU. Hence extortions to make money are on the rise.

Western obsession after the industrial revolution, led to their ascendancy and economic enrichment, though political and economic exploitation of the colonies was there that they managed to grab their political rule. They sometimes pass judgments, on the administered countries and developed western countries, collectively passing judgments on the countries they controlled politically and exploited economically, as there colonies. For some it is an intoxication and an obsession, to live in a make believe world of superiority and in the midst of their maze of hierarchical concepts. They consider themselves more rational, more literate, and more fashionable, in their dressing styles, due to variant and multiple dresses easily available to them pretty cheap relative to other shall ticket items and of course the big ticket items. It is this hierarchical thinking that smears their way of thinking, about various areas of life such as education and college university ratings school district ratings and the like. There also occurs rating of the cities on the basis of fast food courts, eateries, brand retail outlets, density of the stadiums for sports; openness to professional immigrants, tolerance to illegal Latino immigrants; crime infestation, ease of doing business etc,.

The very fact that those who have better per capita income, better per capita percentage of high school educated population, who stays in better neighborhoods and that they originally came from the developed countries, which have witnessed high per capita income, which is comparable to USA and well maintained physical infrastructure, they tend to live in their world of hierarchical superiority. Probably these thoughts make them to believe to maintain segregation and even increase them. If Wabash street in the north

Michigan Avenue road area, is moved about by the American blacks, then Water Tower area of the same Michigan Avenue area in the city of Chicago, are frequented more, by the whites with near absence of the American blacks. Hierarchical thinking is neatly witnessed, in highly fragmented nature of the schools that get maintained for almost a century with local taxes and local funds. Teachers are recruited and laid off by the city administration but they do not take instruction from a bigger city or for that matter the provincial government or even federal government. Teachers in white neighborhoods tend to invariably be whites and that of black neighborhoods black Americans. Little exchange of thought and sharing intellect is remote between teachers of the better neighborhoods and that of poorer neighborhoods. Having being brought up, in inferior schools, the possibility of being selected as executives of nice firms, remain bleak and rejections looking at the school details, is very common in America, due to long drawn racial prejudices. Thus human resource in millions, get discriminated, at multiple stages of the economy, decreasing the economic productivity of the country. Even shops are clearly demarcated as high end medium end and low end and such distinctions are hardly unleashed by corporations in Asia. Americans clearly know and discriminate buying, from inferior chain of shops, such as Marshalls and Marshall Field's, Kohl and Wal-Mart.

In the same sit down nice eateries, if suddenly the white clientele, comes to know that black non-white clientele occupy the restaurant in big groups visit and stay from 5pm to 8pm then the whites adjust their times of dinner from 8.15 pm to 10.15 pm, visiting the same restaurant though at different times. Such is the adjustment to live in a segregated manner.

Democracy of presence of all of the people, in eateries, without any discrimination is reflected, in the fast food restaurants in USA. Such inclusiveness is wanting, even in greyhound coaches, which are patronized mostly by the minorities and the blacks.

One reason probably, why India deals with divides ably, is that divides are created voluntarily or as a part of religious and social sanction for convenience of leading life nicely without frequent disequilibrium, due to shift of trades by specialized trade experts groups. If a few mason families that live in a village move to a distant location, the villagers may find challenge in regard to construction of new homes and repair of the homes, as and when they need services of masons. A few carpenter families leaving the village could challenge the village, as carpenters are needed, from time to time to keep the bullock carts functional for human and merchandize transportation intact. Removal and disposal of carcasses could be a huge challenge if those families that deal and know this item of work, leave the village as all of these professional skills are required, as per village division of labor and are not easy to be switched, by incumbent villagers, most of whom know agriculture pretty well. Basic need of these economic skills, by the multitude in the villages, makes the majority to accord good behavior and compensation affordable to be paid by the payer. In absolute terms, the payee could fix charges, based on aspiration acquisitions, in the current times, as well as to meet basic necessities of life and as an oligarchy with limited competition, not too low prices for their skills could be acceptable to them. The self-sufficiency nature of Indian villages, at a time, when the modes of public transportations, were nonexistent and privately owned transportations, were too slow, life was possible to be comfortable, when divides were to meet the skill needs of the villages and for inclusiveness in general, to humanity. Here the divisiveness in India was born out of necessity, to be comfortable at the village level and to avoid uncertainty, in the supply of skills to individual homes. The divides were also created with some sort of religious and social sanctions. However when some discriminatory elements entered the caste system that part of the caste system needed immediate reform.

8.7 Slavery Driven Divides and American Poverty

In the western developed world, particularly in America the divides were basically created, by trading slaves, in buying and selling of slaves, who belonged to a different category of people, way too poor, of far darker skin, belonging to different races, illiterate, suffering from surfeit of disadvantages, vis- a- vis the affluence and better living standards and better access to quality food. These divides were created, to recruit these poor slaves, to make them slog, without any monetary compensation, on their fields and address agriculture, for making money by those whites, who owned the lands. Cash crops were grown, for reaching the fruits of the slaves labor and any negligence in agriculture, by the slaves, could send the slave owners, to heights of anger to inflict numerous lashes. Even to this day, the poor neighborhoods are lived by those poor slaves' descendants, and many of their young due to drugs are subjected to incarceration, which make men in their neighborhoods running into short supply, for black women. About 73% of black women, per force remain unmarried. In families, where children are born they live mostly fatherless, because of the incarceration and thereafter lack of proper jobs. They tend to live in poverty, as they are raised mostly by single mothers.

In the Indian rural scene, the labor castes, who slog in agriculture, once were deprived of money and lands, which were lost to the landlords, zamindars and money lenders, during several decades of the British rule, developed as the British used to collect taxes from small farmers, through the route of landed gentry, who in turn also collected as per his whims and fancies, the revenue collection charges. During the British period, the rural India was exploited economically and poverty came gushing, in the villages. The British also never started any schools, for educating the villagers in India, concentrating their education initiatives in Calcutta and other cities only. Latent anger against the rich landlords, continued and it took many decades before these wounds, could be healed.

The education was imparted in village schools after 1947 and Indian administration motivated them, to continue their children in their education, without their being dropped out, from the schools. Further, the Indian government, in the state legislature and parliament took special steps, to ensure that given number of seats, in the parliament and the state assemblies, remained served only for the labour castes such as SCs STs BCs and the like. Each political party got into the habit in each election, to nominate the electoral candidates from those constituencies, on their behalf and the winner sat in the parliament and the state legislatures. Government similarly desired the departments, to make roasters of vacancies and the steps taken up, to fill up those vacancies, on a priority basis. In case, qualified candidates were not available, they were directed the states be carried forward and not filled up by forward castes. These aspects being checked by concerned caste welfare department's senior officials. The periodic meetings are convened, by the state legislature SC ST welfare committee and the parliamentary committee for examining the compliance of these rules. The labor castes being pretty large in number, offering jobs in private and public sector of the economy itself is quite a sensible task.

Other welfare measures, such as housing for the poor, internal roads for the poor, assignment of government lands for house sites and also for limited agriculture, income generating, economic support priority lending schemes. Government coming up with highly subsidized higher education for labor caste's children, also offer a huge help for the poorer communities in India.

8.8 India's Thin Slice of the Metros: TV Causing Social dynamics

Electronic media, if it does not conduct responsibly, it could harm the brand equity of the nation and thus make nation unpopular, in the perception of the international community.

In respect of the thin slice of the metros in India, the TV channels, through the TV serials dealing with bizarre social themes of alien stance and afar from the pristine values of Indian culture and Indian lifetime marriage system, could weaken the Indian marriage, in a thin slice of the metros. It could spur marriage break ups and it could destroy the familial cooperation, which is unique only in India, to achieve economy of scale, division of labor less fatigue from home work, more security for children, above all less debt, more savings and the guidance of the council of elders, with lot of wisdom.

In a thin slice of the metros, in India, who are educated and have jobs and a career, like the western women, interest in getting married on time, is on the wane. They are confused at what age, should they be identifying a spouse, to get married, Interest in marriage for them, has been visibly dwindling. Riveted to watch TV's private channel serials, dealing with family drama, their attitude to getting married, is all the more, on the decline. Mindlessly some of the TV channels, have been making TV Serials, on themes that exhibit crimes, within the family, the likes of which would be probably one in 40 millions in reality, but carries the potential, to disturb the young women, generating an antipathy, towards the institution of marriage. In these TV serials, the mother in law is shown to scheme against daughter in law to cause her agony. TV serial producers mindlessly, in the new millennium add these sauces, to make the serial popular. They make the serials interesting, in the negative sense of the term. Any amount of counseling by parents, who raised them, from infancy, is failing to convince some of these girls, in favor of marriage, explaining to them that the TV channels to make money depict, such bizarre themes in relationships inappropriately.

On the other hand, men are also losing interest, in the same vein, in the institution of marriage and looking for girls for matrimony, when they come of age. They are influenced by watching TV serials, in which TV channels depict highly cantankerous young girls, who are too demanding after marriage. They act rebelliously, in matters of dressing, in contravention of the Indian culture. They kind of take sadistic delight, to insult in some ways, the husband's parents, instead of being nice to the new home. In addition, the. men have been losing interest, in marriage, when they see TV serials, in which false cases are filed against the husband, his parents and extended family, for no fault of theirs, by an unscrupulous wife, driven by money greed, for extortion of huge quantum of money, running into tens millions of rupees. Through the route of the TV, the entertainment industry and some related industries, they are aping the moves of the western corporations. The TV serials, some of them mindlessly made, they are in conjunction with the captive media is out to destroy the institution of marriage by, frightening young girls and boys to lose interest in marriage which would mean, for them, a lot of business to benefit the corporations. Left to themselves like corporate America they would like numerous singles, dotting the society disturbing them through programs, to be afar from marriages so that their businesses, more than double in top line as well as bottom line. One wishes the government, in the Information Ministry Culture Ministry Home Ministry and the PMO would conjointly guide the media, to be only a mild entertainer in a poor country like India and not a destroyer of moral hygiene and multi millennium pristine institution of marriage that have received value, form this society for over 10,000 years. Such social assets cannot be sacrificed to satiate the money greed of the India and coronations in India.

As singles, as their financial decisions are more afar for being responsible away from savings more in favor of frivolity of eating out. Such serials would cost moral hygiene and may take a heavy toll on institution of marriage, which multimillion culture of India values, so much.. Too many serials, based on belligerences between the man and his wife, is creating a real mistrust between the genders, in a thin slice of the metros, who are naive to believe what mindlessly the TV shows, unlike most of India where the young men and woman know, that these serials are all artificial as made on the TV for entertaining people. They know how to compartmentalize real life from TV serials, as all of the Indians addressed the themes of films for over 50 years now. They knew for half a century that that film is a film is a film and has nothing to do with social reality of the Indians.

Thus in the metros, in a thin slice of society of the young, unfortunately. a general mistrust is arising on the lines of the west between genders, which never existed in India. Gender divide concept, even in 1990s, was alien to the India and this expression was never in the lexicography of the news media, or in the books or in any literature. Today this expression is casually expressed in the media and incessantly media, is trying to make this artificially, by showing TV serials, dealing with gender divides. Women to earn some acting money, are asked to spew venom in society, talking derisively about men, accusing them of falsehoods, generalizing isolated incidents of insignificant proportions.

8.9 TV Promoting Gender Divide in India, Working with Bizarre Laws, Urban Misuse

No gender divide, existed in India and manufacturing them, on the western lines and legislating is erroneous. Illiteracy in India and denial of access, to formal education, were always gender blind, during the entire rule of the British. Farm work such as cow cleaning work, cow mulching work, storing the seeds and the grains, broadcasting of seeds, ploughing the lands, spraying pesticides, applying fertilizer to the soils, bathing the animals taking them for grazing and returning with cows in the evening, after the dusk by men and the cooking of the meals, offering food and offering drinking water to animals, were indistinguishable duties of human life. None could categorize the duties, as sophisticated and unsophisticated jobs and the concept of chores never arose.

Feminism, in the west, in Europe and America, screamed in the 1960s, treating comfortably staying at home and supervising the workers who cleans the place and cooks a meal as inferior or making meals for family, as inferior. However, going to the office, working with type machine, pen as superior, has been so erroneous. One fails to understand how punctually getting ready in the morning every day, leaving home and take a public transportation, rubbing shoulders with other office goers and then bossed by the boss addressing some office work, with pen and paper and finally coming back in public transportation, only after the office left him, to be a superior job, hierarchically more important. In the new millennium, some scholars have come up, with the theory that corporate America to drive the wages of employees down and to usurp bargaining power, to stop its benefits, propped up the feminists to agitate for more employment of women. The object according to these scholars, was to burgeon the supply of labor, in the market, so that more work output from the family, could be sought reducing their compensation.

This law has significantly frightened men, to get married as the earlier trust, in women looking at few such cases, has heavily challenged them. In India, from times immemorial marriage has been a noble institution and making section 498 a and exposure by the media, has almost made institution of marriage a mockery. It is spreading sorrow and indignity to some families, never known in social India. Husbands are falling into mental depression to recover after a few years, from the metal ailment. Some parents are even suffering from heart attacks, when taken to the prison. Some are even known to have died as soon as they were taken to prison for no fault of theirs., Authorities such as Indian judiciary, executive as well as law making body, need to think deeply, about the issue and act according to the great value, which India for tens of thousands of years, have attached to the institution of marriage, as an integral part of India's pristine culture. The importance of the institution of marriage, in ancient times since the time humanity existed in India, emanated from several factors, as it has noble functions which cannot be done nobly, once the institution loses its heightened value. The marriage institution entwines a man and a woman, into a lifetime companionship, taking care of the procreation of children, absolutely within the boundaries of marriage, and raising children, with morals and rectitude. It is a great index of civilization and differentiates humans from all other creatures, such as animals and treating it shabbily, could have huge negative consequences. In a society, devaluing the institution of marriage, could have disastrous consequences.

In economies, where this institution of marriage, is taken casually, a lot of poverty has shrouded children, who are living with single mothers, with little care, little education and barely the comforts that they deserve, in the near absence of both parents. A lot of them are being tossed in foster homes, from one home to another home, despite their monthly expenditure being met by the government.

Some societies are witnessing tens of millions of fatherless homes, as the institution of marriage, has been taken too casually, by extended family, community society, employers media and finally government, looking absolutely the other way.. Swami Vivekananda's addressed the Parliament of Religions, in 1886 in Chicago, USA and his message emphasized, the need to appreciate the spirituality of India. He wanted about a thousand Indian educated youth, from the universities, to propagate India's nobility and values to the world, as India, since times immemorial, has been a land of spirituality. A link between social issues and economic issues, some scholars fail to appreciate. Through this weird legislation 498a, with slavishness to the West, some pressure groups are intending to get to a thin slice of the metros of India, precipitous social decline, destruction of the institution of marriage and encouragement of divorces through the back door.

While GDP of India, is galloping, a lot of economies that have adopted this pernicious practice of gender divide, to their detriment and are unable to deal with poverty, caused by it, are feeling the envy that in India divorces are less than 1%, when the countries that have GDP proximate to India, such as the USA and some countries of the EU, are suffering from this social ailment of frequent talks of gender divide and runaway divorce rates, exceeding 50 %. US has a divorce rate of 59% and about 40 % of people in USA, who are in marriageable age, from 20s to 80s, are only married and the rest 60% live as singles. They would naturally, not like India to have such a huge economic scale advantage, in the social realm. An idea can be had, when 60% of nation's population, has to live absolutely alone, how much wastage of expenditure, would accrue, in the national economy, from this lack of adjustment attitude, of the average Americans and they preferring to stay single? For 60% of the population, the constituencies that constitute the national economy, be it the Government, corporate America, the industries will have to create incomes, to meet living facilities, such as cars, consumer appliances, recurring gas electricity and heating expenditures, health care expenditures and the like. To this, some more expenditure may be added, due to lonely living, such as more dinking, more food consumption, more mental depression and the treatment, occasional physical ailments, from lack of care, from anybody at home,.

All of these responsibilities, thrust on the national economy, would raise the national borrowings, which are clearly visible, when national budgets get passed in the Congress. How much financial load, an economy with so much individualism, would need to take, causing hurt, to the future generations is anybody's guess, in addition to the depletion of fossil fuels, to use personalized transportation.

One wishes that nations that are dotting with personalized vehicles, now, do not toboggan in future, not even able to meet public transportation for the next generations, bringing in horse driven carriages and horse driven cars. The pictures of 1890s and 1900 unfortunately, should not get repeated, in about 100 years, for the next generation. For the last 4000 years, no hierarchy of jobs ever existed since the time of Prophet Moses and the Old Testament and none talked about gender divide ever. Feminists, in modern times, in the 1960s. after being briefly exposed to manufacturing work, during the great depression and the war years, came to manufacture this expression in 20th century, of gender divide. Only after the construction of formal buildings of the workplaces, the factories, the banks and the insurance companies, which came about in the cities in the 50s and 60s, the so called feminists in the 1960s, started screaming about the office duties, being superior duties. They did not know and they did not explain, how these duties were regarded, as superior and how the duties, relating to enabling everyone in the home, to get their terabytes of energy annually, to supervise the work of the home workers and maids or to attend to some home management duties, as inferior and degrading. One need not forget that beach visits and lounging in the beach, in bathing costumes, in bikinis were termed as great achievements for women and they were celebrated as women's freedom, also began with feminism. The self pity attitude was preached, to the women, for no valid reasons, when none perceived any duties as inferior, in human society. Presumably corporate America, in order to burgeon its bargaining power, with the labor and to enfeeble the voice of the labor, to ask living wages, desired to increase heavily the supply of labor in the US labor market. Increased supply of labor for Corporate America was considered glorious a cause to be supported through the electronic and the print media, so that they could happily reduce the wages of the individual workers, once both spouses, in a family started working. Corporations seem to have banded with feminist movement, with huge resources available with them. Consequently, the feminists erroneously started, depicting the women, as the victims of gender divide and gender discrimination. Hence propagandas, of denigrating the home management responsibilities and extolling the office duties, came to be continued incessantly. The propaganda was misused, in the west, thoroughly to drive a wedge, in human society. It is common knowledge that the cooperation brings peace, in the homes and society and divides bring belligerences and the lack of peace.

This problem is near absent in India, as the concept of gender divide, in most of India, does not simply exist and family responsibilities, are voluntarily undertaken, not by mathematically counting the tasks and halving them for each spouse, as it has come to happen in the west, on the plan of which belligerences on a weekly basis, go on. Temperature controlled homes, its close doors and close windows, in the recent decades, prevent the noise, to be out, to the streets and the neighbors. Misuse of the paradigm of gender divide, has done a lot of harm socially and economically, to societies wherever that paradigm has been nurtured, particularly in the west.

Once going through the mill of being arrested, spending some time for no fault of theirs, in jail and their reputation having been trashed, could lead to a development of indifference and shame that such exploitation, in the name of law, is occurring to them, for absolutely no fault. Thereafter, once society having known, friends and families, having known about the arrests, gradually once the hesitation to be arrested, to go to jail, is likely to be whittled down and some of them may even get, into the habit of indulging in criminality, with a hope that they would manage, to escape and even if, they are caught they would feel less hesitant, to be taken to the prison, probably than before. 498 a. It is a shame that this law has been allowed to be liberally, used, as a tool, to harass a lot of gentlemen and gentlewomen and it carries the potential, of morphing, at least some of them, to be more criminal minded, because of the hurt, they would have felt, when their reputations went to precipice, despite being innocent, driven simply by the excessive money greed, of a woman, the daughter in law.

Such discriminatory unjust laws, where even innocent are taken to prison, for absolutely no fault of theirs, to carry a permanent stigma for one's life, carry a huge potential, to whittle down general law compliance and also citizens being, not so reverent to law enforcement.

For a country, of the size of India with 1.3 billion population, such negative development could be disastrous and there is an urgent need, to rescind the law 498a, which is serving no purpose, only deteriorating morals of women, particularly to speak filthy lies and file false cases and finally weakening, the stolid granite like, multi millennium institution of marriage.

8.10 Gender Divide is a Myth: Creation of Big Corporations and Feminists, in the West

Before industrial revolution, when society was predominantly agrarian, men and women both shared the agricultural responsibilities, the hard task being done by men, such as ploughing the fields, making it ready for broadcasting of the seeds, watering them, taking the cattle for grazing and the like. Women attended to less harder tasks, such as weeding, feeding the animals in the sheds and home management responsibilities. Men and women both stayed in the village in the simple lifestyle. There was no necessity for men to be away from 9 to 5, in the work place and return home after commutes, around 6pm to 7 pm, based on urgency of office work. In agrarian societies, men and women both got enough time for a siesta, and could wind up by 4 pm. The men would go to the village square. Women could go to the neighbors and spend some time.

Hence the hollow talks, of denigrating home management responsibilities, never arose. The women could not talk, as though they are fighting competition, with their male counterparts, extolling the office work and the commutes twice a day and putting down in hierarchy the home management responsibilities. These talks carried some meaning only, after urbanization took place in the urban areas, where men went for office work or factory work and women stayed home for home management responsibilities. Hierarchical thinking always creates social problems. The caste in India, the class in the west, race in the west, gender in the west have created the most novel dimensions of divides and once some people think on those lines, grief follows them.

All jobs are duties to humanity. All humans carry similar souls that are eternal and blessed with divinity by God's blessings, as per Bhagwat Geeta's preaching. Such enveloping thoughts for humanity, as a whole do not create animosities, in thinking and people live in peace. Some earn more and some earn less. Some study mathematics and science and others study liberal arts. Some spend more time away from home. Some spend a lot of time in the home, addressing their duties and responsibilities. The thinking dimension, of high and low in modern times that has driven, a lot of wedge between groups of societies and now between genders, in the west, particularly has been doing lot of damage to human relations,.

Thorough the route of globalization, along with economic globalization, human attitudinal globalization, is also seeping, among the young, both men and women. The dissemination of social attitudes, prevailing in the west, is creating a very artificial divide, between men and women, who should be thinking, in a synchronous manner, to be able to lead a happy married life, as pr Asian culture, particularly., dispensing care to the young and the aged parents, on both sides. Instead, there is a mad rush to be similar and this is causing headache to the children, to the aged, whose care have gone really, to the back burner. Home is not home any more, in the west, in such situations, as it is lonely/ empty from 7 am in the morning till 9 pm, in the evening, all of the wake up hours. With the dusk and darkness that follow, the home lights do not get lit, until about 8 pm or 9 pm, because members of the family, are still in the workplaces or on the roads. Neighborhoods have turned deserted and lifeless. Home kitchen and the kitchen table fun, have eviscerated. No cooking seems to be done, in the western homes and the McDonald plays the parents to kids, young adults and the old people, offering cheap and hot food, at a throw away price, inducing people to hog not eat. People are eating no more in the home, at the kitchen table or at a dining table and eating now is ubiquitous fast food places.. Westerners, particularly Americans are eating on the highways, driving cars; eating at the car parks,; in the cubicles of their offices and in the class rooms, when the lectures are going on; eating in the trains and at the railways stations and of course on the roads, while they are walking. Fast food, which is available cheap, has made this eating revolution, any time and at any place, leading to Americans becoming, heavily overweight to a tune of 70%, including children. Many adults and their children are turning obese, due to sedentary life, before screens of multiple varieties to see emails and operate the internet, the great electronic post office discovery, as it is touted in the middle of the 1980s. The outdoors are shunned and the indoors are lapped, courtesy the birth and accelerated growth of the IT industry, making screens of multiple sizes and shapes, an obsession of the young and a little less for those, who are in their 40s and 50s ad 60s.

So much time, away from homes is spent, by people in the west, that it looks as though they are leading an automated kind of life, where money earning, is be all and end all. Thus emotional relations with the spouse, relatives, elders, nephews and nieces and interaction with the neighbors and their children are dwarfing to an extent, that animate and inanimate behavior are turning indistinguishable. If a computer does not talk to the furniture, as they are inanimate objects, the humans at home hardly ask/ say anything to parents or siblings. One parent rarely talks with the other parent, as mind is replete with thoughts of how extra money, could be earned, how a promotion in the organization could be grabbed and how to please the boss, so that while others go away, due to layoffs, layoffs should not affect him/her. The spouses talk from home, more over phone, than with each other is the indifferent attitude they develop, as both address jobs and commutes, both have bosses to obey, both have hangovers of the job work, both are uncertain about continuance in job and both are highly stressed, with their own matters. Moreover, society and the media address Americans, to be self confident and self centric, which dilutes the tolerance of the spouse and small opinion differences, exacerbate, into solid fights.

Central heating and central air conditioning precludes the fight noise to go outside and it all the more encourages them, to scream at each other and sometimes fly blunt objects also. Window curtains usually, in modern times are closed, so neighbors cannot peep to see, what is going on in a western/American home. Only hapless children are helpless witnesses and their voice are not heard by both parents. In a Hindu joint family, such freedom to fight, with the spouse would not be unavailable, as there are a lot of relatives, in the house, who would calm the situation. Is it any wonder that in the absence of such freedom to fight, the spouses with little adjustments with the relatives in the home, lead a happier life and they are parts of a permanent lifelong marriage? Joint family homes, in India do not have so much inter spouse noise pollution, as it has in the nuclear homes of the west, where only spouses and children are available. In India they do not also have noise insulation and neither do they have central air conditioning available,. Hence the windows are all open and therefore the neighbors could hear the noise and even rush, if the noise in a home is too much. To avoid that embarrassment, from peering neighbors, the spouses do not dare to escalate fights and make up differences sooner. Indian homes on many occasions, do not even have curtains for the windows and inter spouse fighting could be easily seen by neighbors, due to this enforced transparency. Environments matter a lot, for the good of the society, as well its decline. In western and American homes noise insulation of the home walls, air conditioning and thereby closure of the windows and the window curtains, all coalesce to make the home non transparent/ opaque and a home fit for solid inter spouse fights. Jocularly speaking the home environment, is just perfect to scream at each other and thrown pillows or objects at each other in anger, as hesitation that someone from outside, might observe and derive bad impression does not simply arise. Social eye and the phenomenon of feeling ashamed, mean a lot to keep moral hygiene, or throw them. This need to be carefully understood by those, who live in high paced developed economies.

With divorces on the rise, there is not a single adult person at home, to share thoughts, to seek an advice, to smile together and get the peace of a loving home. These, limitations of life tend to frustrate, both men and women, who though for fear of job loss, do the drama of cosmetic smiles exuding to the clients, to the colleagues, to the strangers, to the boss but inside in their hearts, they are not contented and happy. All of these bottled up negative feelings, fall on the kids, who grow with one parent only, in most cases. Single parent, suffering from such dichotomies of life, is egoistic, arrogant and angry, quite a lot of time, in a week. No wonder the children grow up fast, in the west and as soon as they get a part time job, they want to leave and stay independently. Whenever they are down, they visit counselors and start taking anti depressants, at a very young age, which is not so good for sustainable mental health.

Media creates a lot of these divides, one doesn't know why with what gains for them and desires individuals, to be individuals, speak aloud and not to remain in the marriage, if it is not working. In the absence any other adult at home, to share thoughts, with no interaction with neighbors, this TV guy is available 24/7 and is almost psychologically, appear to be a well wishing counselor. What the TV says most of the time in the new millennium, the very young and the young people tend to comply.

That's how media, need to criticize and castigate the divorce, the divorce has not only come to stay, among the Americans but its spread in society, in recent years it is unbelievably galloping. At this rate, in 10 to 15 years, probably all marriages would break in about 6 years, inflicting a huge financial challenge on the economy, besides the society going on a path of disarray. Arresting this trend of rising divorces, is something that Americans and the west need, to pay serious attention and learn from countries like India, instead of Americanizing thin slice of India's metros, in favor of divorce.

8.11 Gender Divide is Perennial Whining by the Feminists

The second half of the 20 th century created easier jobs that require lighter work, writing reports, computer typing using the computers. Most of the work depended on talking, convincing customers, to buy goods and services, maintaining inventory and the like. The shopping outlets and office outlets, were designed neatly, with restrooms attached and carpets on the floor. Premises being air-conditioned in the summer and heating controlled in winter, the work places in the 1980s were easy to address. Women also desired to work, in these places, instead of remaining at home. Secondly, in late 20 century, the feminists started preaching self pity to women that they had to remain at home and they could not go outing for work. Hence some of the women felt that they were sacrificing too much in addressing the home management responsibilities, whereas the men went in the open air, to big and spacious workplaces. This was partially relevant in USA and the developed world, unlike India, by the end of the 20th century, because America and the west, became highly urbanized and in single income homes, which were about 63%, men only had to go to the workplaces.

In most developing economies and also in India most people reside in villages, doing agriculture poultry and animal husbandry and both men and women, work foam home. So this feminism message of denigrating home to women does not hold good at all. In fact, now in America in the new millennium, a lot of people, both men and women are working from home and in video conferencing and teleconferencing, one can hear the voices of the kids and also the dog, if there is a pet. So the message of self pity addressed to women, by the feminists, even in such American homes, do not anymore hold good. Where then is the talk of gender divide, so much valid and where is the need to have gender quarrel, even in the west and US. Why should any constituency egg on people, to get divided and have belligerences, when there is so much beauty in peace, in the home? US and the West have a lot of potential to learn, from India on this point, throw the belligerences away on themes of gender divide and bring peace and happiness to a well populated home..

Thus the loose talk of feminists that they were being exploited by men, started in the developed world. Why would women think that looking after home, which she addresses is hierarchically uninteresting job? Simple home management responsibilities could be shared by two equal companions. Home duties need to include buying goods. A little effort by both spouses, could bring a lot of happiness, to their lives, to the life of their children and the parents. Buying groceries; driving vehicles, generating income, cooking food and cleaning

the home, all constitute home work. It is hard to imagine, why the few feminists thought that earning money to run the home, is not a part of the home management responsibility.

When it came to raising the family, some of the feminists argued that women, were not child bearing machines. Giving birth to the child and training them, have for millenniums, being a collective responsibility of both parents, none have ever denied it. Women holding the baby in the womb, is a natural phenomenon, in this paraphernalia of familial responsibilities and for one baby, it is just, a unique feminine responsibility, once in a life time. when life expectancy is about 80 years why crib about it?. It is not a natural benediction and not imposed by the other gender, so why getting cribbed with the spouse?

Feminists incessantly complained in the west that women are not meant, to take care of the home, which in most cases, none be it, men or women agreed. As much as there is joy to contribute money, to run the home, there is delight to run the home too and it is hard to comprehend how the feminists keep berating, against home management responsibilities? It is also hard to comprehend, why do they tend to extol being in the workplace, which include click the mouse a few times, an a day., sitting before the computer, as a superior job. During the agrarian times, the men and women happily shared, economic activities, in which tough works were, in family, were happily undertaken by men and comfortable works were addressed by women. Dairy and poultry was the domain for women. Ploughing the field, walking through the mud, broadcasting of seeds, fertilization and spraying of pesticides were addressed by men. After harvest of the crops, the bagging was shared, by both men and women. Loading the heavy bags systematically, in the carts in India and tractors in the west and driving the vehicle, to the marketing location, was again addressed by the men. India being a country, with farming done by 60 percent of the population, one could see these responsibilities, nicely shared jointly, by both the genders in India. In the rural areas, no one would one see, the man shirking the hard, farming responsibilities. Even in urban India, those who walk down to buy groceries, the heavier bags are always carried by the, even when the husband is over 60 years young and the wife is given the lighter bags, with affection. This is a common sight in Indian grocery markets. None can be happy living among divides and the feminists arguing, to create artificial divide between the genders, has a debilitating effect in the peace of the human society today, particularly in the west. In a thin slice of metros, in India, too these thoughts are percolating, taken over by electronic media and given a false twist.

Most countries in Europe centuries ago were ruled, by successful queens. Asia and Latin America and Israel have witnessed successful heads of the states. Home happy home captions are no more in the minds of people and this caption is in the least coveted in developed world. Competition among spouses, on trifles triggered by 24/7 TV, has been on the rise exponentially, in recent years, making Americans pay attention to the entertainment, than ever before, away from human values and care for the family. Market ideologues have doped Americans, with addictions of marketing and borrowing, The food courts have been magnetizing average Americans, to excessive eating and acquiring obesity which is challenging people a great deal, to move and think slowly. Americans are manipulated by corporate America through media to be focused on increasing their riches, unnecessarily hiking their ambitions, when in reality, most of the jobs in America are low paying..

Compared to the Indian scenario, where political rights came to women, in a jiffy without even asking for it and where no university ever was out of bounds of an education seeking women, where hospitals are heavily populated, by very large number of female doctors, where revealing compensation by the pay roll, invites no ire, where for being a woman she is never paid less than the man holding the same position, be it in government public sector or in private sector of the economy, where women is not an object of advertising in most of India, where women does not have to be employed, to be married, does not have to be highly educated to be married, does not have to have right credit score to get married and where the man does not expect his wife, to fetch money, every month, to supplement to pay monthly bills, by undertaking a job. However if she is a professional and she wants to work on her own volition she could take up a job and save the earned income. In India, wife receives more gifts than husband buys for himself, during the festivals. It is normal for an Indian wife to quietly save money from the monthly income of her husband, to be offered at times of emergencies for the family needs. She does not spend the money saved by her, on herself.. This is a typical example, of the value of sacrifice that Hindu religion and culture preaches, as opposed to the concept of individualism in the west. If she belongs to a middle class home, she does not have to address even, the home management responsibilities, as she recruits maids. In India, if she is a working woman, her employer would never frown, looking her, in the family way. She would be entitled to maternity paid leave, for 3 months in the government, public sector and most private sectors. In contrast, a western working woman receives frowns from the supervisor, if she is in the family way, and she also has to rough it out with home management responsibilities, at her home, compulsorily with no options. Then she has to commute and take up a job. If she has been divorced, by the man. a western woman may have to take more than 2 jobs and 2 commutes and raise children, in case, she is a divorcee, the possibility of which is very high in US. Unlike India, where she got her voting rights, on the same day, as her male counterparts, in the west and America unfortunately, she had to ask for political rights and she was rejected for 60 long years. She could get her rights, after 60 years of fight for voting rights, which came to be known as suffrage movement. Only in 1920, an American woman was granted the voting rights, whereas the American men were boisterously voting, since late 1700s. The American and the British women had to picket offices, demonstrate for their votes and were even arrested in large numbers, during the suffrage movement. Both in the US and in the UK, they could not study, in top class universities for centuries, though men studied there. Even to this day, both in private and public universities, she is discriminated in receipt of compensation, receiving less compensation than the similarly paced men. In Corporate America, also women employees are paid lot less than their male counterparts. The male employees are allowed to have the last laugh. Any number of representations by women employees fall on deaf years with justice not arriving for years. It's strange that in private firms, once she goes the family way, she not only does not get maternity benefits, and in many of the cases she loses her job. In some cases, when a woman after delivering the baby, does not lose the job, she usually reports within a week to work to save her job. Such is the heinousness of the workplace, for women. Compensation discrimination blatantly, goes to the US labor market, in all of the white collar jobs, which would be astonishment, if Indian women get absolutely equal compensation, for similar responsibilities/ranks.

Human capital caring also includes, giving right pay, for the right talents and not be stingy on the expenditure, on payroll. Human talents need to be appreciated and accordingly compensation, need to be provided. If the US government in conjunction, with corporate help, set up national health scheme under, which health care would be cheap or free, as it obtains, across the Atlantic in Europe, then poverty would witness a substantial southern movement, making average Americans happy. Second best step of the US Government could be for the government to make health care benefits mandatory, for the employers to meet health expenses of the employees, besides directing the pharmaceutical diagnostic and health insurance firms, to act more as service, with reasonable charges than acting as money greedy businesses.

Incentives, like sick leave, annual leave need to be granted, by the corporations, without, taking a negative view, about such gross necessities. With a compulsion to make ends meet, sick persons are not eligible for sick leave. The fear of impending sickness could haunt some of the American employees, as the employees are being denied sick leave. The sick could suffer from health frustrations and this might cause the hypertension to rise and she may even turn him, in the long run, a heart patient. In many firms, the employees feel that the compensation is just enough to keep the body and soul together, and it is a shame in a country, which is a 14 trillion dollar economy there is no sick leave..

Caring for the human capital also, involves updating human resources, from time to time, by inviting experts to deliver lectures, on their specific areas of work and general management. Sometimes the training in management may be once, in a year or two, deputing them for training out of the workplace, for a change and introspection, on their duties, could add value to the job and the organization.. These exercises do not, only help top managers, but also ordinary employees too. This aspect has to be well appreciated, by the corporations.

Nations such as US have been flooding the workplaces, in recent years, of the new millennium, with too many temp employees, with a view to escape payment of long term employee benefits. This move appears to exude their arrogance and bargaining power, to browbeat the employees. Splitting the jobs, for the purpose of, escaping expenditure on health care and other long term benefits, splitting up the full tint jobs, into temp hourly jobs, appears, on the face of it is very unethical. It can be gauged that if employees, find the top management unethical, in their dealings with employees, how loyal and how dedicated they could be expected to be. Managements, these days by indulging in not so ethical practices, do not realize, how deep the morale falls, confronted with unnecessary moves of the cost cutting. These moves are an index of the lack of caring of human capital.

Denial of sick leave sometimes annual leave and maternity leave for women in private organizations in America are all further indexes of the lack of caring for the human capital, which impinge certainly on the morale of the workforce and their covert loyalties. The deceleration of morale can be seen, in the way the corporations are compelled, to recall goods that are defective, sometimes over millions in a year. Merely because engagement in democracy is feeble in this economy the corporations should not be so callous the way the goods are made so defective, in recent years the goods recall is more of a rule rather than exception. This trend of recalls which is negative is going overseas too in Japanese firms and some Indian, as Americana is a fashion..

During periodic economic recessions, with no fault of the employees, the employees are being laid off, and this gesture hurts them. Laying off at the slightest dent in shareholder value or small dent in profits or profit guidance, by investment banks stun the employees, who might have landed the jobs, after a thorough search, applying to multiple workplaces and having faced multiple interviews, only a few months ago. Laying off as an arrogant management style, of the supervisor, could be more hurting. While in the cosmetic sense of the term, those yet to be laid off, work with uncertainty of future job situation and living with the fear, of losing their job in a few months,. These happenings in the workplace could make a lot of the workers sick, with ailments and more so, if they have a spouse and children. Strangely in America, the marriages are too fragile and glass like and the marriages could even break, if the man loses the job and does not land a new job in several months even year or two. Then divorce becomes a likely outcome, with the spouse and the children leaving him, alone, to face job challenges. Every year, several hundreds of thousands of marriages break that are very normal, due to exogenous shocks of the man's job losses. Though the employer knows about these social aberrations, but for money greed and to be able to browbeat employees, on a regular basis, he keeps the sword of Damocles, of the job loss, on the head of his employees. To survive and pay the bills every month and not be castigated, as jobless, people accommodate, without arguing with the supervisors and suffer the humiliation, but not without consequences, of the productivity of the industry and the national economy. Caring for human capital, goes to the lowest ebb, when jobs are temp and are offered, without any security of tenure. Such temp jobs plummet instantly the enthusiasm of the recruited. Lack of promotional avenues that have turned the order of the day, due to layoffs in America, further breaks the morale, of the Average Americans, in the workplaces. Even the joy of getting a job, with iconic American business such as IBM, Dell Computer, GM, Accenture, Deloitte and Touché, vanishes too soon, when the layoffs euphemistically, known as the issuance of pink slips, continue to take place, not on any valid grounds, but on a lot of times, due to serendipity. With their colleagues gone and their cubicles and chairs empty, is enough for the incumbent employees, to need an anti depressant, to get proper sleep. It shouldn't be a surprise that with such uncaring human resource development, tens of millions are in poverty. Over 40 million, cannot afford health care and over a 100 million would never think of aspiring, for a higher education, as the expenses for higher education could be stratospheric.

Economies may be having parties, cutting on the development of human capital, for a decade or so, but soon even in the medium term, they carry the potential of landing into multifarious economic challenges that could result in an economic crisis. These economic systems have come to mirror the feudal times, when a few at the top, led nice comfortable lives and the laity suffered, with frustrations and agony. The only difference is that the visual lifestyle, even at the base level, in current times, look satisfying, in the developed world, compared to poor quality of assets of the laity, in the times of feudalism.

Calling the layoffs, issuance of the pink slips, hardly heightens anyone's spirits. Instead, it is like spreading salt on the wounds of those, who lost their jobs. As the labor unions, are banned, in many organizations in USA, though informally, the labor strikes do not occur,. Otherwise, probably calling layoffs as pink slips, could have brought about the labor umbrage, against the management. In India, derogatory remarks against the labor, could trigger a tool down strike and an apology from the management, to calm the tempers of the labor. A lot of economic challenges, joblessness and recovery of economy, for severe and deep recession of 2008, could all be attributed, to many decades of not caring and developing human capital, properly, in the corporate landscape of America, though in terms of GDP and the number of billionaires, in a year or the list of richest persons in the world, USA is making waves. This is comparable to the British times in India, if we think about the runway affluence of the royalty of Hyderabad, known as the Nizam of Hyderabad, who was the richest person in the world. At that time, in the 1930s 1940s and 1950s, the affluence of the Nizam, that of the princes, his relatives, his ministers in the cabinet and the nobles, may have had a lot of landed property, jewels etc., and they may have been, living in marvelous style, decorating their mansions, with artifacts from different parts of the world, but the laity was fine with farming and making of crafts and working on projects of engineering, but in no way comparable, to the ultra top of the economic pyramid. It could be termed benevolent feudalism.

Today's capitalistic economies, with no security of tenure, joblessness, long waiting period, to get jobs and jobs with rarity of leave, including sick leave and pink slips coming in droves, anytime without notice and without valid reasons, almost mirror the feudal regime of Nizam in Hyderabad India, where the top elite enjoyed, the best physical comforts that was available in the world, played polo, golf, ate world cuisine and went to the developed world for higher education, but the multitude led simple lives.

If human capital, is developed nicely and in a caring manner, leaving them, with little uncertainties of life, rather than keeping them preoccupied with frustrations, of losing a job anytime, not landing the next job after a long wait, the nations would see egalitarianism as the overarching feature than modern feudalism.

Poverty arises due to divisive approach, either homemade or exported by vested interests of the rich countries or mother countries.

8.12 India Suffered Poverty: Exogenous Divide by the British

India saw a lot of poverty, as the British governance in India after 1857, among other poverty generating tools, also pursued a policy of divide and rule. India from times immemorial has learnt, to welcome different ethnicities, into its fold, allowing them to happily settle down in India. When Jews were defeated by the Romans, many of them as early as 2000 years ago, arrived in India and settled down in Kerala. Jesus Christ's disciple, in his own lifetime, arrived in India and many Brahmins got converted to Christianity. Thus Christianity arrived in India and was welcome, before it arrived, in today's predominantly Christian World of Europe. Such has been the antiquity and rich cultural heritage of India. When the Arabs invaded Persia and proselytized the Zoroastrians to Islam, those Zoroastrians, who were not keen to be converted to Islam, left Persia and took happy refuge in India, initially in Bombay and then from Bombay they also settled down in Bangalore, Hyderabad, Pune and Ahmadabad. Today, they follow their own ancient religion of Zoroastrianism.

Islamic rulers knew, the cosmopolitan nature of India's culture and confined their rule, around the national capital of Delhi and the peripheries of the rural areas, by and large were, left to enjoy their autonomous character, merely collecting annual revenue. That is how, the social and economic structure of the village republics, in India was in place, during the entire Islamic rule and there were no occasions of Hindu Muslim clashes anytime, during the pre Mogul and Mogul rule.

Before the parliament of religions, was convened in Chicago, in 1886, the Mogul King Akbar, had convened a conference of people of all religions, where came Hindus, Jains, Muslims, Zoroastrians and also Jesuit fathers, who were Christians. This Parliament of Religions was convened, in Mogul emperor's palace, to undertake deliberations, on spirituality and it was named Din i Ilahi. Akbar started, a spiritual movement that promoted peace and it was named Suleh Kul. Thus the idea of unity of religions, which started with the Vedic concept of Sanaatan Dharma, in ancient times, about 10,000 years ago, also was continued, during the medieval period, as convened by the Mogul Emperor. During Asoka's rule, Kanishka's rule and Harshavardhana's rule, India's religion of right path, spirituality and peace was propagated as Buddhism, preached by Gautama Buddha, and it received universality in China, South East Asia, Mongolia, Sri Lanka and even Afghanistan.

Though Moguls came from Central Asia, they made India, their home and no money was ever transferred, collecting taxes from the peasants in India. Indians, both the Hindus and the Muslims, found it strange when a foreign company, with monopoly of trading powers, started raising army, making treaties with local royalties and sending their troops, to provide security to the local princes, against their own peasants, in case of a revolt by the peasants. A wedge was attempted to be driven between the local princes and their peasants, by injecting a fear, in their minds that their peasants could rebel against them. The company even waged wars and looted the wealth, of the local princes, by siding with one royalty and waging war with another, with an intention to play the favorites, among the princes and driving a wedge, between the royalties. Even annexation of territories was not uncommon, after skirmishes. During the company rule, which was absolutely bizarre, as a company could never be sovereign, a doctrine of lapse principle, was introduced by Mr. Dalhousie, the then governor general, in 1850s, providing for taking over of the royal prince's jurisdiction, to rule, if a male heir was not born, to the incumbent royalty the Raja and the Rani. This move irked the royalties, both Hindus and Muslims. Presence of the skin of beef and pork, in grenades, to be used in the army, infuriated the Hindu and Muslim soldiers, both and the mutiny was joined, by the frustrated peasants, who were taxed very heavily. The Hindu and Muslim royalties and all of them nominated the last Mogul Emperor Bahadur Shah Jaffar as their leader. The company officials were unnerved and nervous. They felt that a strong, military action only, could quell the rebellion. The company very urgently raised big army; from places, where the mutiny and the rebellion, had not occurred, which was Punjab, the Hill Districts and South India. The battalions led by the Brahmin officers and those from the north India, were immediately disbanded. This was the beginning of divide and rule that started with the army. Queen Victoria, declared herself as the Empress of India and took over administration of India, from the East India Company. She wrote a long letter to the Governor General, asking him to ensure that Hindus and the Muslims are not to be allowed to be close to each other. Attempts should continue to create and perpetuate divide to keep the British rule strong. Such clear directions coming from the crown to the Viceroy of India encouraged the divisiveness in India.

The Viceroy started, receiving separate parleys representations from the Congress that represented, all in India and the Muslim League, representing only Muslim cause. Emboldened by the British governance, the members of the Muslim League, were occasionally critical of the Congress and Mr. Jinnah was sometimes critical about Mr. Gandhi, speaking, for both Hindus and Muslims and he desired him to confine talking, only about Hindus. During the wars, when Congress declared Quit India slogan, asking the British, to grant Independence to India, Mr. Jinnah and the Muslim league kept silent, without offering any remarks. Mr. Winston Churchill, who somehow found Mr. Gandhi, too Indian and too ethnic in all matters, including his very simple dress, in which he had attended the Round Table Conference, in London could not bring himself, up to appreciate, the demonstrations, the bonfires of foreign, cloth, the civil disobedience especially, when as War Prime Minister of Britain, he was very busy participating in the Global War 2. He found Mr. Gandhi, asking for independence very untimely, when the War was devastating the buildings, the factories, the academies and taking a huge human toll, running into millions. Mr. Churchill distanced, himself from Mr. Gandhi and he kept Mr. Jinnah, close, a western in style and manners and certainly dressed in suit and tie. But for Mr. Attlee coming to power, who during his election campaign, had promised to grant independence to India, India's independence could have been delayed.

But the beginning of division that letter of Queen Victoria, created in 1857, continued to make the divide of a national family of citizens of India. All of the violence that unfortunately occurred, accompanying the partition of India, would have been completely avoided, had this divide not being created by the British.

India would have not been, so impoverished, at the end of the British rule and it could start, at a much higher level of per capita income. In India's case, the tendency to divide was exported from Britain. Whereas, in countries like USA, where burden of history, by southern cotton farmers, practicing slavery and all of the bad stories of the poor blacks, suffering, from very hard farm work and being lashed occasionally and sold putting them, on auction, like furniture and the captions "furniture and slaves in good condition, for sale," created the divide. These attenuated the overall prosperity, with little inequality, between haves and have-nots. Divides, within the nation, which is homemade, in this case has certainly taken a toll, on its overall economic prosperity and higher standards of living, besides job situations. Several articles that are published about US economy, entitled great divide, would have never come into being. All of that money released from lack of need of crime control, lack of necessity of incarceration and abandoned properties, in poor neighborhoods, would have released huge money. This money could be available, for subsidizing public school education and higher education, in similar institutions, for both the blacks and the whites. Integration efforts are now top down, with affirmative action moves, but bottom up divisive tendencies unfortunately makes the divide, a reality and it certainly has financial implications and loss of overall prosperity and widening rich and poor gap, in U.SA.

In many Latin American countries, the huge inequality happens, between the gated communities of the rich, the middle class and the drug infested, crime infested slums blighting the economy, though they are middle income countries. It is the egoistic attitude of the rich, which Hindu scriptures guide, to shun that locks capital unnecessarily, which some families, never allows, to be circulated, hurting the poor. Release of money, even once in few years, could help the poor, in slums and enabling a large number of them, to join the mainstream. Such moves could bring the poor, to have a lot of gratitude, to the well off, removing the mistrust, between them. The goodwill, thus generated would have got monetized, in a big way, to bring prosperity, in a ubiquitous manner.

Today, the CEOs in India, take about 10 times more, compensation, than the base level worker and this number is 550 in USA. Imagine, if the CEOs in USA, could get this spiritual brainwave, to emulate India and take only 10 times instead of 550 times, how much capital would be freed, in each organization, to bring distribution of better compensation, including even health care benefits, for all employees. How much goodwill would get monetized, in USA, if CEO shows such a gesture, shunning their ego and arrogance. Inclusiveness makes wonders, in economic prosperity, whereas divisiveness increases crimes, incarceration, loss of morale, among minorities, lack of education and tobogganing poverty afflicting them.

It is better to be appreciated by the deprived and move about in a Honda car, rather than be criticized behind the back, by the deprived and move about in Lexus. This would be the message of the Indian sages, of ancient times that brings a no war peaceful paradigm of India. India colonized other countries, through culture and values and never by force and its ships, did not carry firearms and soldiers, but message of peace and spirituality.

The young in America with financial support, from the US institutions, could make a difference, in breaking the walls of divides, learning from inclusiveness and simplicity from Indian way of life

A lot of these problems that cause deprivation, segregation and poverty, would have gone from developed world, if only the young would have been given more opportunity, to address freelance studies, in other countries, from where there is so much to learn, in matters that affect social relations, compared to the sea of knowledge that developed world can pass on, in the realm of engineering and economics today. To make excellent coaches big trucks and aircrafts are the unbeatable talents that belongs to the Americans, which other continents could be taught, whereas spirituality, inclusiveness, trust in those, who are poor and deprived, ability of living without segregation and intense discrimination, and social economy of scale etc, are some of the areas, where India has a wisdom and heritage of millenniums. If the young, from the developed world, are offered an opportunity to learn from India, they would learn heartily. The media in US, has to be made much less green, in pumping hollow ego, among the young, to think elephantine. Instead the US media need to be asked to promote brevity, humility, modesty and moderation, in the ways of life. Media need to act serious and prudent instead of merely acting, as stooges and captives, of some money greedy businesses.

Minds work in the direction of segregation, in USA presumably work with apprehensions that if a white family lives, in the same ensemble, of a high rise apartment or in the same neighborhood, where there are black families live too are, the young whites girls, would be targeted, for marriage, by the young black boys and there would be pigmentation, reducing the intrinsic quality of the white race. Even few American authors opine in their books and writings, with assertion that the purity of the white race and culture would be diluted, if such marriages take place. Probably, there would be very few such marriages, even when, the two races stay, in the same high rise rental apartments or in the same neighborhood. Further, such cases being very few probably, there would be nothing wrong, if such marriages, do take place, as similar and nice natured and educationally endowed, people gravitate together, in dating and marriage, even if the spouses, belong to different races or of linguistic social groups.

India is a great example of how people of different subcultures, could live in the vicinity, speaking different languages, such as Marathi, Punjabi, Tamil, Malayalese, Gujrati, Bengali, Hindi, Naga, Manipuri, Mezzo, Oriya Telugu, Konkani, Kannada and the like, even. eating different food, but marry in an endogamous fashion within the linguistic group. In regard to marriages, globally, those who feel endangered of mixed marriages, could draw a leaf of lesson, from India. It is not necessary or even an overarching reality, that if they go to the same school, the same university, shop in the same market and even live in the same neighborhood and even socialize nicely, there would be mixed marriages. It is embedded in the mind that conveniences would accrue, if the marriages are homogeneous, in terms of subculture and language. That does not preclude a mixed marriage though to happen occasionally, once in a while, but it is an exception..

There also goes on some boisterous thoughts, in the minds of the majority that they are brighter than the poor and the minorities, which is not so true intrinsically, though environments, bring about different academic/ professional outcomes. In India too, there are some false notions, such as the people from Calcutta, Madras and Bombay tend to think themselves brighter than their rural cousins and also their other provincial cousins but all Indian competitive exams for admission to the best academic program, to best professional positions, do not reveal any such skewness in India. There may be some element of nepotism but it does not hurt the mainstream objectivity, as openly people say and accept that in the interviews blacks and Latinos tend to be discriminated and whites are preferred.

In USA, some regional feelings of north and south, based on their subcultures, might exist and in choosing a job, in the public sector or a gigantic private sector or in an international firm, students tend to gravitate to the region mostly. For example, one would see that most from Southern Universities, tend to join southern banks, in southern insurance companies and southern firms, based in the south, whereas those, from the universities, in the east, tend to join firms, banks and insurance companies that are east based. In the south, the feeling appears to be more pronounced. Even if some of the young may like to go to other regions usually their peers ask them, to take a job in the south. These walls of discriminations, and apprehensions, come in the way of excellent inclusiveness, to achieving more affluence and more broadbased prosperity in USA. When a Midwestern boy, from Michigan gets recruited, amidst employees, who are all, from the East, somewhere he finds pin pricks, being given to him, indirectly asking him to quit, so that an Eastern guy could join, in that position. This is more true of administrative positions, in the privately owned universities, where it is a part of fashionably termed labor market, the flexible labor market. The flexible labor market gives the immediate supervisor, a huge authority to call it quits, showing some snags from annual performance evaluation, which could be his figment of imagination. Strangely in the private labor market, once an administrator takes this shot, to dismiss his immediate subordinate, latter in America, has no appeals to the Provost or to the President of the university. These walls can easily be broken, learning from foreign systems, where in formal organizations, such blatant divides do not happen, though at the community level, there may be rooms for informal societal cohesiveness. All of these divides hamper prosperity to be broad based.

People from among the tribal and the labor castes in India, since the constitution was formulated, in early 1950s, work with mutual dignity, not for years, but for decades, holding equal authority and power. It does not matter, if they are less in number, working in an organization, if they hold similar positions. This is something organizations of the Eastern types, who force a Midwestern state boy, to quit, probably could learn for the better. In organizations despite a full fledged HR Department, if the Midwesterners are in majority, a Utah state person may not be supported well and if the organization is based in the east or a western state boy may not be so welcome, unless he is extraordinarily talented. Subtle discriminations even to this day, on a regional basis, even among the whites, go on. These divides go to neglect human capital and possess cost for the economy that people need to be explained, so that all around inclusiveness is promoted, intra white, as well as between the whites and the blacks and other colored.

Life is so much of a happy phenomenon, in a society where "us and they" attitudes in social economic, educational, professional and political realm, are near absent and neighborhood and informal interactions, matter in life.

Stiffness of meeting people, strictly on appointments and inability to distinguish, between a gentle pedestrian and a criminal, in a neighborhood, looking at a colored person on the road or an elevator, with an indifferent eye, may have to go to build better trust result. Inability to accept a surprise, such as an innocuous visit, from a neighbor, who wants to share may be a joke or may like to have a chat over a cup of coffee or tea have to go to oblivion, to be able to build in one's mind, the trust for other people, other races, people of different wealth and income categories.

As a part of moving away from divisiveness, one may have to have to view, a predicament of a stranger, who might be lost and he/she may be asking for a location/an address. The raising of the trust levels and dilution of the unnecessary apprehensions, about other people, may have to be learnt, with an open mind, from people of the Indian origin. People, from India carry the heritage of wisdom, of hundreds of generations of multiple millenniums, embedded in their society and economy. In India it is stated that "AITHI DEBO BHAVA," which implies that the guest, needs to be welcomed nicely. Such loosened approaches to life keep one's mind and body, healthy and opportunities, to share one's weal and woes.

With all of these manners and rigidities, in place, divides are very hard to go, from societal relationships, as these stiff manners and rigidities, play out, in a more rigid fashion, when it comes to (they) while it may be slightly less in case of (we). If a guy who is "they" knock at the door, the door may not open at all, but if the guy is "us", seen from pinhole of the door, the door may half open, with no welcome to take a seat.

Chapter 9

Media, Social Media: Frustration and Future Poverty of the Young

This challenge of poverty, in future is likely to happen, for decades to come in economies that promote media too much, way beyond its utility. The west and the USA, in the new millennium, have gone ahead with 24/7 media, with little gains except, whittling down of serious aspects of life, such as attention to studies, jobs, families and childlike frivolity of the elders. Employers are challenged and so are parents, with such passion of children to screens. Marriages are challenged, with such social media, helping the spouse to remain in touch, with ex friends of opposite gender. On the employment front, the young are challenged with jobs, going abroad with outsourcing and offshoring. Employers are heavily challenged, by not getting enough bright recruits, in areas of academic rigor, such as in math, science, engineering, actuaries, accounting and computer programming Except the personality of repetitive vocabulary that fails to differentiate, between high school dropout and high scholars, university graduates even report writers, have been in heavy short supply. Even in jobs, remedial courses are to be taken, to continue the locals in jobs.

In America, social media and other screens constitute the worst poverty triggers. A paradigm, has developed in half a century that it need not have, to call a spade a spade.. A sick fat man or a woman cannot be counseled, as per this paradigm, to keep trim and healthy. Mediocre student is not permitted to be rebuked, by the high school teacher, to improve results. The system supports, all of these artificial behavioral moves, which think, a guiding comment is not right, but the same system, refuses to recruit fat people and also fires an employee, due to obesity,. The employers also discriminate covertly against fat persons and refuse to offer, a reasonably priced health care scheme, due to obesity. It is also hard at the social level for a fat person, to be able to date Such hypocrisies bring a lot of woes, into people' s lives, when they are unable to develop themselves, or earn well.

9.1 Face Book and Social Media Gobble Time Meant for Studies and Jobs

Face Book, for many married couples, is ruining marriages, as newlyweds are unable, to de intoxicate themselves, from viewing Face Book, late during the nights, when to say the least, the spouses need, to be each other's admirable company.

Face Book gives privacy to the young, when unmarried, to stay in touch, with some friends from opposite gender also, some of whom are emotionally close, some are plays of frivolity and some even write profane inter gender thoughts. All of these are certainly polluting the pure minds of the young, with profanity and heightened senses, for opposite gender. The desire of the young, to get married, is plummeting, in the developed world and also some globalizing emerging economies, as these correspondences on the Face Book are also leading to casual weekend meetings, sometimes in pairs like dating. Face Book is pretty useful, to arrange dinner or lunch parties, at a short notice and to promote friendliness, among the peers. Making friends, away from one's intellectual or professional group, is possible, through the route of Face Book, For some of the young, it is not unlikely that some may lapse, into weaker moments, forgetting the morality, to indulge in premarital physical interactions, thus diluting the purity of mind and body. Once used to physical interactions, with near strangers, could make some men and women, lead that life moving away from pursuing serious aspects of life, such as an academic pursuit or living with a desire to help humanity. These activities that accrue from using Face Book, undoubtedly make the young adults afar, from the idea of a marriage, in the near term.

After exhausting making friends, through Face Book, with multiple friends and vacationing with them, if the money permits finally, marriage loses its luster and it is more of a formality, to live with a companion and procreate. In an Asian society, where one looks up to marriage, for romance and the first inter gender physical interaction and to have a baby, strictly, within the boundaries of marriage, the Face Book could prove to be a highly anti cultural and anti social aspect in life. Hence those trying to promote such anti cultural products, need to know where in culture, a country or a region belongs. It's not like selling Gillette blades or Dutch cheese or French yogurt or even an American car, where a sense of morality, does not figure. Thinking one cloth size fits all, leads to globalization, getting very bad name and the product in a poor economy,. For example, with its time consuming intoxicating value, the social media could hit the academic and professional standards, to make people in such economies, see more poverty. In global societies, where marriage is losing its pristine value fast, even without social media like Face Book, due to rebelliousness of the young and rising tolerance of the elders, against violations of social norms, probably, the social media like the Face Book would do lesser damage, on the inter gender interaction front. However, the negative impact of intoxication with social media like Face Book, is one and the same, as it is with any other kind of intoxication. An alcoholic young or a drug addict, besides, feeling confused and numb, they lose a lot of time, to address any of his serious social duties, whether it is spending time with parents or spouse or children, or attending to a job seriously. So far as the wastage of time component of irresponsibility, from intoxication, with alcohol, is concerned, it is no different, from heavy intoxication of the young men and women with social media, while sitting before a computer. In USA, the Social Science researches indicate that the young high school students are spending, about 5 to 6 hours every day, with computer and most of it is interaction, on the Face Book. Some are spending even 8 to9 hours, on the computer. A person, who is on Face Book for 6 hours, probably, would find it hard, to address serious study of science, math, engineering studies. It would be pretty natural, for a person, who is intoxicated with Face Book, to be not inclined to take up studies, where academic rigor, will be required. With such disinclination, of the young, should the national leaders and parents of the children expect them, to land great well paying jobs and maintain high living standards? It is not a rocket science to understand that the social media, have doomed a whole generation, making them, ineligible for solid studies, learning of trade skills and making them prepared, for any high paying jobs. The fact that the one-liner exchanges with friends, with friends of friends and with friends of friends of friends, is giving a lot of short term kicks, to the social media users. It is not helping the American young, to turn into scientists, engineers, doctors, accountants and researchers or even philosophers.

In fact the Face Book, is making the young unfortunately unlearn, what they have learnt, when there was no PC. Spellings have been forgotten due to small expressions, in communication. Even grammar has been forgotten. How could such outputs of the colleges write reports, for research grants, in a university department or as a part of correspondence, with a lending bank, for a billion dollar loan, for the company. Those reports would be a laughing stock, as peers would not read it, but experienced professionals. The high school educated Americans, are asked to take remedial classes, after joining the firms. Should the lawmakers blame corporations, to refuse to recruit, such young Americans and go abroad to recruit talents, who could write an excellent report, which might need one or two brief editing. They need no remedial classes, to even improve English. Should they not recruit talent abroad, who are good in math and statistics? Should the society and law makers fault them and call them unpatriotic? Are the job seekers, preparing themselves enough, to avail the great opportunity, of working in great firms of America, on a high compensation? Are they not wasting too much time, on social media one liners, replacing study time with entertainment time?

In contrast, in Asia, for a student, under the influence of guiding strict parents, study time per day is 6 hours, outside the school and entertainment time is one hour. in USA, with text messaging, laptops, handheld devices and cell phones having internet facilities, the entertainment time per day for students, has become 6 hours and the study time per day is less than one hour. With such a light environment, awash with entertainment, in USA, is it possible for the American young, to globally compete in jobs. The studies in this era of globalization, reveal that the government and the corporations have come to respect, the global talent, not country talent anymore. With such a disadvantage, of obsession with screens, could the society and the law makers, for long berate the firms, for recruiting foreigners? Partially the corporate America, cannot but be faulted, for being too impassioned with cost cutting and rising profits. However, one will also have to fault substantially, the individual families the parents first, for not minding their children to relax, on academic discipline. Further, the children also have been taking advantage of soft parents, who do not insist much, on studies and are content, seeing their children happy with 24/7 TV, internet and social media. The young need to realize that burning precious time of the present, on the FaceBook or other social media, could give then a life of financial challenge for decades in future, no matter how media proffers their spirits high and talk loud. Such an indifferent attitude to academic rigor and being obsessive on the social media could drown them into uncertainties of life, at a time, when life expectancy would be 80 years. Today's 25 year young, do not continue to be 25 years young, forever and he/she would also live in 70s even 80s of their age and the young of today especially in the west and USA where browsing of the net have reached Himalayan proportions, need to envision that the life needs planning, not only browsing the internet.

Even in a thin slice of the metros, in countries such as India, the social media challenges do affect their quality of marriage. when Face Book users, who are friends, to many from opposite gender, get married and settle down, in a home to raise family, a lot of them, miss out heavily, the frivolity that they indulged in, while they were single. It is found, among some people, belonging to the thin slice of the metros, in India too, write notes from their conjugal beds unfortunately, in the middle of the night, to their strange unknown friends, based on their uploaded pictures, being appreciated, getting kicks out of it. For them, marriage could not be an excitement, not a sacrament, a duty according to Hindu culture and a joy to be celebrated. It is a kind of enforced discipline, on their premarital frivolous life that marriage plays. The character of the spouses, in some cases, have dropped to trenches already, with Face Book being used, as a tool to have multiple friends. Facing the screen without the knowledge of husband, the wife keeps writing to her multiple male friends, the kind of notes sometimes that tantamount to cheating on the marriage and a sin. Men are not behind. They also boisterously keep sending notes, to their female Face Book friends, undesirable notes sometimes, sitting right in front of the wife. With such cheating going on right in the face of the spouse, what love could grow to consolidate the marriage? Both falter in the loyalties and duties to the home.

Should the CEO and the Board Directors not avoid churning out products that has huge potential of making a mockery of the institution of marriage? Feminism adds fuel to the fire. Financial independence that women have acquired, after globalization, makes them feel insolent and they tend to pay attention to the new find freedom, new find career growth, new find bosses and do not feel answerable to inform the home, where they go after office hours and why they are very late, in the night. They take it as affront, if asked about such innocuous information. Other side of the fence appears green. The western feminist, with their radical thoughts of gender discrimination, is gradually coming to impress the oriental women, a thin slice of their metros. A lot of the women from India are unaware that the marriages in the west, are breaking at a very fast, at the rate in 4 to 6 years. They are unaware that women in the west, lead a very tough life, especially those, who go through a divorce, as their incomes are halved. In flexible labor market, they may have to tread to the homeless shelters too, when they lose jobs, along with their children. Women in India at 60, those who come from the middle class, which is pretty big, about 500 million, supervise maids and are comfortable, in a lifetime marriage, with the comfortable by Indian standards compensation of the husband. Her western counterpart at 70 plus years of age, is alone for at least 2 decades, with a divorce. She has to pay the monthly bills and for the same, she has to go the workplace. Children with diluted discipline in the home, due to Parent's divorce, sometimes openly rebel, against mother and talk rough,

They turn physically violent too, with rage, throwing articles. Children, after growing up, often complain and fault mother, for depriving them, of their father's company. They fault those mothers who might indulge in immoral profanity, dating with multiple men and not infrequently bringing them home, as overnight guests, on weekends, right in the presence of grown up daughters and sons.

What regulation can such a mother, impose on her children, when her values are so much in the trenches? Consensual physical interaction, with multiple men strangely, on a weekend, right in the presence of major children, at home is not a crime and don't fall, in the purview of the cops, but certainly inappropriate irreligious and hurtful to the grown up children adversely affecting the psyche.. Until the children are in their teenage, all of these intolerable misbehaviors in the home, they have to tolerate, as they cannot be economically independent. As soon as they get a part time job and they become major, they like to leave home, not because they like to be independent, but because they are spared of the ignominy and the embarrassments which they might be feeling, in western fatherless home.

In the west, it is a huge challenge, to be brought up in families only by a mother, with father never to be seen. Mother has no face, to regulate her children and the same drama continues, with more carelessness, in subsequent generations.

The young women, in a thin slice of the metros in India, are in recent years, enslaved by modern cloth retailers, who are doping these simple girls, offering them, at a throwaway pricey, skimpy dresses, sleeveless, legless dresses, every quarter. They are advertising them to buy them, asking them to live in style. Live in style for cloth retailers probably means live with fewer clothes, baring sleeves, shoulders, bust and legs. In addition, the intoxication from west, in regard to frivolity of multiple screen interactions, regular TV watching, cell phones and the social media are in social place.

How can the girls, known until few years ago, for serious studies, in thin slice of metros in India, be expected to remain pure in mind, caring to the brothers, sisters and respectful to the parents and other relatives, when the social environment morphs so much and so quickly? This category of English articulated women, who are suffering, from intoxication, with wearing revealing dresses, unleashed by the cloth retailers, probably will have more time, for friends of opposite gender. They might be busy, scheduling meetings over weekends, with such friends of opposite gender. They would be seen, outing with friends, clasping them, on 2 wheeler motorbike drives, duly covering their face completely, to move around incognito. After interacting with multiple boys, feeling so casual in revealing, dresses, sharing smokes with them and taking alcoholic beverages, all constitute a sharp conflict, with Indian values and culture. It is no wonder that marriages registered, among a thin slice of the metros are breaking very fast unfortunately. For example, in Mumbai, the marriages that have been registered, have been breaking in 2 years, which is unimaginable, in the holy hand of India that prides itself of a 10,000 years of rich cultural heritage.

Government appears to have become too indifferent, when it comes to retaining, its own cultural heritage. Government is not aware that the cops in America, enforce laws and conventions, in a very stringent manner and arrest the deviants, defined, according to their culture and norms and book cases, with impunity. In the State of Illinois, for example, if 2 people shout at each other and slap, in a public place, the cops book them under law, for which punishment is 10 years of imprisonment. None can hold a beer can and drink beer, in the whole of America, in a public place, either in a bus or in a train or on a sidewalk. The cops arrest them immediately. If on 2 occasions, someone over speeds his vehicle, the car driving license is suspended for 1 year. While the western culture of dress and manners are seeping into India, through MNCs and BPOs and in other aspects of globalization but America enforces its own way of life and norms, whichever social disciplines, it deems fit.

Why then the Indian government and the police take such a liberal view, when openly following a totally contrarian culture, the youth tends to indulge in profanity, which might breed hooliganism, especially in cities, with huge slum population and very limited police force, in the police stations. The Home minister and The Prime Minister's office need to take a serious view, of such profanities and contain the frivolity of being copy cats, of the west, as India's simple and pure social values and culture are ennobling and to be proud of. The cultural practices of India, so unique and pristine, not only need to be retained but launched abroad, to teach the West. The importance of self regulated social values, importance of lifetime marriage and the importance of allowing birth of children only, within the boundaries of marriage, are some of the important features of Hindu culture. The values, which tend to distinguishes the humans from animals, is the sanctity of marriage, within which men and women stay, with moral purity and then procreate children, within the marriage only.

9.2 US Government and Families Need to Promote Education of Rigor for Well Paying Jobs for the Young and Media Need to Emphasize on Sustaining Academic Rigor

The corporations of the developed world need to be sensitive, to reduce unnecessary frivolous ads, on the media and elsewhere and pay attention to corporate governance, corporate social responsibility and strengthen the hands of the government, to make higher education free at least, for those who are financially challenged. Security of tenure in jobs, would give dignity to the workplace, improve morale of the workforce and give the organizations, a dedication unknown, as of now. Government need not be hesitant to make bonus mandatory for the firms, which makes a profit and annual raise routine. If those working in manufacturing in Indian democracy, could get these benefits, a $14 trillion US democracy, could certainly make this happen. Further, such a firm need to be told, to recruit adequate personnel, for better supervision of quality products and respect the family life of family contact and leisure, for the American workers.

Disinclination in recent years of the students in USA, to go for studies of academic rigor, spending, whole lot of time on social media, have led to their taking lesser interest in Science and Math. The results of their being glued to the screens, viewing of social media, for more than 6 to 8 hours per day, are a recipe for invitation to poverty in future, with occasional joblessness and low paying jobs. Spades have to be called spades, instead of talking about promoting the self esteem of the young. Besides, affecting the eye sight, the electronic media screens are likely to whittle down the available time, for home work and serious study. Parents in the homes, have to act with proper guidance, to the children, to stay away from the screens and be at the study table, as their counterparts address in Asia. In a global economy, if the American young will have to compete, in higher education, in science and math and then land high paying jobs, staying at the study table for long hours and being away from fun providing social media, will have to be adhered to. In a non globalized world, even a high school education in USA, could fetch nice jobs that brought some of them, as high as senior Vice President level. As of now, the employers are too choosy and too uncaring, in the light of global choices of the talents required and they do not hesitate, to refuse Americans, if they fail to come up to their official expectations. Media could avoid confusing the young, talking loud, about the screen centric, internet centric products that could intoxicate the young, as much as alcohol does to the middle aged.

Government abhors alcoholics and those, who are wasting precious time, of the formative years of life on the social media need, to be critically viewed too, by the parents, elders, the community and the government. It is not fair to allow them, to be on social media, for 8 hours a day, allow them to neglect home work, expect school teachers, not to rebuke them for neglect of studies. That would lead to the denial to them, of the good jobs, interviewers saying that they are not strong in science, math and number centric subjects. It hurts the young in America, when academic comparisons take jobs abroad and it is unfair too. Hence the young students, need to move away from the screens, to the academic rigor and time, at the study table, like their Asian counterparts. Books have to come back to American homes, if standard of living of future generations, has to be sustained, especially in the globalized world. Even libraries will do well, to remove computers, as one finds in different states of USA, the city libraries have more staff than readers. Further, those who use the library, are not glued to the books and merely read on the computer, Google unedited general information, which does not sharpen analysis of issues and cognitive talents. Cognitive talent development, needs reading of quality books, which have been edited and carry respectable language. Forums, to which the students go, have little to impart knowledge and they are routine tete a tete that too, not without the pollution of ribald language that takes away the scholarliness of a student. Most of the job, requires face to face interaction, the capacity of which thoroughly weakens, because of those hours on screens and the internet. Even vocabulary, is similar without variety, between a people from Boston to Santa Clara, Kansas city to Rockford in Illinois. Sometimes due to internet language interface, the vocabulary in an eatery would be very similar and it's hard to know if the guy is a high school dropout or a high school or have done an undergraduate. A person need to acquire chastening of behavior and language, with university education, which is deemed higher and above all costs, a lot for the students and their parents in America. With a life expectancy of about 80 years, there is enough time for TV and the internet, after seriously paying attention, to the books, scholarliness and paying attention to science and math, in formative years of one's life and land a nice high paying job. That would make further professional advancement easy. In USA and the west, drowning oneself in routine peer interaction, after school hours, on texting and social media frivolities, merely waste precious time, because media is asking the young, to devalue themselves, with entertainment, to make high money, at their expense.

In the emerging world, the students take the challenge of academic rigor, attend to a lot of home work, pay more time and attention to science and math, studying in schools, where furniture lack and one has to sit sometimes, on the carpet sometimes and take a small board to clip papers and write., where misdemeanor of not attending to home work, could land students, to rebuke by the teacher and even suspension, from the class, for few days. The bold challenge takers, in academic work are those, who are raised, in simple utilitarian homes, in an economy like India, where per capita income, could be as low, as one sixteenth of the per capita of America. These academic challenge, facing young from India, for example are liberally recruited, by the MNCs, many a times, to the exclusion of the US educated young Americans. Obsession with the screens, created by the producers of these multiple internet based products and the media egging on viewers, to use them, by giving false promises, of jobs and job contacts, are causing wastage of time, hours on end. In fact, they should be paying attention to the study..

Media has to promote better products, not youth ruinous products, of needless distraction from studies, office work, family life and child care. When the rich, who are educated and socially respected, discriminate against the poor, in multiple ways, it results in the neglect of human capital. In the west, the ripple negative effects of the burden of history, lack of self-confidence and then lack of self-respect, all of these psychological aspects, go in a big way, to impede the velocity of "poverty reduction" in an economy, among the minorities, no matter how much the government tries to achieve, the goals of poverty reduction. Even the good will of the IMF and the World Bank would be of no avail. Even genuine help from developed world would only improve matters marginally. Land reforms inclusive banking, absence of discrimination the feeling of unity of mankind are the legs, on which the table of the poverty reduction has to rest.

9.3 Media and Establishment Criticism

The media need to be questioned.. Why make India look like Libya, Syria and Egypt a country, where hundreds of millions of people toil to develop the country and numerous constituencies make, development happen and have succeeded to bring the nation, in just about 6 decades of self rule, to excellence in numerous fields of human welfare? Should the media not propagate pride, in these efforts of the Indians, to build nation? It has turned a fashion in India of late, among the players of the electronic media, to criticize the government and that too incessantly. It causes huge damage to the economy and also people's trust in institutions, such as the banks. A lot of noise has been occurring, about the criminal background of the politicians in India. While excluding those, who have the charges of heinous crime, such as murder from allocation of political tickets for elections, probably the government needs to analyze, why in the rural areas, the litigation is far higher and so is the complaining attitude of the rural people. It is hard to know even for those, who visit and keep contact with villages, as to why so many FIRs are lodged and in many cases even charge sheets are being filed in large numbers.

Those tried by trial courts, have the opportunity to go to High Court and then to the Supreme Court. There is likelihood for those convicted, by the lower court, to go on appeal to the bench of the Supreme Court. As a result of the conviction, by a lower court, the convicts have access, to higher courts and convictions, cannot be treated as final, probably to disallow them, to contest for MLA and MP seats. Thus disallowing grant of tickets, for contesting elections, as candidates of political parties, may not be fair, when the appeal opportunities, have not been exhausted. Ultimately, judicial decision would prevail and that would be binding on the political parties.

Some in the media have been vociferously, arguing that those, who are in police custody or judicial custody also, may not be allowed, to contest elections to legislature and parliament. When nothing is proved and when no charge sheet has been filed, no evidence has been marshaled, FIR could have just been filed, to create some sensation, and in fact the trial could lead to the court throwing away the case, for want of adequate proof a political party probably being asked by the media, discussing the same in the talk show, not to grant political tickets for elections, appear to be unfair. The respondent may have been in custody to prevent him from manipulating evidence, as per the police version but that does not seem a disqualification to serve in politics, if it could finally be proved as a false case, to damage his political life and reputation.

Indian media has been incessantly criticizing, the government on one account, or the other. Further, the media also appears, to be diluting the role of democratic institutions, such as the judiciary and investigating agencies like police. The media condescendingly thinks that they have to constantly remind, the institutions of democracy.

The media, of late, is indulging also, in chain of inappropriate moves, strangely remaining unregulated by its regulators, to remain within the bounds of law. Many of their moves appear to be flaunting their ego. For example, where a complaint is filed, it needs to be viewed, only as a compliant, and the media need not start behaving like doubting Thomas. which could be deeming a complaint, to be a truth before investigation. Electronic media is seen to start arranging talk shows and loudly treat the accused, as a criminal and speak against him, in a derogatory manner. Before any evidence is adduced. in the court or before a charge sheet is filed, treating an accused as a criminal, tantamount to indecency and playing, with the reputations, of an individual on the line, even, at the national level, and it is so unfortunate.. A matter that should only seize the attention of an investigative agency and a court of law, cannot be usurped by a third party, even if it is the media, and no person's or family's reputation could be trashed, in the manner, it is happening in India, especially due to irresponsible media's conduct, to trash a person, a family or an institution's image. There have been cases, where matter is under investigation and the media colors the view.'

There has been cases, where the matter is sub judice and the trial is going on and the media discusses it in its talk shows. There are cases, where no charge sheet is filed, but the case details reach the nation, through the media. The media in India, is getting away, with such high intensity of misdemeanors and sometimes illegal moves, as the regulatory action is next to nothing.

It is the regulatory arbitrage, which made the EU crisis and the US Economic and Financial Meltdown, happen. It has been acknowledged, by the US Congress and the US President. In India, even persons holding adjudicating positions, high in authority, where incumbent or retired may have been addressed, in the talk shows by the TV person, in the most derogatory manner. In the functioning of, democracy, one has never seen, till the new millennium came, such moves. The media, strangely, is celebrating the negatives, the discomfitures of those, in authority. Merely because some complainant has gone to the police and has filed an FIR, the person complained against is insulted, in the view of the whole nation, by being called names, as a criminal. Media knows that the complaint could be true or false, and it could be filed, by a biased person and he/she could be biased, due to caste divide, economic divide, personality divide, provincial divide, linguistic divide, political divide. A bad case can be brought against any person, even against an innocent person. Media has been calling names, even when no investigations have been done or no charge sheet has been filed or not even accused has been examined by the court of law. How could the institutions of police and the courts, be diluted in this fashion and everyone looks the other way?

Enfeebling government, by incessantly lionizing issues, making a mountain of mole hills has been going on, for years now, in the media, in the new millennium. A nexus between corporations and the media, to reduce regulation of corporation, by the government, in India appears to be discernible. To an extent, this has happened in America, enfeebling the role of government, as a regulator. After economic and financial meltdown in 2008, it has been stated even by the US government that the crisis to an extent, is the outcome of regulatory failures. Intelligentsia world over has acknowledged a link between global economic crisis of 2008 and regulatory failures.

Media's job is not to incessantly spread, negative energy that could demoralize the officials and politicians, to turn disinterested, in implementation of the development schemes. Their commitment, to the schemes of poor welfare, could easily turn halfhearted. Whenever among the hundreds of thousands of the politicians, some politicians are found, to be involved in corruption, politicians as a class, are attempted to be denigrated, by the latest Indian media, which appears unfair. When some financial irregularities are noticed, in a couple of Ministries, all Ministries are attempted to be painted black.. There are about 76 departments in the union government. How on earth, irregularities in 2 out of 76 mimicries take the form of multiple weeks and multiple months of discussion on corruption of the entire government machinery, calling repeatedly talk shows spewing venom, against the government and trying to weaken regulation, in the economic system. Why should the Minister for Information and Broadcasting, not appropriately guide the media and the media regulator, to play its role with maturity and not act incessantly with negative euphoria?

One observes electronic media, in India, is busy celebrating negative news, about the establishment. It seems to revel in embarrassing, the incumbent government. It appears to be in an intoxication and hundreds of millions of people, who are in poverty could be frustrated, by such 24/7 negative news, dinned into their ears, along with a lot of TV soap operas, which uncensored or inadequately censored are spewing a lot of belligerences in the home environment. The dramas shown indirectly, have the potential of triggering a lot of belligerences in real homes, in cities and in villages, because of the ubiquitous coverage of the electronic media.

Media by showing belligerences in Hollywood films and TV soap operas and talk shows have for decades, now heavily influenced the home environment, in the west. US TV is an obsession into midnight and belligerences have risen by leaps and bounds, particularly between spouses, roiling their marriages. To the disadvantage of moral hygiene, detrimental to the caring of the aged and the children, both infants and teenagers, the western families of the developed world, are heavily challenged by divorces and debt disasters. Personal finances have tanked considerably, in the last quarter of 20th century, a lot of, which can be attributed, to the spread of media, particularly in the new millennium, making it mindlessly 24/7 and keeping this industry off adequate regulation.

India in several realms of development needs, to be the leader of the world and not a slavish follower, of the west anymore. Instead the media, with a huge slavish attitude to the west, is influencing Indian viewers, to adopt negatives, which with media influence, is bedeviling the west, for decades now, without a solution, in sight..

Government need to take steps, to make electronic media, move away from its 24/7 negative infliction, which is digressing the young and the students, from seriousness of studies. The media, as of now, has been bringing the negative influences, from some of the news talk shows and some portions of the TV soap operas, which are brought into homes. Interpersonal communication between spouses, between parents and children between siblings and inter generations have ebbed, because of the electronic screens, available seamlessly on a 24.7 basis.

This has come from the west and the Government of India need to take the global leadership, to send pristine thoughts and practices from India, to the developed world, priding itself with its ability to run its economy, banks, educational sector in fine shape, when the developed countries are grappling, with numerous problems, on all of these fronts and sometimes have no clues, how to address them. Indian politicians and the bureaucrats need, to delve into studies made by Nobel Laureate scholars, about India's plusses to effervesce with pride and lead the world.

Media, by giving incessant coverage of Mr. Anna Hazare and Mr. Ram Deva, the TV Yoga teacher, at Ram Leela grounds, has made India look in the perception of the international community, the likes of the capital cities of Libya, Syria and Egypt. Government need to very seriously think should the media be allowed to trash the image, of such a great country, in this manner, merely obsessed with its sensationalizing news and talk shows, for them to survive, in their livelihoods. Can a nation of a billion and a quarter, be taken for a ride, by an industry that benefit a thousand business owners and a few thousand journalists, spewing venom, with news/talk shows, days on end, celebrating all of the time, negative news against the country?

That does not take away the fact that corruption is evil and needs to be checked and law enforcement authorities and institutions under the constitution, need to be always seized to contain and eliminate the same and judiciary to punish the guilty. I am only saying that corruption, an evil item need not be a theme of entertainment, for arm chair crocodile tear jerking middle class people, among whom, many of them soak themselves, in illegal money making and induce people, to take bribe to jump the ques and like to point fingers to other professions and people. Media's mindless obsession, to remain in criticism of the establishment and frustrate the young minds, whom world is calling demographic dividend, in India, is reprehensible.

With brand equity of the government trashed to deep south, by the media criticism, how would tens of millions of families, how could its citizens add value, to its economy or even increase productivity of the economy. Once a society gets demoralized, by news statements that the rust in the government plummets from media, and it is very difficult to enthuse them to be optimistic and me them address professional work, to make developments happen and a new job addressed well. Poverty reduction in a situation so confusing, would go out of the door and poverty increase would be the natural outcome.

9.4 Media and Western Influence Through Globalization : Media and Fear Generation

Media in India appears to generate a lot of fear, in a society that faces, a huge problem of the consequences of exploitative 200 years of the British rule. During the British rule, in India, it is a common knowledge that the revenue was collected, by appointing private agents, for collection, who were given huge freedom, to fleece the peasants. In addition, the private agents could collect any amount of money, for himself as the revenue collection charges. The farmers fell naturally in despair, needed personal loans, which were permitted by the British, to be granted by highly money avaricious, private money lenders, the land lords, zamindars and even the rajas. They charged usurious interests, which were reflected in the huge opulence of the raja's lifestyle, palaces unknown even, with monarchies of the west. Thus the British and those supported by the regime, enriched themselves, apart from the revenue, being sent to British exchequer. In addition, at a very low cost, the British army grew in size, with millions of recruits. They were recruited in India, at a low cost to go and fight the global wars. Between the two wars 2.5 million Indians lost their lives. No pensions were granted to the families of the soldiers. The army was used also to checkmate Russian expansion to Afghanistan. and the Russian expansion to India in early 1900s. This was in no way beneficial, to India and its people, but it was a part of the British imperial policy. A lot of expenditure was done, to spend for war in Afghanistan and a lot of Indian soldiers were added, to the British army, to fight war with Russians in Afghanistan. The British neglected agricultural modernization in the rural India. They did not create employment by implementing, the employment generations schemes. Little was done to irrigate the land in the rural areas. No efforts were undertaken to expand literacy or health care, in the rural areas. Education even elementary and primary levels were totally neglected, so was the electricity generation and its transmission to rural areas.

Despite all of these neglectful moves, by the British, the current media has remained quite mute, to criticize the British rule. Instead, it occasionally praises pre 1947 India. Free market ideologues, such as Milton Friedman went to make such erroneous observations, talking about advantages of free trade, knowing well that India, heavily suffered from the British protectionism, at the British territories and free trade at the Indian territories and no encouragement of Indian industries. Instead, the British took upon themselves, to kill Indian industries, as an easy way to kill competition for the British industries, particularly in the area of textiles. All of this, is kept pretty much under the carpet, by the international media. Indian media also has turned pretty slavish, since the advent of the new millennium.

Media, since 2000, after privatization, appears, to be doing little service, to India's development and is found most of the time, celebrating negatives that are magnified to lessen and blight the reputation and brand equity of the country, which is a country sprinting ahead, with several development positives, when a lot of the world is sleeping.

Media is busy castigating, national institutions such as politicians, to identify a few aberrations and is in the task of arrogating to themselves, the tasks and duties of other solemn institutions. Yellow journalism is at the peak and is used as a plank, on which the private channels want, to increase their viewership scores. The Indian electronic media want to address, all of these, for themselves, at the expense of demoralization of those, who struggle to develop India, with projects, working, under the scorching sun and keep India by and large peaceful, by a constant dialogue with the masses, The masses are motivated to be educated and then to educate their children. The public leaders and the politicians as a group, rub shoulders, with the poorest of the poor, who live in mud huts, endear them, smiling and laughing with them, taking lunches with them, in traditional style of sitting on the floor. This is what the leaders address, as a routine. I am sure the urbanites, who populate the media, would find it very challenging, even to lunch or dine with them, in such poor conditions, eating the food, cooked by poor people, sitting on the floor, even on a cosmetic basis. The problems that people face, are so big, as a result of 2 centuries of British neglect, of the rural masses that the budget required to plug the gap, may even take a century, The fact that the development of colonizing countries predominantly occurred, only after centuries of economic enrichment, of those countries, through their leveraging the colonization of Asia, Africa and Latin American countries, few from the media appear to understand. The cost of construction of a water supply scheme for 20,000 population or a concrete road for a mile or an irrigation scheme, to irrigate 10,000 acres of land, or repairing a tank that irrigates a few hundred acres of land, is rarely known, to the urban educated, even college/university educated people and also the electronic media. The budget per capita requirement of these schemes, once relayed for the entire India and analysis made objectively, for the whole of India, which has hundreds of thousands of villages, the media would understand that a video coverage would not make it anywhere, near the developed world, even in a century. With this impatience, to reach the category of a developed world village, the media is all the time, talking about lack of development in the villages and coming up with their figment of imagination.

They need to ascribe the lack of development, for a lot of deficit in government revenue, in government not setting the taxes for a lot of constituencies, who are enjoying the government kindness and disinclination of a lot of constituencies, to pay the taxes adequately and in time. Astonishingly, the media merrily criticizes, the government in India incessantly for the lack of development, at the pace at which, India to develop, in a condescending manner, to the leakages of funds, alleged to have been swindled, by political people, in different layers of development architecture, with indifference and sometimes with the collusion of the officials. Talking about specific schemes, carry the potential by investigation by investigating agencies.

Quite irresponsibly, more often than not, wild guesses are hazarded, with serious lies, such as hardly 40% of funds are reaching the villages. Some say hardly 20 % of funds are reaching the villages and some even pride their own self assumed honesty and dedication to the rural India and particularly the rural poor, screaming that 10% of funds, released by the government hardly reach the villages. Some of these people, who aver such falsehoods, with little evidence, have been known to be, perennially criticized, by the general masses. The media need to understand that such loose talks heavily demoralize the politicians, who with a dedication to the principles of democracy and remaining in constant touch, with the masses, resolving even their basic issues at the village level, the land issues. Moreover, the officers undertaking development works, for the betterment of the rural India, working under the scorching sun, get demoralized by criticism by the Media. Such loose talks are repeated in the media, spreading more salt on the wounds of those, who work in the grass roots.

Fear is generated, in the atmosphere and a chasm between the developers of rural projects and the beneficiaries in the villages, which carry the potential of deceleration of development works. The projects are not completed, sitting in ivory towers of the comfortable air conditioned electronic media studios. Instead, the officials and the politicians need to sweat in their sweat shirts not suits and ties, the slavish western dress, which the people in the media are given to. The politicians move with the masses. the incessant talk of the lying that funds supposed to be meant, for the villages are leaked, could disturb. Apart from the masses, some of whom may even believe the lies and try to disturb the execution of projects.

In a highly populated countryside, the media is aware, as to how big is the challenge of law enforcement, to be able to bring order, if such chaos is created, at the venues of the projects and how efficiently those, who are committed to development, the technocrats, officials and politicians could safely work in the villages.

The TV news and talk shows in Hindi, English and regional languages same news broadcasters incessantly could drive a serious wedge, between the governance and the people, for no fault of theirs, but due to sudden emergence of an exogenous factor called the 24/7 media in the new millennium, in a poor country of extremely low per capita income. People need to work incessantly, to develop the nation and not sit by the side of the TV screens, to listen to the 24/7 programs. Neither the information ministry thought this issue prudently nor the media, while lapping such a broad time, that these broadcastings, could be detrimental to the time management of a country of 1.2 billion. To cater to the ads of its promoters, the corporations, the media went a thousand miles, to gobble this 24/7 arrangement, with slavishness to Americana, in mind.

In recent years, the Indian media has gone, on to show violence and the crimes on the screen, which no media in the developed world, ever show. The politicians are shown in the media sometimes, getting manhandled by some people. Sometimes, the law enforcement officers in uniform are seen attacked, by the criminal minded people, causing injury and that is depicted in the media on a 24/7 bass, so that the whole nation could watch it. All of these do happen in the developed world too. In high schools of US, there occur quite a few situations, where the high school teachers, are manhandled disrespectfully, by a bunch of students, but never a single visual, of such incidents are shown, by the media on the TV. Not even such weird incidents discussed on the TV talk shows. A small column somewhere, in the daily news, is made, which could easily be lost sight by the TV viewers. Such is the maturity of the electronic media of America, which the Indian media fails to internalize. However, some negative aspects of the western media, gets immediately lapped by Indian media and slavishly implanted. Matured media in USA, never show a mutilated body, either a result of accident or a crime, unlike in India where mindlessly violence related scenes, get depicted meeting no purpose. New find enthusiasm of the private channels, are causing a lot of harm to India, which need either self-regulations or regulations by the ministry of information and broadcasting.

The media in India and its private multiple channels, granted in early 2000s, is too excited having come to existence and in that excitement, appears to have forgotten its role that would add value, to national peace and development. It appears unable to handle its new find existence since 2000. Mindlessly, the manhandling of a principal of a school /college or a politician and even people, beating policemen in uniform, are shown liberally, as though they are celebrating this negativity. One is surprised that regulatory authorities, the information and broadcasting ministry looks the other way. In one case, the Chief of a District, the District Magistrate was shown being injured by the irate mob and he was shown helplessly, running to his car. Does the media understand the severe damage done, to law and order where such onerous authorities, who protect people, even the media and their families are shown so helpless, to the people viewing the TV. One does not know if the TV channels are in their minds, when they trash the national dignity and national brand equity to garbage, exhibiting such visuals mindlessly. They need to be alert and cautious when such visuals are rerecorded leave aside showing them to the nation and to the world, on their TV channels. In the name of transparency, the unity and integrity of the country, cannot be thrown to winds.

The damage is done, which is very toxic, as the goodwill in the masses, which we see now in future could turn, ill will with misunderstanding, if such canard by the media, is continued against the politicians. None of the media personnel probably, come from political families and neither are they probably motivating, any of the younger members, in their families, including their children, to go for politics. They are aware, about the huge challenges that elected representatives face, at the grass root level, with a workplace that is highly distributed, among villages, where the duties involve moving from one village to another, walking around in the scorching sun, talking to the masses, dealing with their frustrations and celebrating their joys with enthusiasm, where the clients are not educated, not English speaking and not sophisticated. In politics, the interfaces are required, with extremely ordinary people, who are poor and not even in many cases literate. This comes in sharp contrast, to the air-conditioned studios, in which the educated personnel work, media responsibilities, with occasional representatives talking from the site for few minutes and the interfaces, happen to be again well dressed middle class, English speaking educated people.

So the media people know very little of the grass roots, live most of their working life, in urban areas, feed viewers with negative news and indulge in yellow journalism, to make a lot of money, from the corporate ads. They are in many cases, promoted by the corporations, flaunting corporate ads, after every 10 minutes, so that corporations have their bottom line and top line, cared for, by the media. To an extent, criticism of the development projects is fine, as it keeps the development people also on alert. But talking utter non sense, about the leakage of funds, knowing well that funds are used, properly and meticulously and moreover, the funds are highly inadequate, to cover even 30 % of the needs of the villages, because of the hoary past of the country, which was financially heavily exploited, by the rich feudals in India, with the support of the British regime, which many a time were not even accountable, to the British government in London.

Some media persons inebriated with celebration of negatives, over one decade, since these private channels were born, as a part of globalization and privatization of the media industry, may question that if they have to be away, from trashing India's brand equity by celebrating its routine negatives, then what could be their role. Their role probably would be, to entertain and inform, though once or twice a day, news about the country and the world could be fine. They need to refrain from restlessly identifying a topic for 365 days in a year, which naturally cannot be of importance and value. The time that they have exacted, by request to be either plummeted, to eliminate talk shows days on end. The topics would be otherwise be heavily in short supply, for 365 days a year and the time of a lot of adults, adolescents and even children, would be grossly wasted, with this 24/7 TV, that is already roiling the professional and academic standards in America.

The information and broadcasting ministry has to seriously think, of shrinking this time that is harming a lot of seriousness to professional world, family duties and academic concentration. The TV industry having been, located in a country of very low per capita income, will have to be content with few hours of broadcasting, instead of showing garbage in many channels, 24/7 for 56 weeks, in a year. The TV has a serious element of causing intoxication of a kind, not very different from alcoholism, from where it is hard to withdraw. It is not dissimilar to the nicotine in the cigarettes, which asks the individual to smoke again. Other categories of intoxication include alcohol and smoking that damage health and cause many physical ailments are no different from obsession with screens including 24/7 TV. Few in America tend to realize that the TV could cause obesity, improper food intake, neglect of job/ family and finally mental depression of a severe type, if the person lives a lonely life, as it happens, more in the west and then TV programs supports a lonely life. In no small measure, in America's high density of overweight, highly obese unmarried people, suffering from severe loneliness and occasional depression bouts, are on the canter, if not gallop and this is because of obsessive TV viewing. It is due to the ubiquity of TV, in all homes, all sports bars, all fast food places, all auto repair places, most eateries, all lounges of offices, all cafeterias of hospitals. It can be observed that the health of the average American have been in recent years, in a downward trend. People of all ages are obsessed with TV screens and the screens of different smaller sizes. They have forgotten the outdoors, have lapped the vitamin D deficit, staying indoors for most of the day, every day. They now lead a sedentary life of laziness in general, for over 15 to 20 years. This correlates exactly with the period, in which the US inequality, between the rich and the poor, has widened immensely and the poverty has increased for both the poor and the middle class, drastically.

US has started to witness poverty, almost of the types of great depression of 1929, 1939, except a green spirit that within a few years, all will be fine economically. Time will however tell the truth. Could something be more bizarre than this ubiquity of screens, with some mutterings, all the time? Does it make sense for the media, to ask everyone, to succeed in life and achieve American dream of a living standard that is nice? How many in USA are watching the TV, most of the wake up time and also few hours into the midnight, not going to sleep. Could one achieve American dream, in such a negative scenario? There is no need to be, so slavish to 24/7 TV of the US type, and instead, it is better for India to keep the timing moderate, say 3 to 4 hours on a single day. Otherwise the frivolity and a lot of misinformation of western TV, would get introduced, in the Indian media industry.

The media prefers to be pretty mute, on the excesses perpetrated by the colonial powers. The poverty that one sees in India, today is significantly the making of the exploitation of the Britain and that fact instead of being shown, once in a while, India's negatives are overblown by the media The glorious lifestyles that the British officials enjoyed in India, were a matter of envy, even for the Britain based government and corporate officials, because they did not have, even half the luxuries that the British officials, in the colony of India availed, by almost fleecing, the villages. Some of the governor generals were known for, not even maintaining development expenditure accounts properly and impeachment proceedings had to be brought against them, by the British parliamentarians. One such major example was that of Mr. Warren Hastings, the governor general of India, in the early 19th century. These pieces of information, in contrast, during the British period, need to be highlighted by the TV, so that the green excitement, about the west, among the Indian demographic dividend, gets corrected knowing about the ethics in politics and foreign relations the western powers tend to follow.

How nicely representative is the democracy, in India, the media need to uphold, instead of a few oligarchs, grabbing political power, in other parts of the world. Even in the developed world, those making big money through lobbyists, tend to influence the law makers on their side, while no interface is visible of the senators or congresswomen, in poor neighborhoods. India's plusses need, to be highlighted to the people who are very young, self ruled nation of 60 and odd years, by the media and not berate its achievements..

The politicians of today are drawn from the villages, from all communities, such as forward castes, labor castes, trading castes and while the constitution provided, for reservation in profession and education for castes initially for 15 years, but that period was extended, with the initiatives of the politicians. The politicians in India, generally hail from villages and they generally belong to the farming communities **So** the Parliament, all the State Assemblies and the District Zila Parshads, reflect a mirror image of the Indian society. In other words, such a combination of law makers, indicate a fine index of nicely functioning democracy. Associated with the Parliament and the State Assemblies, there are functional committees such as Finance Committee, Industries Committee, Committee over viewing Affirmative Action, in regard to welfare of the Scheduled castes, Scheduled Tribes and Backward Classes, Women and Child welfare Committee and the like, within the Parliament, In these committees, the members examine different aspects of development, sometimes, travelling to the institutions and their branches, in the States and in the Districts. They also advise the administration and in case of dereliction of duties and responsibilities, fault them, duly taking action, against the administration. Officials. These committee meetings are pretty long drawn and the officials are asked a barrage of questions. I wish the representatives of the media, watch some of these Legislature and Parliamentary Committee meetings, as to how effectively; the officers are reviewed, by the representatives of the people. Wherever, there have been unnecessary cost overruns, due to delay in completion of the projects, disciplinary actions against some senior officers/ engineers/ doctors, as well are initiated, as per the deliberations of these meetings This is however not to state that there could not be exceptions of some money greedy politicians.

Democracy is expected to have open minded media persons, never indulging in loose talks, without adequate exposure to the villages, where the projects are taken up and then coming to wildly wrong conclusions that funds meant for the poor and villages, are not properly utilized. Probably, the media need to think, as to how vociferous the general masses, could be, in the villages, as they have the gut intelligence, in India's effervescent democracy, to keep a tab, on what has been sanctioned and executed. They have a kind of gut sense, intelligence that few in the non rural areas can comprehend. Swindling of money by few, from few projects, even have the potential of the mass leaders in the villages, turning violent against the officials and the politicians merely on suspicion. Besides, government has been remaining alert, with its administrative, vigilance and policing to contain corruption, wherever it occurs.

9.5 Media and Noise in Married Life

Media is also generating a lot of fear, in society, to endanger the peace of the family, egging on married couples to complain, in case of a quarrel, between the spouses. They are rushing to the urban neighborhoods, as soon as they receive a phone call, which in most cases have been, a phone call from the woman. They cover a video clip of what she talks, washing dirty linen in public, about quality of her marriage and how husband has been arrogant. Then the media in an inebriated manner, also seeks the husband's views and he also spews the venom, against the wife. After media team is gone, by evening many a times, the neighborhood people report that both have patched up their differences and are seen by the neighbors, going for outing happily, in a two wheeler. But the damage is done. Neighbors have come to know of the entire nuisance in the life of that married couple and they would view that couple disparagingly. It is flashed either live or non-live, to all of its viewers, not only in the city, but all of places, where the channel has the outreach. All of the married couples of all ages now talk, as though they can blackmail each other, fight virulently, with each other, show heightened anger and even abuse each other. The media instead of confining their scope of their duties are intruding, into private lives of people, in a slavish manner, probably, learning some aspects from the west, where they are aware that family and marital values have gone south considerably.

They tend to give ads, to contact a phone number and keep egging people to report, to complain, in case of belligerences with the spouse. Egged on continuously, some more women and men, are likely to spew venoms to the media, all of such activities have, the potential to trash the multi millennium pristine Indian culture and values to the trash, finally hurting the lifetime features, of the Indian marriage system that the world appreciates and raves about.

Now the families stay in fear, when would the spouse frame them, through the media? Media on the lines of the western media, has been coming up with TV serials, with themes that were leveraged for viewership, by the film industry, making a mountain of a mole hill, of mother in law, daughter in law adjustment minor challenges, by amplifying mother in laws misbehavior, making the script look like, husband's mother was a monster, ready to beat his wife. The regional channels also, to an extent like Hindi chancels, are exhibiting such unnatural weird theme centric serials. In the theme, usually the husband is depicted, as supporting his mother, at least in a benign manner, making the wife feel all the more, harassed.

As a result of believing, in the themes, continued in such weird TV serials, a lot of young women, in the urban India, fear to get married. People openly express that they find their daughters, watching these TV serials, seriously as though, they are depictions of real life and it is hard, to pull them away from TV, to take even dinner or lunch, in time until the serial is over. They feel frightened that they may experience such horrendous life, after marriage and they feel frightened to get married. This fear is universal, ranging from those, who come from different economic backgrounds. Thus interest, leave aside excitement in a marriage, which used to be ubiquitous in marriage among the young in the last few years in the new millennium with TV receiving mild regulation, has plummeted in a thin slice of urban India.

Another type of TV serial, depicts modern English articulated women, to be fashionable, by western sense of the term in their tight fit jeans and tops dresses, revealing more than covering the sensuality. They are depicted as rebels and right by the media. They are rebels and talk rude with the elders, in their own home and in the husband's home. Such women are shown, economically successful, acceptable to the labor market and disrespectful to elders in the home. Particularly, they are shown to be intolerant, to husband's parents. On the basis of the education, she is shown to slight other family members, which is never true, among women, in real Indian society. She is depicted as very rude, with her husband, in conversation in the way, she manages her own money, mostly saving it and expecting husband, to run the expenses of the home. She is shown to care only for the career and not to raise the family and not to have children, in the near future.

Media seems to be trying to sculpt them, as one, intensely on western lines, the likes of which are hard to find, in real society, even in urban India,

The rudeness of the fashionable women on the TV, is alien to the Indian way of life. In reality an Indian woman, is an epitome of values and qualities and besides being professional, she knows her family responsibilities,. One hears about Indian working woman, happily supporting the family, in addition to the duties in the workplace and these aspects have been off and on, aired by women holding CEO positions also such as Indira Nooyi the CEO Pepsi, Chanda Kocher, CEO of ICICI and the Dr Arundhuti Bhattacharya, Chairman and Managing Director of the State Bank of India, effectively, to give a few examples. But strangely the Indian media, tends to depict her in the garb of some of the rebellious women. The effort is to show how the Indian women have turned closer to the western women, leaving children to the care of others most of the wake up hours. Even western women too know the challenges of ignoring the family in reality.

The women and men, who in their adolescence, have been happy to get married, even until recently. Until the 1990s they were used to look up to marriage, with lot of excitement, in urban areas. In the 2000s, the media incessantly appears to egg on them that they need to be rebellious, instead of following the cultural norms. Some weird TV serials, bordering on criminality, are chosen for broadcasting. Out of millions of peaceful happy homes, are chosen some very weird themes, and women's exploitation is deliberately depicted, to create a gender divide. The attempt here, is to get surfeit of themes, with gender divide on the lines of the west. Attempt is to enable corporate India, to make pecuniary gains from such divides. That appears to be the intention, of a number of TV channels that exist because of the support of corporate India. In the background of some original stories, bordering on crime, where women are insulted in the family, the serials embolden the female viewers, to misbehave with husband and his family, in real life. Such weird divisive themes, shown on the TV, fits well, to egg on creating gender divide, which has done a lot of harm, to the western society and economy, creating huge mistrusts among people, within the families and in the community.

Women, in a thin slice of urban India, are pretty riveted/ glued to the TV and some of the female viewers, tend to believe the stories, spewed by the media and also morph, to be rebellious and enjoy the freedom of being unmarried, as long as they wish,. Such women are in the vanguard of indulging, in inter-gender friendships and to an extent feeling the Americana, while distancing from the Indian values. Such women deem Indian values, to be conservative and obsolete.

TV serials dealing with such themes are also polluting the minds, of male viewers. Some men are seen, to express view that marriage could be a liability, if it is fraught with such an uninteresting belligerent life, with the wife and if it could cause also so much indignity, to his parents and relatives. He gets certainly frightened by such TV serial themes, where wife is shown to harass husband and in laws alleging and filing false criminal complaints, to extort money from husband, asking the husband to sign on a mutually agreed divorce. The media in India in the new millennium, is certainly successful, to influence a thin slice of urban India, to be a part of Americana, such as late marriages, belligerent attitudes as spouses, a break up in a few years and then a remarriage. All of these are so called popular themes, of the media. Should the information and broadcasting ministry not guide them, to remain in consonance with what most of India is and how pristine is the multi millennium institution of marriage is in India, for thousands of years, not a few centuries.

Should they not be one with sages, like Swami Vivekananda, who appealed to the young Indians, to launch a cultural leadership movement, to lead the world?, In the realm of culture and spirituality the Indian media need to be guided that the west is certainly, not to be copied but led by India, with its spirituality.

Let the TV producers and actors and the channel owners not financially gain, at the expense of the loss of the India's moral hygiene that is a multi millennium phenomenon and to be retained and preached to the world, including the developed world, where moral hygiene is heavily challenged though physical hygiene is excellent..

In both types of TV serials, the themes move about only one gender, to desperately create a type of divide, which has been wrecking the values in the western world. In India, men and woman in their marriage, have always liked to be happy individuals, since millenniums, living together with endearing children. Sharing duties in life that make a family life dutiful and responsible to each other, to the children, to the parents and the elders has been the age old Indian practice.

In the new millennium, the electronic media is hell bent trying, to cloud the minds of both genders, egging on them, to devalue the Indian lifetime marriage, from multiple dimensions. Ministry of Information and Broadcasting Ministry, Ministry of Culture, Ministry of Family and Child Welfare and the Ministry of Home need to work, in sync, to keep in constant interface with the channels, so that they do not impair the pristine family values that have come to this generation, from times immemorial. Values in the Vedas, in the messages of Lord Buddha and that of Lord Mahavira and in Bhagawat Geeta are not meant, only for chanting, in the places of worship and not meant only to be remembered, during festivals. They are for everyday life, of rectitude, for the Indians and the Ministries need to sensitize themselves and sensitize the channels, before it is too late, in the impairment of culture, through globalization/Americanization.

Based on very few negative, social occurrences/crimes, emanating from inter gender anger and wrong behavior, extrapolating the same to the whole country, the lawmakers in India have passed a law in 2005, reflecting a general gender divide, making false assumptions, about the relative differences of conduct, of the 2 genders in India. This law, unfortunately has indirectly provided for a wife, to approach the Court, in case of wife's perfection of physical and mental harassment. It has converted for some women, in a thin slice of the metros, an opportunity, to consider marriage as a business, to enrich themselves overnight, by threatening husbands that unless a few million rupees are handed over to her, she is going to blackmail him and his family by giving a false report, to police. This bizarre law also appears to have come about, without adequate due diligence, under the pressure of some activist groups, who slavishly think, following western themes, which is in sharp contrast with Indian way of marital and family life.

This law has been misused, by many women, in metros and big cities specially, for extortion of money, from the husband, by raising false allegations or threatening to file false FIR. Even the advocates and law enforcing authorities, openly aver that by misusing these laws, many women, have converted marriage, as a ticket to be overnight rich and have made marriage a business, through filing of false complaints. Thus many of them are uttering falsehoods, against the husband, without any fear of perjury.

These cases overnight, after 10,000 years of unbreakable Indian marriage system, have downed the image of the institution of marriage. Because of heavy money greed of some women, such false cases have caused enormous damage, to the lifetime pristine noble and honest institution of Indian marriage, which was deemed to be the most happy occasion, in human life so for, in India, be it a man or a woman, even until the 1990s. The adornments of the bride and the bridegroom, the happiness of the guests, on both sides, illumination of the venue of the marriage, adornment of the house and the feast that accompanies the Indian marriage, the music and the dance, the Barat, the bridegroom's journey to the bride's place, are all indexes of how much of value, is accorded in realty, to the institution.

It involved huge sacrifice, to be loyal to each other forever, to raise a family and spend most of the time, with spouse children, outside the workplace. Life in India, for a human, always surrounds, the institution of marriage. It called for the delight of duty, to the children, to the spouse and family. New families for both were a source of joy and even extended relatives, on both sides, are treated courteously and time spent with them. Indian bride and the bridegroom constitute the most adorned married couple, in the world. The number of guests, who come to attend the marriage, are the largest ever, known in the world and the amount of jewelry that the bride receives, as a gift, from her parents and her family and from her in laws, make her look like a princess or a queen, unlike a bride, in any part of the world.

Such a beautiful institution is being trashed, by misusing 2005 law, by some women in the thin slice of the metros, to make huge extortion of money. She injects fear in the husband that his reputation, built over decades, could be trashed in garbage, once she goes to the police station and lodges a false FIR, with false allegations of mental and physical harassment.

Writing these 2 words makes, it seems, mandatory, for Station House Officer, to register the FIR and to arrest her husband, her parents in laws and other relatives, on her husband's side. Whoever she names, dooming everyone's reputation, of numerous decades, to garbage and to avoid it, she expects her man, to prostrate before her and to pay whatever money she demands. Such a bizarre law, assuming that one gender consists of the angels and the other gender consists of the devils, have been passed mindlessly and it is implemented, in this manner. Relying on a mere averment of a woman, once she names her husband, files a complaint of harassment, it is enough to cause the agony, to the husband, no matter how innocent he is, how nice has been his conduct always, how pristine is the reputation of the family, for generations and the, arrests are made. A woman's voice accordingly, appears to be a gospel truth and no investigations seem necessary, before arresting her closest relatives, her husband and his parents.

In India, the principles of natural justice and the rule of law, prevails and in such an environment, how is it that at the instance of a woman, with no evidence produced by her, a man has to face, such indignities, in many cases, without reasons? When the husband and his parents are arrested, presumably, on her false complaint, to make extortion of money, the money seeking woman, has the last laugh.

This is not to say that any man should go scot free, after causing harassment to his wife. If the alleged complaint is found to be true, after investigations and by the court of law, he certainly deserves to be severely punished. But arresting husband, on a mere complaint, filed by his wife, with no evidence adduced and without police even, taking up any investigations, appears too much of an agony and is reflective of intense gender divide in store for years and decades to come. It needs to be kept by those, who decide, in mind, that India is an ancient country, where gender divide never existed and children revered both parents equally, whom they saw together for a life, unlike other parts of the world, where marriages are too fragile to their disadvantage. In India judiciary and the administration including the police need to think that both parents command equal respect from their children. There is no need like the west and America, to have a separate Mother's day and a Father's day. In India the employed children come home and see both parents in one go, spending pleasant time, with them and thus expenditure, is limited whereas in most families in the west and America, the adult children have to plan separate visits, incurring twice expenditure to travel, to meet father and mother annually, at 2 different places, as their parents are divorced and they do not stay together. This is the plight, not only of the parents but also of their adult children, both socially and economically, hurting them and is a consequence of manufacturing artificially, for corporate America's higher profits, the concept of gender divide. The feelings of gender divide, whipped incessantly in the US and the west, have made divorce, a rule now and staying in marriage, turning into an exception.

Marriage in India is one of a lifetime, as per the culture and religion of India, though law permitted a divorce since only 1955. This nuisance of divorce, caused by the money greedy spouses, is happening to families, in the new millennium, after the law of 2005 was enacted in India. Such is the mindless enacting, of a law that seem to be destroying the purity, of Indian Hindu marriage system, in a thin slice of the India's metros. In the realm of society, law makers in India, will have to act, in the Indian context, as Indian culture and values, are based on spirituality and pristine moral values, which have little in common, with other parts of the world. India needs to take a leadership, to launch a cultural movement that would make families strong, worldwide, not only in India, which would make child care and care of the aged a pious duty, not only in India but worldwide and where unity of mankind, will be the essence of human life, and not divisiveness of any kind, including gender divide.

Such nuisance is happening, to a lot of people, of nice character and repute, known for nobility decency, for generations, to their family and public at large, in different professions, which include, being a doctor, a minister, an engineer an architect an academic, a police officer an attorney, professions, to which husband and parents in laws belong. Men are feeling artificially gender divided and humiliated, for no fault of theirs, on several occasions. In India, there is astonishment, due to this bizarre law and this law is viewed as a trigger for immorality, except in a few genuine cases of husband hurting his wife which is rare.

In India, small boys and girls, playing together, in the family, as brothers and sisters, respecting their parents equally and respecting aunts and uncles, and getting endeared equally, in the extended family, are growing up suddenly, to find that India has a bizarre law of 2005, which treats them differently. They are aghast that this bizarre law, believes one and disbelieves another and a half page complaint; on a piece by wife is enough, to doom husband's reputation in family, community and among friends. He is addressed, as a criminal, in correspondence and arrested without any investigations, due to a complaint from his wife, who adduces no evidence of any wrong done to her.

He is aghast that until yesterday, he saw entire humanity as one and today, a bizarre law is suddenly looking society as 2 different genders, with a divide between them, carved artificially by some vested interests.

West has come up, with the concept of a highly erroneous concept of a gender divide, for quite some time, which can be traced to several centuries but India, has no such discriminations. India's attitudes, even in electoral politics, where the entire developed world, very haltingly gave political rights, to women, where admissions in the western universities, were also haltingly agreed, after several decades of fighting by women, have been the most progressive. For 200 years the British ruled in India. in their own country, the British treated the 2 genders differently, by disallowing their women, to vote for a long time, despite decades of suffrage movement. In contrast, as soon as India became independent, from the British rule, in 1947, India's Constitution provided for absolute equality of men and women. The Constitution and government in India gave universal suffrage, to every human being, to vote for all elected institutions, such as state legislatures and the national parliament. Even in first elections in independent India, the men and women voters, with pride marched to polling stations, to vote for the Members of Parliament and State Legislatures. In India, not a single year, not a single month, not a single day, the Indian women had to be on the street, to beg the government, to grant them voting rights, where as her counterpart, in the western world, in Europe and USA had to struggle, as a part of suffrage movement, for over 6 decades, to get their voting rights. The women in USA got their voting rights, one hundred and 55 years, after men had started voting, in the year 1920.

Chapter 10

Family and Social Values and Poverty Reduction

In some of the developed world economies, inter gender interaction, before marriage and the young women and men bearing children, without the institution of marriage, has caused multiple challenges, to such economies. Bearing children outside marriage that is considered deplorable in Asian societies, has been so much accepted, in certain segments of the developed world economies, particularly inner city neighborhoods of many cities of the developed countries that tens millions are getting born, in this manner. This has created a large and ever bludgeoning institution of single mother families, in America. Single mothers are discussed, by all political forums of different political parties, as the constituents, who suffer from economic challenges and poverty. It has also led to numerous teenage mothers, who are themselves, children. While economic challenges, faced by such women, who have borne children, outside marriage, tend to be huge, which compel them, to neglect children, as they start working, at a very young age. Being a single mother, compels them to neglect furtherance of their own studies and also compels them to take very low paying dead end, hourly jobs, which do not help them much to pay their monthly bills. Hence all of these single mothers, who have been irresponsible, to raise family, at a very young age and that too flouting the social norms and derecognizing the importance of the age old institution of marriage, face a very uncaring flexible labor market. The employers, who want work efficiency, are ready to pay only very low hourly wages, which veer around minimum wages. This leads to these singles getting wages below the living wages. and that is way below the average cost of living.

Cost of living and its standardization in America, and high labour force participation rate due to the women having joined the workforce, in large numbers, since the world war 2 years have come to make 2 income families, a broadbased reality. Bearing children outside marriage, enforces the lives of the single mothers, around a single income. That's how single mothers, so well known in the USA, are unknown to even the intelligentsia, leave aside the laity of India, where marriages are sacrosanct and the children are born, only within the boundaries of marriage. Indian way of life though requires a lot of social responsibility and social discipline.

Thus the irresponsibility of raising family, outside marriage makes these children, face a life of neglect, by their mothers, due to their economic preoccupation, with multiple jobs, multiple commutes, every working day. Some of these single mothers also work, during the weekends, which further challenges these children, along with the disappearance of a father figure, in their life. While they grow up and turn teenagers, they are severely bewildered, to find their father not around, to guide and motivate them. In such a large country, with relocations associated, pretty normal with job changes, in a flexible labour market of America, it becomes difficult even to locate father, in many instances. Where children pine to see their father, even if their mother in the initial years, knew the whereabouts of the father, his address might have been lost to her, due to movements from job changes. Unfortunately, in many cases their mothers might have had a casual relationship, with a casual acquaintance, to give birth to a baby and in such a case even the name and contact address might remain, unknown to their mother, in the first instance. Here, locating father becomes not possible, in many cases. All of these challenges, affect the psyche of the children certainly create a lot of confusion, in the minds of children, who in an ideal situation, would have liked to see and meet both of their parents, while growing up. A lot of these tantrums and elements of social irresponsibility, in the name of pursuing modern fashions of parents, in the developed world, cause acute agony, to their hapless children. These agonies are unknown to their cousins, in the Asian societies, where child happens to be the focus of social responsibilities, of both parents and this responsibility in hierarchy, stands far ahead, of the responsibilities to the employer. Unfortunately, in America the responsibility to the employer, takes the form of 'be all and end all' of an American way of life.'

Children, in the families of single mothers, miss out on the absence of father figure and rarely see their mother too, due to the single income configuration of the family, in a society where costs breakeven, when 2 incomes are generated. The chain of consequences, which follow, including various dimensions of the flexible labour market of USA, are quite stolid.. With such neglect, the children belonging to single parent homes, waste a lot of time, loitering around, in their neighborhoods, pay less attention to their studies in schools. Many of them, turn to gangs and start keeping guns. These gun totting youth, belonging to many single family homes, particularly of inner city neighborhoods of the cities, like New York Chicago, Los Angles, Detroit, Pittsburgh etc with little family contact, family care and living in an environment, of near absence of the interaction with parents, sometimes go the criminal way. Once prosecuted, convicted and incarcerated, to undergo jail sentence of few years, drive many of them, to a life of despair, severe economic downsides, social stigma and repetitive criminal offences. To deal with these challenges, the government at the neighborhood, city, state and federal levels are compelled, to make provisions in the budget, to continuously spruce up, law enforcement and also maintain and add incarceration facilities. A lot of avoidable expenditures, come to be spent, all due to, lack of social responsibility, in settling down nicely in marriage in time and women bearing children, outside marriage, at an age, when they should be attending to studies and building their economic futures and then men also indulging in casual affairs, with women, outside the institution of marriage and enabling the children to be born, with little or no intention to own the responsibility of raising the children, as a father.

President Obama, in his Presidential Campaign, on a Father's Day, reminded this responsibility of men and women towards their children. He called upon men to be good fathers, duly paying attention, to proper growth of their children, Coming from someone, who later became the President of America, after the Presidential Elections in 2008, it assumes significance, how the institution of marriage and caring for children, need to be considered in America. Raising family on time, after settling in marriage on time, has a moral connotation but it also has a very important economic connotation, for an economy. The absence of settling, in marriage and raising family, on time or indulging in multiple courting, owning little responsibility toward the economic and social future of their children, and the like could trigger a challenges of poverty. Further, men and women, bearing children, outside marriage, all of these could have far reaching economic consequences, on countries. Another type of social imbalance that one sees among educated men and women, is to remain single for many years and delay raising of the family. This lack of social responsibility, which goes in current times, camouflaged as a fashion, could in a few decades, may reduce the number of children drastically, in upper echelons of society to be able to support an aging population. This phenomenon could add another dimension, to the country's economic scenario. An economy might even head for an economic doom, when the ratio of the old, to the young that could work and support the old aged population, starts skyrocketing. That is what is making Europeans concerned now and increasing number of countries are coming up, with incentives for the young weds, to have more children. Child earned income credit annually at a rate is granted, to citizens in America, to encourage people to have more children. Such financial incentives should have been in place and all of those negatives that have generated, a trend in the developed world, in the last half the 20th century, in the name of fashions, could have been avoided. A lot of frivolity and irresponsibility that society, economy, media and the corporate world have indirectly and directly promoted, has now been causing, a lot of economic challenges, in the developed world. It would be hard for these countries, to keep their GDP sustain, their living standards flat and above all to be able to fund the care of the bludgeoning old population. One solution could be through importing, whole lot of foreign workers, both educated and uneducated, which in the case of Europe will have to be from North Africa, due to its geographical proximity, especially from the former colonies of individual countries. That would be at a cost of a huge adjustment challenges, with the incoming population, challenged by their difference in race, religion educational levels, development levels, religion and culture. Despite governmental cosmopolitanism, the traditional racial religious and cultural, differences, in the society, would be too much of an obstacle, for the differences, to be ironed out and develop a working relationship developed, with foreign workers. Foreign workers, knowing the helplessness of the deficit of the young workers, in the developed world, could be probably less courteous than the immigrants today, because they would know the economic affluence, they could bring to the destination countries. Hence Europe may have to face the challenge of immigration in large volumes that too pretty arrogant immigrants, once they fill up the economic vacuum, due to the deficit of young workers, in the importing countries. If Europe has to face less of these challenges, it has to seriously address the potential of a huge deficit of young workers, in a few decades now, by learning from Asia the importance of family values, moral hygiene and uniqueness and aver importance of the great institution of marriage that Asia venerates.

10.1 India Teaches West to Nationalize Banks

Parents in India set apart money, for celebration of children;' marriage and they are very happy to spend on marriage. Except in some families, in some states, where woman's family spends money, in most Indian weddings, the money is spent by both families and the events photographed and video graphed. Weddings are attended by relatives. Invitees outnumber relatives by a factor and it could, vary from 500 to 2000 attendees. There are elaborate function halls, beautifully decorated that are taken for the celebrations. For a man and woman, marriage is a huge event and bride and bridegroom do not have to spend money, as the parents sacrifice, to spend money on children's wedding. Unfortunately, American children are challenged and they are expected to share the expenses and parents appear to have a hand off approach, which one thinks is unfair. In India, once parents in middle class homes reach the middle age, a chain of sacrifices they pride in such as to setting apart money, for marriage celebrations of children and for boarding expenses of higher education, which is subsidized, by the government. Eating out, movie going, buying spree of new dresses, vacations are happily sacrificed, by the parents, as the parents reach an age that calls for making sacrifices, for children. Voluntarily, they use much less hand expenses, after the middle age dawns. Indian scriptural guidance provides for sacrifice, as a great family virtue and especially for progenies and the aged. This scenario makes it easy to understand, why the young Americans tend to delay their marriage celebrations, fearing the expenses, especially during the recession years and get into live in arrangements. Justin Wolfers observes," The recession has taken a toll, on the institution of marriage, we keep hearing. Young adults, according to this narrative, have less money to spend on a wedding and are less eager to enter into a lifetime commitment, during times of uncertainty." This observation is understandable, in view of parent's indifference, to meet children's marriage expenses in USA.

Live in arrangements, is equivalent to saving money, from an arrangement of living apart and dating with each other and brings about some economic advantage of the social economy of scale. However, lack of accountability characterizes, a live in arrangement, and the moral discipline that accompanies a marriage, is near absent. In a live in arrangement, one could stray in other inter gender friendships and suddenly drop out of a live in arrangement, without any notice and without assigning any reasons, leaving other person in trauma. Live in arrangement, where even children get born, outside the marriage, could dilute moral hygiene and it could set a bad example, for future generations, when they come to know that they were not a product of a regular marriage, of their parents, but were born outside the wedlock. As a child, it hurts that one is a child of unwed parents, though parents may think otherwise and convenient, sometimes, in the western societies. All of this departures from social responsibilities, have serious consequences to contribute to high intensity of poverty in economy.

During recession, it was far more difficult, for high school young to land jobs, relative to those college educated young and logically the recession would negatively impact those, who have not gone to university, in adhering to timeliness to get married, on time. The Pew Research Canter noted that, for the first time, college-educated 30-year-olds were more likely to have been married than were people the same age without a college degree. The news was interpreted as another side effect of the recent recession.

It can also be seen that runaway profit greed, of the corporations, have led to making the employees live, pay cheque to pay cheque and even managers are compelled, to tread to pay day loans, every month, denying them the health care benefits. All of this has been causing a delay in marriage. For a happy man and a happy woman, not suffering from financial discomfitures, to think of settling down happily in a marriage and bear children is normal. Drowned in the uncertainty of being, unable to pay monthly bills, leaves the young mind, unable to think of a romance, marriage and honeymoon. In no small measure, social dysfunction is arising, from corporate neglect of citizens in America, for paying them too less a compensation with no benefits.

Marriages are delayed in America, as wages have become low and health care benefits are unavailable. In addition, the cost of living has not changed. While few industries pay well but most industries, pay too less, for men and women, to view marriage between them as an expensive proposition. Expectations of leading comfortable life, after marriage is ubiquitous, but employers are too passionate about, cost cutting, to impress their shareholders in a big way. At best, they pay the labour a living wage. Some organizations do not hesitate to give less than living wages and give wages around minimum wage. Hence low wages are certainly a deterrent in USA, for the excitement of marriage, between men and women, to have evaporated. Keeping the health costs so high, in the name of quick scheduling of surgeries, has almost kept 38 million Americans outside the health care system, except in emergencies, when they are treated in the hospitals and a fat bill is sent to them, for payment. Such a high cost of the health care, coupled with disinclination of employers to give health care benefits, further decelerates the desire, among men and women, to get married until they luckily land a job that pays health care benefits. After adulthood, when men and women continue o be unmarried, for over a decade, they get quite used to living alone, though occasionally feel lonely and that plummets the fear of being divorced, once they are married and lead a married life. The caution that obtains in young couples, not very young though, to keep the marriage unfailingly, which obtains in socially traditional countries like India is near absent, as they have already being habitual before marriage, over a decade to deal with living as a single.

Hence the factors that delay marriages in USA, are also the factors that indirectly contribute, to the downside in the quality of marriage, leading to high frequency of divorces, occurring in a few years of marriage in USA. From financial point of view, the economy of scale in case of 2 income families, are almost not availed, during the long delay in getting married and thereafter, after the breakup of marriage in about 3 to 6 years, for the rest of the life. The possibility of failure of marriage is pretty high in America, in respect of second and third marriages and that explains, why most people who are divorced, once remain single for life. About 60% of marriageable Americans remain single and about 40% of marriageable Americans lead a married life. We are looking at a picture of about 60 million adults, remaining single, with all of the concomitant problems of lack of care in case of physical or mental ailments and also lack of social discipline, hurting their physical and mental health. Casual friendships barely help one to survive in life and inherent desire in a human, to interact with a fellow human, at an inter gender level is natural. With so much focus on the short term, in America in multiple dimensions and certainly in the social realm, melancholy dawns, when one of the singles, decides to snap the casual friendship and the other single wants, to continue the friendships. Such breakages of even casual friendships, cause heartaches and mental depressions. Very rarely a divorce or a casual friendship breakage, is mutually felt and it is mostly one person, who is hurt and that makes the population of those mentally depressed, in America due social reasons, pretty high and make the American psychiatrists, in so much demand, enriching them to the stratosphere..

In USA, in the 1950s, a typical marriage involved specialized roles for the husband and wife. Usually he was in the marketplace, and she was in the home, and this arrangement led to maximum productivity, nice one income compensation, no student loans for children ability of parents even to fund college education. But with both spouses in the workplace, extra busy for career growth, the quality of marriage, is on the decline, as dependence on each other that used to be the case in single income families, have dwindled substantially. Marriage need to contain dependence on each other, as well as passion. The researchers indicate that mere passion cannot hold a marriage together for long, once initial glitter of courtesies are supplanted, by a life of reality. One hears all the time a joke from young newlyweds, the wife saying that the guy took a lot of care, when he was dating and pleading her to marry him and also vice versa. In such conversations, one is basically talking about passion. A Harvard Professor in his research study article mentions that American marriages are failing fast because they think marriage is a matter of passion, whereas

Indian marriages consider marriage a duty to spouses, to children to the aged and to society and their lives tend to depend a lot on each other, besides of course having the component of passion, which makes those Indian marriages, a lifetime marriage. US society and economy will have to generate an environment, where marriage has leisure and time for each other and a lot of dependence also for each other and keen sense of duty. To an extent, too much of density of eateries, fast food places and corner sports bars, have reduced the home activities, to the minimum, making it a place merely to hit the old sack and retire to bed and early morning again get ready for the workplace. Isn't it too much to expect, from a marriage that contains such minimal interface between the spouses? With such an environment, one wonders if there would be any friendship, between the room mates in a room, in the dorm of a university. How could marriage carry any meaning, in its incumbent configuration, in USA?

In fact, interface with team members, team leader and business clients would consume a lot of time, during the day, for both the spouses. Then the time is spent, at an eatery, to finish dinner, before going home. All of these times put together, would be the time way ahead of what remains for the spouse and children and the aged, at the end of the day. Capacity to smile, after smiling all though the day, as a part of protocol, in the office and with clients, would usually evaporate, by the time, one reaches home, after an average commute of about 90 minutes. What is normally left is, frown by each other and small talks, about running the home. Such a marriage, in highly busy schedule of both spouses, would be uninteresting, in any continent, including in Asia, where marriages are for a lifetime, With such lack of attention, one does not know, what would be the duration of such marriages, even in other continents. Hence what one calls fashionable, the so called high paced American life, is the enemy number one, of the quality and duration of marriage and any other factor comes later. Corporate profits have come to determine America and the gigantism of MNCs and not the quality of married life, at the individual American level. If in Asia, the marriages survive and if in India marriages survive, to the hilt, it is predominantly because the negative factors are strongly reined in. The social eye regulates individuals and government regulations fetter corporations, from damaging marital life of employees, as against the USA, by exacting excessive work from the employees and paying too less relative to the cost of living in the economy.

A lot of Americans, do not seem, to realize, that another important factor, which is causing the American marriages, to get delayed and the raising of children to get delayed, is the result of immigration and especially illegal immigration, led by the illegal Latino immigrants, from southern border of USA. With tsunami of illegal immigration, occurring from southern border of USA, to a tune of about 1 million every year, the wage configuration for the local Americans is further tanking. This serious wage decline of the local Americans is happening presumably, not without indirect liking for the illegal immigrants, by the business owners of the small and medium enterprises, in USA. The American business owners appear to very keen to make solid profits and therefore covertly, prefer to employ, the illegal immigrants, at a very low wage, The wage structure, especially in the border states, have been going deep south and for an American, with that wage, it is very hard to survive.

Here the poverty is striking Americans in two ways. One, the wages are going so deep a south that renting a studio, buying groceries and paying for the gas in a public transportation deficit economy, is making him/her, living with perpetual credit card debt, Secondly, his/her hesitation to get married and have children with such low wages, has been disallowing him/her, to take advantage of the economic theory of the economy of scale. Neither the regulator nor the business owner seems to think, about individuals in America and his/her plight.

The Latino immigrants survive, as they come at a very young age mostly and live in a ghetto with their spouse, left in Mexico, for years and each room is shared, on average, by 4 Latino workers. For an American man or woman, to share a room at the rate of 4 persons, would just not be comprehensible, though in big cities like New York and Chicago, due to poverty even among the middle class, it has become common, for the Americans, to share an apartment, each room to oneself. The immigrants have heavily depressed the wage structure, even much lower than the minimum wage sometimes, in firms that employ illegal immigrants, in large numbers. In some industries, thus the jobs of the Americans in droves, increasingly are being replaced by the immigrants. The only exception occurs, when an American forces himself/herself, to suffer with the same low wages that his exploiting employers pays to the Latino illegal immigrants. Such a poor wage structure challenged by illegal immigration, the marriage, absolutely remains, out of the doors, for eternity, not for a decade, unless one turns suddenly lucky enough, to land a job that gives American wages. Hence it is no wonder that a lot of people, who used to be living in middle class in America, only a decade ago, are moving to the poverty levels, with little hope of climbing back to the middle class again. As a family of two spouses, a lot of challenge could be scaled and economic prosperity attempted, but a lone person does not find it easy, to achieve socio economic mobility.

With workplaces, dominated by both men and woman, since the second global war and number of homemakers only 37%, in USA, both spouses run the possibility of men and women getting close to inter gender innocuous interactions, turning sometimes, into a desire to marry each other. In workplaces like India, which looks more like pre war US, where workplaces have only men, the possibility of a colleague straying, with an opposite gender colleague or a client, for both spouses is conspicuous by its absence. The divorces therefore could be counted on finger tips, in most of India. Even in metros, most of the metro population believe in solid lifetime marriage. Hence the poverty from the marriage break ups that has been on the gallop in America, is absent in India.

In America, while delay in marriages, is a reality even for decades and high intensity of marriage break ups, only in few years of marriage, also has become a hard reality, but one positive fact remains, that in so far as getting married, is concerned, a large proportion of the marriageable men and women, go through the process, of getting married.

Currently about 81 percent have married at least once. This number used to be higher earlier and it peaked at 93 percent in 1980. It can thus be seen that marriage remains an important part of most people's lives in America. To reduce American poverty from social causes corporations and the government, could work together, to ensure that low quality of marriages is addressed, along with breakages in marriages in about 4 to 6 years. Another aspect that would reduce poverty is to ensure that those who delay in getting married are given right incentives, to get married in time, to take advantage of the economy of scale in living happily in a marriage that too, with enough leisure and devoid of workplace stress.

In recent times, marriages are breaking, on average in about 4 to 6 years. Overconfidence of the female spouse, to be able to get the child custody, in most cases, is not deterring, the women much, from breaking their marriages, as at the emotional level, children, she thinks, would be her asset, even after the divorce.. She feels less challenged, by an impending divorce, as she almost knows that she would get the custody of the children, whose company she could adore, despite the divorce. If child custody is broken down, in judgments to 50:50, If half number of children are accorded to the father and another half to the mother, then there might arise likelihood of a lot of women, to keep the marriage with minor adjustments. In many cases, in America, she makes adjustments, such as with her parents and siblings and maintains a lifetime relationship with them, why should she not make minor adjustments, to keep the marriage, like her Indian counterpart from India.

If the custody of children is flipped, to men totally, then there could be substantial decline, in divorces, as women would find the idea, of losing the company of all children, for all of their childhood and adolescence hard to accept. This is not, as though the nation and its institutions, cannot reverse this trend of divorces on trifles, in about 4 to 6 years of marriage in USA, but there has to be a solid will, in this regard. It is no rocket science, to be able to make institution of marriage far more important, in America and reduce the divorces, to the minimum, to address the poverty issue, provided the social institutions, the church institutions, the government and the corporations coalesce their efforts, in this direction..

Economists always talk of the role of incentives, to move people's altitudes. Incentives certainly work in morphing people's behavior. Thus the financial incentives, probably could work, to achieve earlier marriages and even to achieve lifetime marriage. The Counties in America, could come up with cash awards of $100,000 for marriages of 10 years duration, with cash award of $200.000, for marriages of 20 years duration, with cash award of 300,000 dollars for marriages that celebrate silver jubilee (25 years) and for silver jubilee marriages of 25 years duration, another 50% tuition waiver, for their adult children, who are to go to college/university. That would put a moral pressure, on the parents also, to see that their children's education are improved and some pressure also coming from the grown up children, on the parents, to stay together, at least for their academic future and peace among parents. If any county has large number of married couples, eligible for cash awards, but having fund shortages, this could be addressed by the concerned state governments. to provide incentives, to arrest the tsunami of divorces, every year, which is 1 million now.

Similarly, the 50 years duration marriages could be given, a cash reward, to a tune of half a million dollars. 25% amount of this reward could be allocated for the adult children, who might have had sobering effect on the parents, not to break a marriage and be loyal to each other. American children are pretty frank and independent in their attitudes and they could exercise nice and sobering effect, on the parents, talking to them in case of disputes, about the value of a pristine lifetime marriage.

In such a case, the extra expenditure that a lot of the adult children, in USA, have to incur would be saved, in meeting father and mother annually. For many adult children, whose parents are divorced, they have to go to two different places, to meet them, which require absence from work twice in a year, as well as 2 airfares. He/she may have his divorcee mother, staying in New York City and his divorcee father staying in Miami, Florida. Isn't it a lot of saving of money, to remain in touch, with both parents, only visiting one place, in case of lifetime marriage? When one's parents are in marriage, he/she would save on 2 airfares to the 2 locations of the 2 parents, besides seeing them happy together, at one location.

Driven by monetary incentives, as well as their own savings, on an annualized basis and also to see their parents happy together, they would probably play a sobering familial role, on the parents. Lifetime married couples have more money, more leisure time and longer lives to spend together. They can contribute in a positive manner to even adult children's lives too. The importance of leisure and idleness, so emphatically talked about by Mr. Bertrand Russell the philosopher, cannot be overemphasized, in a happy lifetime marriage. In USA also there are lifetime marriages and I have noticed them happy too but the need of the hour to reduce poverty, is to make that number of lifetime marriages gallop, in USA, not canter. And it is here, while they violate the message of a great philosopher Bertrand Russell, who talks about value of leisure and praises idleness; a lot of times, divorces are skyrocketing in USA.

These financial incentives might work, as the marriage break ups in America, do not necessarily happen, only due to social irresponsibility and lack of adjustment abilities of the spouses alone. The marriage break ups that happen cannot be blamed only on the young men and women, not valuing the institution of marriage. A lot of exogenous factors tend to work against marriageable men and women, to delay marriages and thereafter to break the marriage, in a few years. For example, due to highly challenging flexible labour market, where people lose jobs in droves, even working with large gigantic organizations, for no fault of theirs, could simply throw away, two spouses, living happily in marriage, to two different job locations, after landing new jobs. Then the long distance marriages, tend to break, as they do not properly meet, the needs of the marriage. I have known one of the spouses, in a marriage, deciding to go for a new job, to a distant location, indirectly frightening the other spouse, who thought that now could be the time for the marriage to be challenged. It is known that long distance marriages tend to fail in a few years. This is the predicament of a 2 income family structure, in the US economy, coupled with flexible labor market, both benefiting only one constituency, the super rich corporations, at the expense of a happy married life of the two individuals. Blaming only the spouses, to break the marriage, would be unjust, when there are such strong negative exogenous factors, which tend to break marriages, not with a hammer, but with a bulldozer. Once a person turns single, poverty cannot be escaped, as economy of scale in a marriage is gone.

Betsy Stevenson, an economist, who has done extensive studies, on marriages, in America and the divorces mentioned, "In the old days, opposites attracted; an aspiring executive groom would pair up with a less-educated bride. But today, that same young executive would more likely be married to a college-educated woman, who shares his taste in books, hobbies, travel and so on. Indeed, marriage rates for college-educated women rose sharply through the 1950s and '60s, and have remained remarkably stable since. These women tend to marry after they have finished college and started their careers."

The marriage has a meaning when the children are cared for and the aged receive attention, as per Indian values and culture. Probably, it could be true elsewhere, in the developed world also. If the marriage survived in America and was of the older type, when the opposites attracted then a sense of mutual dependence would have kept the child care and care of the aged in place and not outsourced to the day care and the old age care public institutions, where home joy and life, is missing. In marriages, where hobbies and education career desire synchronize the home life gets out of the doors, not only windows. Then the child care and aged care sees the severe neglect. The love of parents in 2 income families, got transformed into heavy expenditure to buy gizmos for the children, to keep them diverted, with too many gizmos screens of computers, DVD players, hand held devices and the TVs.

With no time to ask questions to the parents and nicely interact with them, their ethics levels tend to have rooms for additional knowledge. Further, the children grow up, with soft skills of exposure to too many screens, far too many hours, neglecting academic rigor of science and mathematics, with no one in the home, during their wake up hours, to monitor their seriousness in studies. Attending to home work also could go to back burner. Giving them long lectures, to compete with India and China and other global competitors and to focus on science and math, makes little sense, when at least one of the parents, is not ready to sacrifice, for making them globally competitive professionals. Despite marvelous school infrastructure, with money to buy books and tools of education with privacy of an exclusive room in the home, the quality of education has tobogganed and the American young lack skills of academic rigors, particularly number skills. These negatives in education, at the minimum, has been due to a couple of factors. The parents are held responsible as they pursue their individual careers, during the entire wake up hours and neglect them in the most impressionable years of children's lives. This is happening, in the single mother's homes, as well as two parent homes, where both parents are busy earning extra money, pleasing the boss overtime, for career growth. With so little importance to family, it is hard to build a fine generation of skillet professionals. Only vacations, with children are not enough. Neither it is enough to give them good pocket money and gizmos. Where they are going in life, need to be watched and softly guided. Parents need to be around, to restrict their screen exposures to the minimum and increase exposure to study of math and science and see that they are in the company of books, rather than being obsessed with sending and receiving one liners, from the peers though the interface of social media..

Due to severe neglect of the parents, with both parents busy, in ther respective careers, the children turn out to be more mediocre, less interested in academic hard work and neglectful of rigorous academic disciplines of science engineering and mathematics. Most of them educated in unskilled jobs, are turning into victims of high bargaining power of the employers, who have turned gigantic and indifferent, to the plight of the young men, entering the workforce. The employers pay hourly wages, with no long term benefits, causing poverty and debt seeking conditions, for tens of millions of the young Americans. Those hailing from Asia, where one parent is in part time job or a household parent, to monitor the child for academic rigor, in a short while coming to America, grab high paying jobs and live a nice life style.

Layoffs by the employers hurt. the paid. The laid off employees, face economic uncertainty and indirectly it also challenges the wedding strangely in America. In India it evokes sympathy for the laid off spouse and also of increase in love and care for him. Whereas in America, the data shows that after a spouse is laid off and it happens to be the man, if he takes several months or over a year, to land a new job, the wife might suddenly lose the patience and walk out of marriage. It would mean that the jobless laid out employee would lose his job, his spouse and also his children. That is what, the recessions every few years in America do, to many families, leaving the men forlorn and lonely, with a divorce slapped on them. Woman also suffers from divorce but seems, to be taking it slightly better, as she does not lose, the company of children. It really baffles one why, in times of crisis, the spouses in America fail to be together and the divorces rise. Poverty for both spouses accrues, after the divorce takes effect.

The societal tolerance, for a divorce in America and the west makes, it easy for spouses to make a decision, to divorce each other. When societal eye is pungent, against a marriage break up and a divorce is looked down upon, the spouses strive hard, to adjust with each other and succeed to remain, in marriage. Misunderstandings also evaporate with some flux of time. In India, breaking a marriage is looked down upon and is viewed as a social taboo. This social acceptance of single living, has further roiled the value of values of family and marriages in USA.

Those who are less educated, and are in teens, they tend to avoid marriage and casually produce children, as a teenage single mother, in large numbers. In USA in recent years the teenage single mothers are also on the rise raising the level of poverty. Some of them after they drop out from the school, probably have a lot of time, to indulge in romance and they get married, in their teens no matter what the law of the land says about marriage age. A lot of teens get married in America especially in the inner cities and produce babies. Those who get married at an early age do not seem to make mature decisions about marriage and they revise the decision when they turn more aged. There arises then a justification that the match selected during the teens is not right. It is this justification that trigger divorces among many women

During the US Presidency of Mr. Ronald Reagan, approved the law of "No Fault Divorce", where fault of a spouse need not be proved, by the divorce seeking spouse. Earlier, divorce seeking cases, used to consume lot of court's time, but mutually agreed divorces, cut short the divorce granting time, for the judiciary. However, it was noticed that once this law, came into force in US, the number of divorces sought and the number of divorces granted, increased, by leaps and bounds. President did not like the increase in the incident of divorces, accruing from the law. It was also clear, from the data that over 90% divorces were filed by the women and a small number by the men.

The statistics of poverty indicate that since the 1980s the poverty levels increased significantly and among other factors the increased number of divorces also increased the intensity of poverty, in the social landscape of USA. This again validates how a number of exogenous factors, have destroyed American marriages and not merely the tantrums of spouses, as misunderstood by some superciliously and divorces have certainly augmented the intently of poverty in the US economy.

In a lot of single mother homes, in USA, in inner city neighborhoods, a lot of the young after dropping out from high schools, are seen to peddle drugs. The law enforcing agencies being vigilant, such members of the young, getting incarcerated has become common, Once incarcerated, they generally lose employability. Thus both male and female categories of the average Americans, would face dead end jobs and some of them after incarceration will be castigated, in the job market. That is why occupy Wall Street movement, the numbers 1 and 99 percent turned very popular, not very far from the stark reality, in terms of financial health of individual balance sheets of hundreds of millions of Americans.

This is not to say that the economic downturn has had no effect at all on domestic life. According to the Census data, the number of unwed couples, living together rose sharply after the deep and long recession after the 2008 economic crisis. This is not a happy trend because cohabitation, without marriage, works against the institution of marriage, which has its own merits. In cohabitation, the moral hygiene, has a potential to go south, as both man and the woman need not be accountable to each other, unlike in a marriage.

Chapter 11

Poverty and Size of the Government

Poor people in a democracy, when engaged thoroughly, indirectly where put pressure on the government to be of good size. In other economies, where the middle class and the rich maintain a distance, in not trying to influence the government, on their side or especially feel very indifferent to the poor, the government is likely to have more role in the economy. India's freedom movement, led by the principles of non-violence and truth, took a representative path and not a combative path, under Mahatma Gandhi's leadership. All of the freedom fighting leaders banded together, with Mahatma Gandhi and his principles of non-violence and truth, became the essence of India's freedom movement, from the British rule. Mr. Gandhi and Mr. Nehru, having access to the governor general, representations, continued to represent to give India freedom, from the British rule. That India did not like the British rule, was amply evident, because in 1929, during the Karachi Congress, under the Presidency of Nehru, a resolution asked for complete Swaraj (self rule) for India. There goes a saying that after Mahatma Gandhi, returned from South Africa, where he started the Satyagraha movement, in 1884 and he was fighting for the rights, of the colored people, against racism, practiced by the white apartheid regime of South Africa. In South Africa, he was also regularly preaching the importance of sanitation to the poor and during plague, even participated in cleaning their neighborhoods, with them. Gradually the poor people for small problems, in life approached the lawyer, in the personality of Mahatma Gandhi, who had his heart always, with the poor and the masses. He came to India and in the early decade of 20th century, after analyzing the negatives of foreign British rule, he started educating the masses, in the villages and fought on their behalf, for social and economic justice. His leadership was such that the poor instantly responded and in large numbers, started participating, in the civil disobedience movement, burning machine made clothes of the British origin and preaching to spin local cloth. It has been said and acknowledged that the congress party, which before the arrival of Gandhi, on Indian political scene, was a middle class party, taking causes of the middle class got heavily democratized, with leadership of Mahatma Gandhi. The poor in India joined, in very large numbers, to protest against the British rule and the movement for freedom from the British, widened extensively, causing a lot of inconvenience for the British, to continue control of India. It is this ubiquitous presence of the poor and congress handling the problems of the poor, with dedication led, to the congress adopting a socialist veneer, with initiatives of Nehru and other young leaders. Socialism came to be a paradigm, in the minds of those, who would later constitute the India's independent government. The British granted independence to India and India as a country turned free, on August 15, 1947. The Constituent Assembly formed the Constitution Drafting Committee, under the leadership of Dr B.R. Ambedkar, who was 16th child of a poor family, belonging to the labor caste. He had seen through his childhood, challenges of poverty, yet had the desire for higher education. He went to the University of Columbia, USA, an extremely scholastic university, to address his Doctoral degree in Economics. He had the exposure of US Constitution and other constitutions of the developed countries and he knew how the poverty challenges of India could be addressed. Under his leadership, the committee came up, with an inclusive constitution, with democracy, independence of judiciary and sufficient checks and balances that will make the government function, with important roles of legislature executive and judiciary. Fundamental Rights got clearly defined, in the Constitution and so were the Directive Principles for guidance. Affirmative action for the poor labor castes, was an important component of the Constitution, providing for not only inclusive welfare attitude toward the poor, but also formal reservations in admissions in educational institutions and reservations in recruitment. Probably, at the micro level, those who had the assets and influence as forward castes, may have not so much welcomed the reservations, though agreeing with other pro poor measures, government was determined and proactive, to adhere to the public policy on reservations, to be reviewed after 15 years. However every 15 years, the reservation in education and employment, was continued. Those settled well in life covertly felt that the government was extending the reservations, due to the vote bank, but these provisions and pro poor measures gave, voice to the people, gave the fair wages and more than minimum wages, fixed by the government. The poor people from their families found their brethren, working as chief of the police station, an agriculture extension officer, a doctor of the primary health centre, sometimes a revenue inspector, an educated member of legislature and an educated member of parliament. Deputy collectors of revenue and deputy superintendent of police, who mattered in the district level, for welfare of the people also gradually, came to be drawn in proportion of the population of the labor castes. All of these socio economic changes gave the poor confidence, which enlarged their knowledge to improve their income, to apply fertilizers and pesticides by those better off than, among them. The better off in the villages, while employing them looked after them better, and were not rude while exacting work from them. They paid the labor well as they knew that India's administration now, is far more inclusive, than during the British rule. For development of human potential for economic growth, rising of GDP and general economic and social condition of people from poor, the stance of the government was extremely benevolent. Social distinctions in the cities with combined transportation and combined living, in most neighborhoods, practically disappeared. In the villages, there remained some feelings but a realization dawned that the labor have to be paid well and also they have to be treated affably.

The British always sided with the rich and the members of the forward castes and opened universities, only in Presidency towns and very few big cities. They did not even start elementary, primary and high schools in the villages. Their goal was to rule the masses, keeping them uneducated and illiterate and collect runaway taxes for Britain and also to keep the hold of the rich, on the poor, by not fixing any collection fee for the taxes. This arrangement gave the rich indirect support and made them distant, from the base of the economic pyramid. Mahatma Gandhi's leadership to the poor, in the freedom movement, adoption of pro poor socialism, as a paradigm in the Congress Party and administration as per the pro poor Constitution, gave a very nice direction to economic development, not only of the middle class and the rich but also for those, belonging to the base of the economic pyramid. It is in this context, it is interesting to notice the role of government in a democracy, to achieve all round development, with inclusiveness to those who are deprived. An inclusive democratic government is a unique arrangement for an economy to function because unnecessary fear of the authority that precludes human potential to full fruition is supplanted by an extraordinary enthusiasm, at each level of human society. Riots and rebellions become unknown words, as mental depressions and stress. In India a reasonably educated person, does not know what stress means and what depression means. Even highly educated people, know only great depression of 1930s and not the depression that every other citizen of a developed country, suffers necessitating counseling, in the college, university and in the clinics. In America, a lot of depression patients wait for multiple weeks, to be able to see psychiatrists, who charges about $300 to $400 dollars for half an hour, session per day. Sudden neglect by others and sudden uncertainties in jobs and inter personal equations land people into depressions to people of all ages, ranging from 18 to 80, of both genders. The US media, cooperates and the general public all acknowledge that US economy is a market economy. The reigning paradigm, as per US government, is to encourage free markets, with government paying little role. Even democrats, who believe in more role of government, in the US, believe and reiterate that US is a market economy, with role of government, only when felt necessary.

The World Bank, and the International Monetary Fund work to accelerate the economic growth of the economies. It has been seen that these multilateral institutions, tend to help the successful economies in the world, which pursue appropriate public policies, duly encouraging economic activities and sincerely addressing economic development. Such of the economies are provided with the initial push for economic growth by the World Bank, by financing its projects and providing them technical knowhow. In building the institutions, the political and economic institutions and developing the competencies, such as managerial competencies, professional competencies, legal competencies, financial competencies, educational competencies and the like, the government plays a very important role, especially when the self-rule is new.

In building a cadre of entrepreneurs and for incumbent businesses, to expand their businesses, the role of government becomes important. The bureaucrats help policy making to run the economy, in an orderly manner. There is a lot of apprehension about central planning, among the free market West European countries and also in the United States of America. The word central planning is considered synonymous with communism, but if central planning is done, taking into account the backwardness of the regions, taking into account limitation of financial resources, right allocation to different sectors of the economy, central planning can be really helpful. Government plays a very important role, when economy is dormant and is just about to take off. To push the economy, government need to build management competencies. Once competencies are built, the government need to roll back and allow the private sector, to play its role in the economy. As and when there occurs market failures, the government intervention yields nice results for the economy. When the businesses become too money greedy or try to exploit some constituencies, based on a constituency's deprivation and lack of education, government could play an important role to fetter not so desirable moves of the businesses. When some businesses indulge in financial irregularities inquiry and charging the case in the court of law makes government role important again. The government has to keep regulations in place, to prevent perpetuation of racial discriminations, against the minorities, In order to regulate the businesses, in a fashion that some selfish self centric businesses, do not become a menace and function in a proper manner, competing in the market place, the government sometimes need to assert. Once there is a serious market failure, naturally there is need for the government, to intervene in the economy. Occasionally, the government may have to effectively regulate, the private economic entities, if the latter tries to defraud the economy. When there is no exploitation of any constituency, by the private economic entities and the market is functioning fine, the government should allow the market to function, on its own. Market allocates resources efficiently, where it functions, in an economic environment, where the ethics are significantly high.

When ethical standards toboggan, when the blue collar and the white collar crimes, start to rear their heads, then the government may have to play, its legitimate role. India has been an example of how government, when at a time it had to play its role, acts to govern the economy, to build the educational competencies, the managerial competencies, professional competencies, legal competencies and the like. Government in India also pays attention to the stock market, so that businesses have an opportunity, to raise the capital, from the equity market, issue IPOs. The secondary markets are also supervised, to be in place, so that stock investors, have opportunities to invest. In addition, the banks are in place in India. The government saw in the 1960s that the banks were confining their activities, only in the urban areas and that too only to provide loans for businesses, when over 75 percent of Indians lived in the villages. Neither the bank owners, desired to expand banking, nor the bank officials had the enthusiasm, to relocate to rural areas, where living conditions were in deficit, compared to the cities. Then government in 1969, had to take the leadership, to nationalize 14 banks and gave a guidance that they need to expand rural banking and finance agriculture and rural industries, to develop the rural areas with equitable focus. The bank branches came to be opened fast, in the rural areas, to build saving habits and to provide loans, not for consumption of goods purposes, certainly not to buy consumer electronic items, such as televisions, radios. Loans were not provided for housing or to buy autos. But loans were only given to those, who needed to set up economic activities that would generate return on investment, in different areas such as modernization of agriculture, poultry, sericulture, dairy schemes, and opening of the general stores, brick making and the like.

Blacksmiths, washer men, carpenters, goldsmiths and other such trades like activities, were also encouraged by the commercial banks in India, under the guidance of the government, duly providing bank loans to be repaid, in regular loan installments. Agriculture and rural industries came to be supported, by the cooperative banks and the nationalized commercial banks. Hitherto, when the banks were private, the rural people in India until late 1960s, had not seen a banker ready to help them with loans. Those who are too passionate about the market efficiency and free markets, to be given a free hand, need to observe a practical example that in such a big country, with most population in India located in the villages, though the private sector of the banks existed, but they only supported a few shops and industries, in and around few cities, wholly neglecting the villages. Small lending by the banks, to buy a few cows and buffalos and to construct sheds, to keep them and money to buy a village mode of transportation, bullock carriages, in which agricultural produce, could be sent to market yard, for sale made, a great difference across the length and breadth of the country. India set up National Dairy Development Corporation and in each state, State Dairy Development Corporations. A technocrat, very dedicated to development of national dairy, Mr. Kurien headed the national dairy initiative, to make India, the largest milk producer of the world.

In the democratic governance of the nation, as much as it is, in the area of economic development, India has achieved significant distinction, in which so much confidence of individuals and institutions is reposed. As a result of this confidence, inter business disputes get resolved, though objective impartial adjudication. Thus judicial wing of Indian government's democracy, plays a very important role, in matters of equity and justice unavailable, to many developing countries. India is characterized by independent judiciary. An independent and fair judiciary accords businesses, the confidence, to run their businesses confidently, earn income, pay taxes and create employment. They know that any wrong can get corrected, by approaching the court of law. Similarly, educational institutions were set up in small villages and then in a few years, on the request of the villagers, they were upgraded, from elementary stage, to the primary stage. Government also set up numerous high schools, running into hundreds of schools, in a District. Even today 93% of educational institutions are run by the government, duly subsidized. Government provides primary education up to high school, absolutely free of tuition. The joy that a village gets and celebration it addresses is seen to be believed, when the District Magistrate, after examining the proposal, finds it convenient to upgrade, an elemental school to a primary school, in some villages and to upgrade primary schools to high school, in some villages. These schools are accessed by the rich and the poor alike, as no tuitions are charged. However, physical infrastructure leaves much to be desired and there exists no furniture, in the building. Students, while studying sit on country made carpets. As per government rules, the teacher has to take up residence, in the village, but in some cases, the teacher tends to take up residence, in a nearby village, which has a bigger infrastructure and he bikes a few miles, to teach in the assigned village. Such transgressions are not taken seriously, as he takes interest in teaching. High school building and university, bachelor's degree colleges of science arts and engineering and medicine, have relatively better infrastructure, though nothing compared to the physical infrastructure, of the developed countries. Many authors in the west, today feel aghast, at the state of the schools, in the developed world, which have nice infrastructure, including spacious class rooms, nice elegant furniture, vending machines, auditorium, enough backyard and front yards spaces, but suffer from heavy dropout rates sometimes over 30%. Even academic results, in many of the high schools, located in the developed world happen, to be average. In India, in contrast, the elementary and primary schools have the physical infrastructure, of only two rooms with tiled roof and abetting veranda, where over 100 students study. Homework rigor, even in such surroundings, are significant and teacher is tough, enough to find fault, if some students, take studies easy. Even in the poorest homes, the parents are aware that education is a ticket for economic opportunities and given attention to studies, in the highly socially and economically mobile Indian economy, any one of them, could rise to be a business owner, a doctor, an engineer, an attorney, a scientist as all of these education degrees, are based on merit and are heavily subsidized. One can finish one's degree education in science or arts spending $1/100^{th}$ of what their counterparts spend, in America. Degrees in engineering and medicine can be had, for about $1/50^{th}$ of what an American youth, has to spend, that too in USA, by heavily borrowing student loans, which take on average, 20 years to repay. No one among the Indian youth, has to take any student loan, in a country of 1.2 billion, as higher education is very heavily subsidized, by government and small tuition left is, paid by the parents. Does it not show how important has been, the role of the government in India, in the life of a person, duly allocating freedom to market forces, where they have interest to invest? However, the businesses have to function, ethically and regulations are in place, to rein in the businesses, only when they defraud, or exploit labor.

Simplicity centric state funded infrastructure, of the public education, led India, to possess the second largest human resource in the world, next to USA. Engineering education came to be privatized, since 1990s and All India Council of Technical Education (AICTE) accorded permissions to, open many private engineering colleges, following the accreditation norms. With this supplemental private efforts, India churns out tens of millions of engineers, to support India's manufacturing, IT areas of economy and also the global economy, particularly US economy that looks forward to employ them in a large numbers.

The city of Bangalore, churns out more than 100,000 IT engineers, more than churned by institutions in USA. Numerous engineering and science programs, both Master's and Doctoral programs are pursued, in most American universities, by the Indians and the Chinese, with locals representing, a small percentage. It is the simplicity of life, taught by sages and seriously internalized by Indian people, both young and other demographics for tens of thousands of years, which help India, be at the forefront in education. As much as the Americans, like cars, the Indians like education and to acquire university higher education degrees. India accords since times immemorial, importance to becoming educated and acquire knowledge, which has brought India this glory, in just about 6 decades of self rule, after the British granted independence to India in 1947. All of this educational achievements of India were achieved, wholly with the government support, without any private initiative until the 1990s, when they came on board, enthusiastically, to promote engineering education and management education.

11.1 How Poor Brought Indian Government Nearer to Them

The poor remain constantly, in touch with the government, raising individual and village issues to be solved. Government at the same time, remain inclusive, to the poor not only in budgetary allocations, to their welfare, but also to receive them, well and be interactive. Visits of the senior District Officials to the villagers, are a routine, including the Revenue and Police officials. Any issue raised by the poor, where their lands have been brought, under dispute by those better off than them, are dealt with rebuking those, in higher economic categories, after the inquiry reveals their fault. Bore wells for water supply, abounds in the villages. In many villages, mini protected water schemes are implemented, with piped water to the homes. In other villages, which are bigger and have higher population, steps are taken to implement major protected water supply schemes. These moves bring lot of joys, to the villages. As per the availability of budget, the street lights are provided and extended from street to street, in the villages. Fair weather roads are replaced by, concrete roads in many villages. Homes in most of the villages are provided with lights and wherever there is shortfall, steps are taken to cover all of the village homes, with electricity facilities. No electricity charges are collected from the farmers, who use electricity free of charge, for irrigation purposes. There is a cross subsidy scheme, wherein the industries subsidize the electricity charges, collectable from the farmers. Further, the farmers do not have to pay any income tax, on their income. The exemption from payment of income tax from 60 percent of India's population, who are related to farming and also providing free electricity, for irrigation purpose are two major benevolent steps that government offers to the agricultural sector, where most of the poor are engaged in farming in India, is an occupation which is in ubiquity and land holdings are small and medium. Rice at the rate of 5 kgs per person per month, is made available, subject to a maximum of 25 kgs a family, for Rs 2 per kg, while the market rate would be thrice as much. For one individual, free elementary education and primary education, are provided free of tuition, in the village school with teachers, who have graduate qualifications, in addition to an undergraduate degree in education. Math and science teachers are ensured, to be available in all of the village schools. Government spends maximum amount on education of children. If a comparison is made, with all of the other development departments, in so far as the pay roll of teaches, is concerned. Government teachers are paid well, they have have security of tenure, in their jobs, are transferred from one posting to another, every 3 years, so that no local interests, are developed by them, diluting their teaching duties. Being an educated person, in emerging economy, the villages, he is also an informal mentor, for the adult villagers, who come to him, for information, they want to seek. Village is administered, by an elected body of the village council, consisting of village head and council members. Community hall usually arranges a community TV and now each house, would have a color TV. Cell phones have become a part of each home in villages, in India, in the last few years. In the light of so much help being extended by the government, which even a member of a family, would not be able to extend government, is kept in admiration and reverence by the villages. Several children are studying in city science engineering colleges and some working abroad from villages.

The urban middle class, can take care of themselves and they have little, work with the government. Some of the members of this class, egged on by a lot of misinformation, about government schemes, unfortunately spread by the electronic media, after multiple private channels came about, in the new millennium, have started shedding crocodile tears for the rural poor. The same is seen on the TV, when the talk show managers, who have probably not visited villages ever and probably have rarely, talked to villagers, seems to have very limited idea, about the progress in the lives of rural people. Coming from middle class, they probably deem progress, as equivalent to playing tennis, attending parties in star hotels, celebrating birthday with 25 friends, decorating drawing room with expensive sofas and cashmere carpets, wearing umpteen dresses and the like.

For talk show organizers, this level of rural development in 60 years of self rule in India, brings crocodile tears. One of their pastimes, is to repeat talk that the government is not allowing, grants issued by the government, to reach the villages, that is personally misused by the politicians and such venom is spewed without a basis. It will be interesting, to know how many relatives of those, who organize talk shows, are serving the government as politicians and how enriched they are, in their skyrocketing economic status. It will also be interesting to know how many children, nieces may and nephews of these talk show guys are preparing themselves for the service of the nation to be politicians.

Media, since the early 2000s, with the influence of globalization, has been playing, toxic role to blight the mind of the average slogging Indians and blighting the morale of those, who slog under the son, to create public goods and spew venom against government sitting in air-conditioned studios. The British policy makers in India remained indifferent, to broad based schooling and criticized the rural people and their backwardness, duly spending nice party time, with sophisticated English educated lawyers and doctors and the rich in Calcutta, and one would not hear the contrast, between school infrastructure in 1940s and decades thereafter and how glorious has been the ubiquity of educational institutions, in India. Instead, the private media celebrates, criticizing the current government, while they live in cities, themselves, speak slavishly all the time the Anglican language, hobnobbing with westernized friends and then shed crocodile tears for the rural poor, as a ploy to condemn political workers. They are not sensitized that those, who start their political life, moving with people, understanding their problems, representing their problems, both individual and collective, with officials at the District and State levels; then address party work, to endear with senior political leaders and haltingly get promoted to higher party positions. Through serendipity someday some of them, may run for members of legislature and be selected as a Minster, while the multitude among political workers, remain political workers for life, in rural India. There is no mention of the contributions of such people, who enlighten the common masses, during their interface with them, about democratic governance, as per Constitution, who make them acquire the gut knowledge, of how to elect a party and how to reject it, if the party forgets rural interests. Media does not inform that the budget of only few Ministries will be enough, to take up some schemes and a lot of Ministries, both in the Union and the States will have only meager budgetary allocations All the efforts of political workers, to make democracy happen, never get mentioned, in the electronic media. One only wishes that information rather than misinformation, would be the dissemination, to a nation that has had enough challenges, to be one of the top ten countries today, in the world in so far as national income, is concerned.. The nation was fleeced by the British, for over 200 years, the media need to remember, when it talks about India's politicians and development scenario.

11.2 Poor in Rural India Neglected by the British Government Came to Get Sunshine from Government of India

So Constitution of India was a great equalizer, which made no distinction of gender, education and property ownership, in so far as elections are concerned. Astonishingly, the poor in India, have remained unlike the poor in other parts of the world, actively participating and got engaged in freedom struggle. The poor became a part of Indian governance. India achieved freedom, from the British rule. Politicians have to depend, every five years, for the vote of the electorate, which included all of the adult poor. The poor in India, unlike the poor in other parts of the world, have been extremely engaging, on national issues that affect them and welfare. Out of necessity, to be popular, with the rural masses, the political parties, also keep close contact with the poor.

To this extent, the Constitution embedded in the fabric, a very close relationship between the democratic government and the poor. Despite lack of formal education, many a times remaining illiterate, they had the benefit of oral education passed on, from millennium through millennium. Thus they tend to acquire a unique gut sense, to confidently deal, with their lives. Their informal education left them a gut sense to deal with crises, face calamities, when they befall on them. The government in India gradually expanded its role, made efforts to correct the injustices, to the poor, through dedicated professional work. Injustices had emanated from the special interests, that came to be supported, by the colonial Master, the British, for centuries. The British had a tendency, a propensity to continue, to exploit the poor. The poor in India during the 200 years of the British rule, had to face a lot of problems. Elementary and Primary educations were deliberately neglected, in the rural areas, by the British. The aim of the British was to recruit those, who could run, their offices and collect revenues and perpetuate their rule. That demand was met by those, who were educated city dwellers and they were recruited by the government. They felt that there was no need, to educate, the masses in the villages. Even in the 1950s, a District having hundreds of thousands of population, had only one high school, which was generally located, in the District headquarters. Sometimes, the students from several adjoining districts, also came to study, in the high school, located in another District headquarters, as in their Districts, the high school was conspicuous by its absence. Such was the paucity of high schools, as the British paid little attention to promotion of education in India. With government of India's attention today in 2014, there is effervescence of learning, with several hundreds of high schools, dotting every district. Today elementary schools and primary schools are available within the village. No child in India is excluded, to study in a school and admissions are on merit, no matter which neighborhoods he/she comes from. It is the State government that funds education, in all of India's about 700 Districts and not the city administrations' local taxes, as it obtains in America.

Indian educational system promoted, by the government is uniform, with the same syllabus and same books and the teachers, similarly endowed in learning, with specialized bachelor's degree and bachelor's degree in education. The teachers are uniformly paid, in all of the schools, as they were State funded, by the budget of the State government. This arrangement is unlike the US public education system, where there is large standard deviation, in the compensation of teachers, in different public schools. The richer neighborhoods school teachers, tend to get far higher compensation, relative to the teachers, teaching, in the poorer neighborhoods. In the US, in the public school system, unfortunately, there is huge fragmentation and the poor quality teachers, as per this arrangement, teach the poor kids, thus indirectly, perpetuating the rich and poor divide, in the quality of learning. When they grow up, it is no wonder that the children of richer parents, land jobs that are high paying and the children of the poor, because they were educated, in the poorer neighborhoods, by the teachers, who received far lesser compensation and naturally were of inferior quality, gravitated to very ordinary jobs. The skewed funding of the public schools perpetuated, the poverty, generation after generation, with little correction and style of living of one generation, only differed slightly from the earlier generation, unlike children from high and medium neighborhoods, where the next generation could even take a quantum jump. System in India with uniform funding, for compensation of the teachers, by the State government shrunk, on the other hand, the gap between the rich and the poor through education. Probably, the US would do well, to imbibe this aspect of India's primary education system.

In an article, published in the New York Times, dated, November 4, 2011 entitled Poverty Inequality in America Paul Krugman observed, "The larger answer, however, is that extreme concentration of income, is incompatible with real democracy. Can anyone seriously deny that our political system, is being warped by the influence of big money, and that the warping is getting worse, as the wealth of a few grows ever larger? We have a society in which money is increasingly concentrated in the hands, of a few people, and in which that concentration of income and wealth threatens, to make US a democracy in name only." He added, "From being a middle class society US, with inequality, going through the roof is gradually turning into a top 1 percent and rest 99% struggling to pay monthly bills.

Paul Krugman emphatically stated, "The budget office laid out some of that stark reality in a recent report, which documented a sharp decline, in the share of total income going to lower- and middle-income Americans. We still like to think of ourselves as a middle-class country. But with the bottom 80 percent of households, now receiving less than half of total income, that's a vision increasingly at odds with reality."

As against the spread of education, at a galloping speed in India, after British left India, a very inequitable public funded school system, has been kept in place that has accelerated socio- economic mobility, unbelievably faster. Labor's children from small interior towns and villages topping National Civil Service Examination List, National Chartered Accountant Certification Programs stuns people in India, from the middle and the richer classes. Through education and social mobility, the next generation of the poor, are achieving the social status, dignity and opportunity, to qualitatively serve the nation, in increasingly large numbers every decade. Such was the abysmal neglect of the education, during the British rule of India, and this is very clearly mentioned, in the seminal work entitled "Discovery of India" written by Mr. Jawaharlal Nehru the first Prime Minister of India. Mr. Nehru points out how the British neglected elementary and primary education in India deliberately, to keep the masses ignorant of the goings on, in the country by the British. Such was the poor condition of education in the rural areas and no attempts were made even to increase literacy. The need for credit, to attend to domestic consumption, the rural population was left to the mercy for those, whose duty was to pay obeisance, to the British authorities. They were the ones who collected the taxes from the farmers and pass the taxes on, to the government. The rate of taxation, due to the government, was in advance intimated to the zamindars. The rich farmers and the zamindars, were allowed to retain, the tax collection service charges, separately collecting the same, from the farmers. However, the British had not capped any ceiling, on how much tax collection charges, they were to collect, from the agriculturists. There was a practice, among the zamindars and big landholders, to behave like a lord and browbeat the common small farmers. British had created a money avaricious class of zamindars. They were also lending to the poor, at exorbitant rates. In modern times their lender equivalent would be the issuers of the credit cards, where the interest rate is high at the base level, and interest keeps galloping, in case of credit card default, all over the developed world. Government hesitation to cap a ceiling on collection charges on tax collected, for the British was akin, in the past in India, to current hesitation of the government and the central banks in the developed world, to cap a ceiling on additional interest charged, on the card holders, in case of loan repayment defaults particularly in America. There were also moneylenders, who could lend money to small farmers and the British government placed no regulations or restrictions on them. The interest charged, by the moneylenders on the loans, extended to the poor, varied from village to village, in a province, from province to province, based on their whims and fancies. Within the village, the interest on loans to the poor could vary, from one defaulter to another, based on how the borrower, made out a case in his favor. The British government here again, had not capped a ceiling on interest on loans, to be collected from the poor. No relief was given to the rural borrowers, from such brutal exploitation of moneylenders, to charge varied interest rates, from different areas and within an area, from different defaulters, without justifying the same. While in London we notice the British government, was introducing several measures of justice. Magna Carta providing for citizen's rights was in place and there was importance of Bill of Rights, casually emphasized. Another scenario quintessentially mirrors a market economy, where market is allowed to play out, with no government intervention. There was no regulation by government and yet how soaked, were the woes of the rural farmers, is writ large probably, to the free market fundamentalists/ ideologues could observe and pontificate. They tend to extol the role of the market, in functioning of an economy and wish the government, to play hands off role. In reality, how free market plays out causes justice can be seen, when they are given a free rein. Ronald Reagan's government came to power in 1980, in USA and the President gave a popular slogan of bringing about, a small government, but ended up leaving a huge budget deficit, at the end of his two Presidential terms. It will be inappropriate, if the developmental efforts of the British are ignored, to be discussed here. The British Government took up some irrigation schemes, in the rural areas, some electricity generation and distribution schemes, in rural areas and also set up universities in Calcutta and other Presidency towns, to built nice buildings for the museums and national library and the like, which exuded the glory of the British government, in the urban areas. In other words, the British created pockets of prosperity, in urban areas surrounded by abysmal negligence of the rural areas, where attention was waiting, both in and financial expenditure particularly in the realm that adds value to people. Later on the national leaders were very inclusive, towards the poor and also rural India.

In the past, the rich people in the villages, who paid obeisance to the British, were condescending to the poor. The government politicians and the bureaucrats, took upon themselves the responsibilities, of ameliorating the conditions of the poor and to bring sunshine, in their lives, once the country, became independent, from the British in 1947. The Planning Commission of India was set up and it was felt that planning for orderly development of the rural areas, with focus on agriculture and industries, the nation, would require 5 year plans. India developed systematically, drawing on the development of the 5 year plans. Thus started, the First Five Year Plan in 1951. The developed world deem planning as a bad word and the developed world continues, to celebrate, when a nation moves away from central planning, thinking planning is counter to the capitalistic march of the nation. After 11 Five Year Plans 12th Five Year Plan is in place in India. India is a country that receives worldwide attention, for its industrial, banking, legal, engineering and scientific competencies, besides being the largest democracy in the world.

Is it not necessary, for the free market ideologues, to revisit their aversion, to planning and see, if there are substantial payoffs, from planning in economic outcomes? The planning can be done, within the ambit of the democratic governance and capitalism. Once the focus on poor, was set in the planning process in India, welfare of the poor got institutionalized, in various layers of the government of India, state governments and the local governments. It also percolated to District, development, block and village levels. In each village, the panchayat is now an important decision making body. Cities are governed by, headed by the municipalities, with an elected chairman and elected councilors, representing different wards of the cities. When the poor sit in these decision making bodies, the decision outcomes reflect their welfare. Overarching inclusive culture of India also helps the effective participation of people, in decision making bodies. This is unique in India. In the developing as well as the developed world, if the poor has to achieve dignity, they need to have a voice, to frankly express their opinions. It is one thing to live with material comforts and it is another to speak aloud, when injustice is perpetrated against the poor. The poor need to keep his/her chin up and should be able to apply correction, through democratic mechanism and not indulging in the incidence of crime. The crime among the poor, in the developed world, has been causing a lot of inconvenience, besides increasing the cost of incarceration, of increasing number of criminals by the State. By institutionalizing the voice of the poor and their contribution in decision making, a lot of crime that takes place, due to the frustrations of the alienation of the poor people, in the developed world, would probably free the capital from expenses, on incarceration. Funds so released, could probably be used in a better manner for expansion of education among middle class and the poor. The big government is likely to be good for the poor, when the type of the governance is civil and, with a limited tenure of the head of the State. National leaders need to have clear understanding of the paradigm. When some constituencies are hijacking the government, against the multitude, the government should be capable of protecting the interests of, the poor and the middle class and not have hands off approach. Regarding an inclusive government, with a Global approach of PPP, Public Private Participation, be it for infrastructure, education or any welfare schemes, for the base of the economic pyramid, it could do wonders to keep the nation happy. There could arise the sunshine, in the lives of the multitude, without deduction from the life of the well off. Thus the government plays an important role, if the ideology is one of democratic governance, allocating equal importance to the private and public sectors, with significant focus for the welfare of the poor. That could add tremendous value, to the economy especially, when the economy is in the developing stage.

Seeing the absence of drinking and smoking, in most of the middle class homes, they advise their men, not to cause ill health to themselves, by smoking and drinking, a sobering effect comes. Since she does not ever smoke or drink, on her own volition, her words on her husband, has many a times, a salutary effect. Wife is a marvelous disciplinarian, in Indian homes, be it moderation in food, abstention from drinking and smoking, keeping the house reasonable clean, no matter how small it is, taking a bath every day, and be in bed on time in all the economic categories of Indians, the rich, the middle class and the poor. As she is sober, she is capable of injecting that quality among children and among men.

Slum is again the link between the village and the city. The village folks learn from those, who have migrated to cities, listening to the anecdotes for hours on end, when the urbanites spare time and visit their villages, for few days, at least once a year. All of these things that they have learnt from their employers, they happily pass it on to their relatives and acquaintances and they then discipline, their homes by teaching the discipline that is quintessential rural. Focus on education, in the manner in the last half a century, has gone to stratosphere, with a desire not only to educate the children but to send them to university for current academic discipline of academic rigor.

Those who work in official positions, in the government, in the developed world, as well as in private firms hail mostly from big cities such as London and few from suburbs and practically none from the outliers, the rural farm areas. The patterns would be the same for Chicago and Los Angles too, in USA, mostly coming from nearer suburbs of Chicago and probably none from the farm outliers. Interviews with government officials and private executives, in India, including the recent IT industry one, would be pleasantly surprised that most at the middle and the top layers of organization pyramid, the engineers and the managers, come from the Districts and the villages of a State and not necessarily from the State headquarters. So is the case with civil surgeons and superintendent of the hospitals, doctors, working in even private nursing homes and corporate hospitals.

Today even all of those IT professionals who are working in New York, Chicago, Madison and Minnesota are from the districts and villages of India and few from metros, though they have had their few years of the academic exposure. In the metros also in these years, out of 16 years of study, for all one knows, 12 years have been in farm areas and the districts. It implies that a very important trigger to come up in India, is realized throughout India, It is thoroughly understood by the rich middle class and the poor families, both in the cities and in the villages. This is an important reason, why India is making waves, in several parameters of economic development. A child surrounded by books and notes is deemed a good child and a child with MP3 hanging from his ears and his eyes all the time, on computer screen, is viewed normally, in an average Indian family, as straying from serious way of life that India adores, along with education. Not everyone in India, who considers himself or herself a computer geek, ends up, being an IT executive and he invariably finds it hard to land a job or could land an ordinary low paying job, in India, as he has neglected his hard core skills of science engineering and math, which Indian institutions employ or value.

One feels good that such screen focused children are very few, unlike in America where almost 80 percent of children are seen glued to the TV or a computer, and hardly anyone with a book, to read at least in the public places. Even among the adults, reading seems to have evaporated, or have gone to the back burner. In Europe, one finds quite a few adults, carrying a serious nonfiction or even a fiction, reading on the train, on the coaches or while sipping coffee or tea in coffee/tea places.. Even the paper that is available in the fast food eatery of a town in US, is seen to be perused, only by those men and women, who are past 70 years. The paradigm appears to be that no reading, after high school, for most, is required until the age of 70 years. Libraries are lonely, in America, with only staff awaiting readers, who are never to land. Those who arrive in the library, without even looking at the new arrivals of the books, rush to the computers, to check their emails or be in social networking and the age group would be from 19 years to 50 years. None appear interested in reading, even a few pages of the books. There are no alerts, asking people to read books, either in pamphlets or on the bill boards and definitely not on the TV. Where have the corporate and government social responsibility, evaporated is a big question mark, to keep the nation learned. Auto companies are learning to make small cars. Cooking is back in American homes. rather than eating out few times a week Reading habits and pursuing studies of academic rigor such as math science engineering and medicine so fastidiously addressed in India, could inspire Americans someday, learning from academic discipline in Indian families.

Manufacturing needs to come back to America, to give spur to well-paying jobs and high education, in science, math and engineering education is important. This opinion is strongly held by the American leaders and now with reluctance accepted by the laity. Public works bring jobs and need investments by Government. Government ownership of firms can certainly add value, in addition to functioning of well performing private firms. An Indian paradigm is reflected, in the US Government in 2008, helping the big US based banks, to get over financial challenges, in preventing home foreclosures, for average Americans. American economic and financial crisis has shown that irresponsible lending, by the mortgage lenders, is to be abjured, a paradigm followed by India's public sector banks.

As much as India, has been learning business ownerships, entrepreneurships, urban development from USA and the west, the US would also do well, to internalize some of the practices that the current Indian paradigm values. For example, the social and economic practice, of the borrowing and living beyond means, is deemed irresponsible and shameful, as per the paradigm in India. Probably sooner America learns, it would be better for individuals, as well as the banks and the lenders. Moderate size of the firms, has the potential of regulation, both self-regulation and government regulation. It would do the American firms well, if through the process of globalization, US based businesses tend to learn, from Indian business landscape, not to live beyond means. Similarly, in the social realm, the marriages are made, to be kept for life and not to be dumped, at the altar of tenacity of individualism, belligerence among spouses, to the detriment of the nice growing up of the children. The ancient thought of Indian sages and rishis (saints), could teach the developed world, also the fast modernizing, westernized thin slice of the Indian metros and also that of the other countries, in the developing world, to look for the long term approach, to life, be it marriage or a job or a business ownership. Divorces are not only bad moral decisions, with release of frustrating future for hapless children, but are also a trigger for financial challenges, including poverty and the downsides, which, can probably be averted, by studying Indian permanent marriage system. Care in the home, needs resuscitation, probably on the lines in India, if financial savings, have to be effected and if the corporations have to be saved, from the declining ethics of the top managers.

It is important to realize that through the process of socialization, the children tend to learn ethics, both its theory and practice, by asking questions, to the elders, such as the parents, the grandparents, the other close relatives and the neighbors, who tend to reply, explaining the events that are in doubt, in their minds. When the concept of neighborhood disappears, in the excuse of a busy professional schedule, when grandparents are, on average, guests for about a week annually, again, when the family is a 2 income family and both parents work, with busy professional schedules and they are unavailable for children, during most of the wake up time, right from their infancy, where on earth the lonely and forlorn children, would learn the ethics from? The gizmos give very short term entertainment and do not teach ethics. The gizmos may be expensive, because 2 income families, would need them, for children to burn time, in the absence of the parents in the home.

Children, being literally, raised by institutions such as day care centers that are run mostly for profit, where children, are huddled in large numbers, for over 16 hours a day, under the guidance of a teacher, who is paid some kind of an hourly wage, until he/she gets a tenure when supported by teacher's unions. The children, who grow up, with such utter parental neglect, may have less comprehension of the ethical issues..

If the children have to be given, more value addition, in their lives, besides happiness and ethical values, the developed world, in the realm of home, will have to g, to the basics. It will be happy moments for the children, at least, if one parent happily, spends time with children, guide them for studies of academic rigor, keeps them off the screens of TV and other handheld devices, keeps them off the clicks, of the computer, arrange books in the family shelves, so that children develop, interest in, reading, other than text books and allocate set number of hours, for rigorous studies, before going to sleep.

A lot of learning in Asia, takes place from, living in proximity, of the grandparents. The Americans may have to learn to leverage, the priceless wisdom of the grandparents, to be passed on, to the children, by not treating them, as annual guests, for a week only. They could from, a part of the family, with multiple room family homes, in America, like joint family, living under one roof, in India's not so big homes..

The British were aghast to see, about 500 local rajas their opulent life styles, their palaces, their gorgeous way of dressing up, with the rajas wearing embroidered clothes and even gold ornaments and attending a lot of paraphernalia of the symbols of royalty. There was standard deviation, in their size of jurisdiction, their status and their wealth and even ruling styles. In other words, the jurisdiction of about 500 rajas was pretty fragmented, including the tax rates. Hence the British might have thought that allowing fragmentation among 500 rajas, could be quite challenging to them, as they thought of seeking suzerainty and obeisance from each one of them. They must have felt that fragmentation, in the ruling style in the 500 local raja jurisdictions could lead to anarchy and rebellion of subjects, against each raja, at different times, could not be ruled out. Even inter raja conflicts could not be totally ruled out, among 500 wealthy rajas, with exclusive jurisdictions. Hence the British offered to collect taxes from each raja and in lieu of which the British government assured them of protection, from any danger, which included from public and other rajas. In some of the vulnerable big rajas, the British representative gave some armed protection, to deal with any miscreant rebellious situation. It was a kind of safety and protection, for individual rajas. However, the cost of keeping the force, with the raja had to be borne, by the raja himself, which meant another dimension of extortion, from the poor hapless farmers and the agricultural labor. This arrangement offered an opportunity, to the political leaders to learn the art of policing, a big jurisdiction in which, there may be hundreds of small fragmented power centers. Once country became free, in the reorganization of the police administrations, government of India internalized some of these techniques. The British had the cunning, to tell the rajas to remain independent or to amalgamate with India or with Pakistan. Most rajas joined India. Some who were recalcitrant, were suitable dealt with by Sri Sardar Patel, the tough Deputy Prime Minster of independent India. All the rajas lost authority, except their personal wealth palace and artifacts therein. They were granted an annual privy purse.

The rajas offering their sovereignty, to the republic of India, was a fine step for the poor, to be administered, by a democratic inclusive governance that helped the economic growth of the nation, economic development and improvement in the conditions of the poor, across the nation, with uniform anti-poverty welfare programs, of the Government of India and Governments of the states.

The rajas had little goodwill, with their farmers, because they used to collect taxes, for the British and also the collection fee, for themselves and money, whenever there were celebrations in raja's family. They sided with the British always and during the wars. under the British instructions, the rajas collected money and they handed over money to the British, which during the global wars, were a huge burden of pauperization, of the peasantry. These rajas never contributed funds, to the India's freedom struggle and they had practically no interface, with great political leaders such a Mahatma Gandhi, Subhas Chandra Bose, Rajendra Prasad, Sardar Patel, Pundit Jawaharlal Nehru and the like. Their loyalties continued, with the British all along, strangely though. It could also be necessitated, by their survival, as they had only small army and tiny jurisdictions. Individually they were no match to the British armed forces in India, which were located in different linguistic regions. Rallying so many rajas, for India's cause, would have been a herculean task. When in 1947 India got freedom and the Raja who were hitherto reliant on the British administration, for even their protection, if the peasants rebelled felt it would be nicer to join India's central governance, renouncing their authority, to rule their tiny jurisdictions. As they collected taxes for the British and also for themselves, to maintain their status, the peasants had felt impoverished. They knew Rajas took a decision in pursuance of Deputy Prime Minister Mr. Sardar Patel to join the Indian republic. Peasantry felt a sigh of relief that they will be part of a strong democracy, where they will have the voting power and they will no more, be a part of the raja's despotism, which certainly had more potential, for being in poverty.

11.3 Repeated discriminations of the blacks, put them down, in poverty, to Lag in studies, Employment, Wealth and Income Generation

While a lot of talk, goes on in the international community, for developing human capital, but in reality, even in the developed world, such as the US and the major countries in EU, much remains to be addressed. It is quite baffling to observe, how the human capital gets neglected, even today. Rules, though are in place, such as affirmative action laws in USA, but they, are also sometimes followed more in breach, in some organizations,

As per the law, in the US, no homeowner can lie that a home that is put up on rent, is already rented out, though it is not yet rented out, responding to a black home renter face to face or even talking over phone and discerning the black conversational style of the caller. Strangely enough, discriminatory moves are undertaken, by the majority community, on many occasions, when the blacks, who earn well, and they are capable of paying a high mortgage, want to move to a higher end white neighborhood. Such treatments, being meted out, to the fellow residents of America, who are around, there for over 4 centuries is strange though. The blacks naturally feel hurt and some of them tend to lose confidence, in the economic and social system. Their melancholy sometimes passes, to their children and grandchildren, in some ways, to anticipate the racial divide, from generation to generation..

Not only such refusals are made, but they justify their stand, on speaking the lies, citing economic grounds that the prices of homes, in the locality, would have moved south, if one or two black families, would have been rented out homes or would have been sold out homes. These loose conversations of discriminations, against the back minorities, do a lot of harm, to the black's cause, because with internet, such loose talks, move far and wide, to different States and a bad illegal practice acquires ubiquity, in white neighborhoods, in other States, even if, it was not the practice earlier, in some states. Even in published books and on the TV serials, mentioning these appear against inclusiveness and integration of American society. Even in TV serials, in a routine manner, such events are shown and justifications aired, in support of such illegal discriminatory moves. These remarks should invite ire of the law enforcing authorities, which does not occur.

Such remarks, in the media and face to face talks in social circles of the majority not only embarrass the blacks, but make them feel, hurt in the country, where they and their several ancestors, were born and lived. It kind of revives the hurt, they used to feel in the past, when suffering as slaves, by their ancestors, used to be their grandma's stories. All of the past and the slavery wounds, come afresh. These illegal and wrong pronouncements, are like rubbing salt on the wounds and making those wounds fresh. Ethnicity matters, for a whole lot of humanity and when an ethnicity's image, is blighted repeatedly, they lose confidence to rise in life, substantially and they feel the frustration ridden anger, against the social and economic system. All of these discriminatory moves accentuate poverty of the minorities and such poverty has the potential of sustainability too.

187

Realtor, is another constituency, who seems to thrive on racial divides. For their business gains, to earn more profits and to make the housing market more liquid, they have consistently, for decades, been keeping the story of nexus of crime, poverty and race alive. They informally categorize the neighborhoods, as high end, medium end and low end. Most black neighborhoods, are bracketed as low end neighborhoods, not rightly always. Similarly, there is ample discussion, both formally in literature and informally, by the realtors, while discussing with clients, about the high incidence of crimes, in the black, low end neighborhoods. The attempt here, is to convince the client, to move to the higher end neighborhoods, to lead, a life, fearlessly, in a crime free locality. While such stories repeat in all of the 50 states, the homeowners are egged on, by the realtors' indirectly, to buy a new home, a more expensive home. The intention of the realtor, here is to egg on their clients, to encourage them, to buy homes every few years and thus to keep alive, the realtor industry. As. home sales transactions rise, more successful would be the realtor industry. Many realtors even make, high 7 figure earnings, at the expense of the reputation of the blacks, which again tend to, hurt them and make them feel helpless, about denting of the reputation, from multiple constituencies.

Though slavery was abolished in the middle of the 19th century, the discrimination against the blacks and treating them inferior, continued in Southern parts of America, until even the middle of 1960s. They were excluded from transportation initially and they had to rely in their life, on human energy, to scale distances by walk. Thereafter, the blacks were permitted to use public transportation, but they were assigned specified sitting places, away from the whites, in the rear. In case, the front seats were vacant, they could sit on the front seats, until some whites, at a coach stop, got into the coach. Then as per law, the blacks were, to go the rear, giving the front seat, to the whites, making them feel highly inferior. One can imagine how embarrassing would it be for any race, to be compelled by law, to act so servile, in this manner. It is this concept of inferiority of the blacks, slapped by the majority community that was questioned by Ms. Rosa Parks and she courted arrest by the police, by not moving to the rear, to give the seat to the white, at Montgomery, Alabama. Further, there were exclusive white drinking water fountains, meant for the whites, which the blacks could never use, under law. Similarly, there were exclusive rest rooms, for the whites, which were out of bounds, of the blacks, under law. In rail journeys too, such segregations were practiced. Such transportation segregation was also a part of apartheid white regime of South Africa and despite holding a railway journey ticket of first class, Mr. Gandhi was asked, to leave the train, as he was not a white. It is this discrimination, which made Mahatma Gandhi to protest, against racism practiced, by the apartheid white regime, in South Africa, as early as in 1894 and called this agitation Satyagraha, which he translocated to India, asking the British, to be just to India and end their colonial rule. In southern states of USA, no one could join the police department, unless he was a white, under law. Thereafter a change occurred, showing inclusiveness to the blacks, and the minorities such as the blacks, could join the police force, However, a black policeman, under law, could not arrest, a white accused and he /she could only report the matter, to the white policeman, for action. Such ridiculous laws, were framed in South of America and these laws were brutally practiced, with pride by the whites. Thus the framing of laws, itself was fraught, with open and daring exploitation, of the blacks and then in the later years, despite law, the justice was not accorded to the blacks, in many cases and boisterously, the laws were violated by the whites, particularly, by the southern Americans.

Though slavery was abolished, no political rights were granted to the blacks. Blacks could not seek a political office, either as law maker in Washington or in other States and not even City Councils as mayors. The blacks did not have any right to vote, until the middle of 1960s, after about 100 years from the abolition of their slavery, by Sir Abraham Lincoln, the President in the middle of the 1860s. Denials of rights went on, in America to the blacks, without any feeling of guilt, by the whites.

In 1965, influenced by the marches and agitations by the blacks, under the leadership of Dr. Martin Luther King, Jr, the government took the dynamic step under the Presidency of Mr. Johnson B. Lyndon in 1965. Dr. Martin Luther King, Jr, saw this justice happen, to the blacks, though he was unfortunately assassinated in 1968, for taking up, the political cause of the poor blacks and for ensuring their victory, in getting the ballot, like any other whites. However, a caveat was introduced that grant of political rights, will not be unconditional and the voting rights shall be reviewed every year, by the government. Hence even in the eyes of the government, a discriminatory approach against the blacks continued.

The concept of school districts, though it does not appear so, seems to be a tool to perpetuate the segregation, among the white and black children and to keep the young blacks and the whites, segregated, for years to come. Neighborhoods, were made the basis of admission to the public high schools and not the merit of the students. A very average student, even a duffer, from a neighborhood x could join in the x public school only and no other school, no matter what was the academic standard of the x school. Similarly, a bright student y could only study in y school, no matter how low was the academic standards of the y school and how high was the academic standards of the x school. Such queer school district law was made, to perpetuate the segregation also, in the process inferior education, for the black children, up to standard 12th, the high school. It has turned out to be such a monolithic law, of school districts that some Americans, who were non-whites to make their children get better education, went overboard to pay a much higher home mortgage per month. They remained content with much lower savings, for the future and obtained much higher credit card credit limits and such cases, were very few and far between and included some legal immigrants from abroad.

The black children knew clearly that the education, which they were receiving, from their neighborhood schools, are far inferior, compared to their white counterparts, in the elite neighborhoods, the latter, had better lab facilities, better quality of reagents to do lab works, could do science and math under good teachers. The blacks in their neighborhood schools struggled, with very poor lab facilities, deficit of teachers, for some subjects and very low paid teachers, who would, for economic reasons, be of lower academic caliber. This concept of school district, which blatantly exploited the poor blacks, in the realm of education, emerged, from a deliberate public policy of funding them, from the fund allocations of the city administration, from the city taxes. As the city taxes, in the poor black neighborhoods, much depended, on how much the parents of the children earned, the funds for the public schools, in the minority neighborhoods, were far lower than the funding of the public schools, in the better neighborhoods.

In white richer neighborhoods, as the city taxes paid, by the parents of the children, were much higher, they maintained better infrastructure in the public schools and also higher academic standards, appointing quality teachers, paying them, far higher salaries. In other words, public policy clearly and covertly averred to the children, through these measures," If your parents are rich and they pay higher taxes, then only you will go to a better public schools, with better infrastructure, with better academic discipline and with better quality teachers; If your parents are poor, earn less and pay less city taxes, you would be saddled with schools, of lower academic standards, as the teachers would be ill paid and they will be far less scholarly."

It has been, a well-known fact that due to a combination of circumstances, the black parents earn, far less than their white counterparts. Knowing well that this weakness in finances of the black families and their inability to pay higher taxes, are driven by not only the endogenous factors, but also due to many exogenous discriminations, over centuries, the school districts have been institutionalized, in an unjust manner, and an educational system divide, between the rich and the poor for eternity, has been brought in place. This has the potential of reining in, the development of most blacks. In other words, the professional and economic domination of the white social groups, over the black social groups, came to be solidified, through the school district concept, throughout the length and breadth of the country.

If such segregated discriminatory educational system, exists, how could there be any level playing field, when the blacks go to the college for higher studies or the blacks go for interviews, for employment. It is the interviewer, who would feel, biased against a black candidate; because the loopholes of the education system would be known to him, as he would have very low opinion, of the high schools, where the black candidate studied. Naturally, the white youth felt emboldened and the black felt weakened, in their spirits, to rise in life. The blacks feel frustrated, as they see the gap of academic standards, in their own schools and its contrast with the schools meant, for education of whites. How the products of such a system, can fare equally well, when the system is so faulty and appears to have been designed, to keep the blacks educationally down.? As though, this was not enough and time and again, people are allowed to talk and write about black indifference, to ambition in life or hard work in life, terming them, many a times, given to laziness. One can imagine how sensitive many blacks would feel about ~~rubbing~~ salt over their wounds, in this manner. In the realm of public policy, in education probably, the US could draw inspiration, from highly inclusive stance of India's funding of the highly subsidized almost tuition free public schools, for all segments of the Indians, which are uniformly financed, from the budgetary allocation of the respective state governments. Compensation levels, all over the country, are the same, for all the teachers in India and the teacher's academic abilities, are of a high order, with graduate degrees on the subject and another graduate degree in education. Their jobs, which the state is liable to relocate, every 3 years, so that they remain riveted to their academic profession. They have security of tenure of their jobs and they are judged by the authorities, from student enrolments and high school results. High school examination board, is an independent board and examination papers, are set, by an independent body of paper setters. Before examinations roll numbers are allocated, to the students and in their answer sheets, only roll numbers appear, preventing the examiner, to know the identity of the examinee. At designated centers, under the effective supervision of the district education authorities, the answer sheets are evaluated, for several days, with hundreds of teachers, descending on these centers. The centers in which, the students appear for examination is different from where they studied, to maintain objectivity and even the invigilators are not their own teachers, but teachers from other schools, whom they do not know and the examinees have never seen before. This measure is also to ensure transparency and objectivity. The answer sheets are again evaluated, by not their own school teachers, but teachers from a distant place, to maintain objectivity. In India, Government ensures that the teachers are actively in place, for subjects of academic rigor, such as math, science and language. Minimum 2 languages are learnt by the students and one of them is English language, including its grammars. All of these features of education, are disseminated to all students, hailing from the rich and the poor families, hailing from all states, hailing from all castes and linguistic origins. No discriminations of sorts, in state public schools are allowed, to differentiate education from one student to another, based on any divide such as caste, language province or economic status. Probably, the US could internalize this education model, with some flux of time, to create an even playing field, right from childhood. Most public goods in the US are equalizers, in life's pursuits, such as community pantry, community parks, sidewalks, nicely laid out roads, fast food places, which offer reasonably cheap food, affordable to all races and those from the middle income and the poor families. Similarly, the access to giant retailers, like Wal-Mart, where goods are sold at low prices, both for the rich middle income and the poor, non-categorization seat centric coaches and metro trains, where rich and poor travel together, with no segregation are other examples of segregation free outlets. If in so many activities, the economy provides segregation free outlets, then why funding of the schools, should be done, in a segregated manner. First step that US could adopt is, to fund the teachers of all public schools, from the state funds and recruiting them, on par of academic standards and that in a big way, to pull up the poor and create an even playing field, to a large extent. The schools could be the same, to begin with, not so nice infrastructure, where neighborhood people may study, with of course segregation of physical place of study, between the blacks and the whites, but they could at least learn, from the teachers of similar caliber, everywhere in every neighborhood, in every public school. The blacks would need, to adjust initially, for a decade or so, to be academically trained, by the white teachers, as well who are highly learned, in some schools for what of highly learned black teachers. This challenge will come, because all these decades, they have developed comfort, being taught only by black teachers.

Chapter 12

Slums and Indian Cities

Slums indirectly encourage feudalism. While personal attendance in the homes of urban Indians, at an affordable price, comes from the slums with a nice network of public transport system. It makes lives of a lot of urban middle class, comfortable but too many people in slums has the potential of making urban families, lazy and reliant on personal attendants. It is now becoming common, in many young married families to have 3 personal attendants. With increasing supply of labor, in slums and increased density per square feet the price of labor takes a southern turn. When such families recruit more than 1 personal attendant all of the home management responsibilities, cleaning mopping, cleaning of artifacts, gardening, cooking and deriving is taken over by the attendants. All of these attendants spend most of their wake up hours, in nicer cleaner environments, in the homes of Indian urban families due to trust between the middle class and the poor and also very limited incidence among the poor.

While assistance of some maids, makes life more attentive to intellectual and business activities or more interactive with family members, but moderation in recruiting, them would be nicer. The labor thus gets employed, earning wages and possibilities of their next generation, coming up in life, through the route of subsidized education enhances. The employees tend to see master's inclusiveness too, but it makes urban people slightly sedentary in their life style, with little physical exercises. At the macro level, with increased density of people, in the slums, the physical hygiene deteriorates, in numerous slum areas, sometimes leading to the spread of bad epidemics and downside to health care. Further, these slums could become breeding grounds for criminal activities, if the law enforcing authorities, do not keep a solid watch and also remain incorruptible. With so many people living in slums, some slum leaders could act without education and sobering guidance from knowledgeable people, in a rough manner with mainstream population, making slum dwellers behave, with intransigence, in many areas of urban life. These slums dwellers might learn, to flout the laws and in case of intervention of law enforcing agencies, could misbehave with strikes and agitations, paralyzing the life of the city and causing a lot of economic losses. These slums thus, in some respects, could be a, nuisance for authorities. If misdirected, their minds could turn combustible, with slum leaders asking them to rebel. Some vested interests for pursuit of the furtherance of their self-interest could use these vulnerable groups, sometimes to the detriment of city discipline.

While some slums are unavoidable to align with culture of inclusiveness and they have economic value, in India, but allowing new slums, to come up in every few years and pumping hundreds of thousands of new people, into existing slums, have been creating enormous downsides to the Indian cities, from aesthetic and hygiene points of view, unknown in any other parts of the world.

It is interesting to examine, why slums in urban India attract more people. The caste system linguistic group system plays an important role. The cities are known to have more and better quality of the public goods. Educational facilities that are cheap and funded by government abound in the Indian cities. These cities make no distinction among students coming from different neighborhoods. Since these schools are funded by the state no locality can stake a claim to the schools located in a neighborhood. As the fees are minimal and heavily subsidized by the government, the educational institutions are highly democratic where the middle class, the poor and even rich children rub shoulders. These institutions are an epitome of inclusiveness of the affluent to the other classes. Lack of standardization in housing in the Indian cities, also spurs faster socio economic mobility among people. The road norms in Indian cities have a wide cleavage, between the developed world and India. Petty businesses robbing the aesthetics of the cities, unlike western cities, set up on the sidewalks inconveniencing the pedestrians, but generating employment, for supporting a family. He pays for no infrastructure, unlike shopping arcades and pays no taxes, creating an informal economy for the poor. Political support exists, to the increase in slum population, as an urban vote bank.

The role of political parties, in sprucing up the urban administration has been poor, while they have many credits, in keeping democracy, in place in the states and in the country. Unfortunately, the cities have suffered due to uneducated law makers and leaders in urban areas. Allocating lawmaker seats during the elections, for the state legislatures and the national parliament is understandable as 60 percent of the country's population lives, in the rural areas and they are also engaged, in agriculture but in the cities, denying seats, in the municipal councils, to the suave educated people is hard to comprehend.

Allocating urban seats to the slum leaders, unfortunately, by the major political parties, despite the availability of many qualitative educated professionals, who might be willing to contest elections to the municipal councils and astonishingly to select candidates, who know very little about urban administration, makes no sense. Initially the aesthetics of the cities were randomly blighted by bringing a lot of uneducated rural poor to encroach on the vacant government lands, The political parties to derive the goodwill of the poor, encouraging at the city's cost was not right and then to choose slum leaders, who are barely educated and are rough in disposition, to give tickets for elections to the municipal council baffles the educated urbanites. The least the political parties could have done, is to have municipal councils of cities, packed with qualitative educated people. It is no wonder compared to South Eastern Asian nations, even the cites in India, wears a poor non aesthetic look and the cities, the political parties need to understand, are the first impressions about a country. It is rightly averred by Mr. Narendra Modi, the current Prime Minister that the cities have to look far better like that of the cities of the developed world, if India wants to be viewed as a developed country in the decades to come.

Chapter 13

Debt and Poverty of the Developed World

Debt has become an overarching problematic reality, in America, which is not confined to one constituency. It has assumed the dimension of ubiquity, unfortunately. At the national level, debt is problem, in terms of the quantum of debt, already incurred, being incurred on an annualized basis and the possibility of escaping, from this liability appears, remote at the moment. Firms, instead of running businesses, with more equity and less debt and consolidating their businesses, to gradually increase the debt component, act aggressive on borrowing and land the firms, to multiple challenges. When the higher order institutions, such as the national government and the businesses are not indifferent, to borrowing, the banks want to make the public at large, captives of debt, so that they earn extra dollars over and above their compensation levels, show a prettier balance sheet, for the banks and knock away solid incentives, by nice and courteous talks with clients, duly making them big borrowers. Debt has been turning, in the last couple of decades, a very important trigger for poverty, in American families. A lot of families are unfortunately, breaking as one of the spouses, is magnetized to borrowing, with irresponsibility and the other spouse is prudent, not to borrow. This becomes the point of friction, among many married couples, before landing in divorce.

13.1 Debt is caused by Low Compensation and in Turn Poverty is Created by Runaway debt, at the Individual Level.

Gigantism of some of the organizations, have resulted, in dwarfing of the power of the smaller boutique businesses, who are suppliers to the gigantic firms. Here there is no level playing field, as the suppliers, have no place, to go to supply their items. When economic landscape in America, was not characterized, by gigantic firms, in an industry, there were many medium sized units and then the group of suppliers, had the level playing field, and with the buyers of the items and it was a competitive scenario. If one medium sized buyer was acting arrogant and cutting the price, the suppliers could turn to other buyers. But in retailing industry, when the boutique shops or industrial categorized slightly bigger shops, were closed, as the giant retailers appeared on the scene, the suppliers felt helpless and they were compelled, to sell the supplies, to only one or two retailers. The level playing field was completely missing. Similarly, for employees, when there were millions of boutique shops, traditional relationships in small downtowns, made difference in compensation. In some of the boutique shops, where the employees were dependable, honest and sincere, in their work, the owners sometimes even paid $14 an hour, before the Wal-Mart became really gigantic. Now Wal-Mart would pay somewhere around $8 an hour, with no sick leave and no health care benefits. Here again, the level playing fields, are completely missing. As Wal-Mart has resulted, in the sudden disappearance of those boutique shops, to which the employees could run, to ask for higher wages are all gone. The employees either would have to be jobless or take Wal-Mart jobs, at the terms and conditions of Wal-Mart, which is very harsh, relative to the cost of living. Culturally, the teenagers used to do work, in small shops, which were so many, in numbers and now with their businesses closed, the teenagers are seeking jobs, with giant retailers. Those who have retired, but want to delay taking social security and who are not entitled, to any pensions and find their social security check, too small, to meet ends, are also seeking jobs. Women once got used to working, in depressions times in 1930s and then during the second global war again, when men went to war as soldiers, found it difficult to stay at home. Egged on by the feminists that home management responsibilities, are inferior, to going to the workplaces, spending time on the commute and meeting team members and team leader, many women found it fashionable in America, to go to workplace, which provided, in most cases, only extremely low paying retailing jobs. With so many constituencies, lining up for retailing jobs, is it any wonder that Wal-Mart calls the shots, to pay low hourly wages, no bonus, no annual raise and certainly, no health care benefits? In addition, it boisterously issues a pink slip, to about 90% of the employees comes, at the end of working for 9 to 10 months, in flexible labor market of USA.

It is not known, why extraordinary bargaining power, has been given, since the 1980s, to the managements, to ride roughshod on the employees and the workers and it is hard to understand, how the lack of level playing field, which is so huge, is unseen, by public policy makers, the decision makers, at the board and top management levels of the companies. All these have been done, neglecting human capital, in this manner, and it has a huge cost, in the long term, which is showing up, now after about 3 decades, in the form of economic bubbles, being busted in different industries. The US economy has been thus, seeing the downturn and poverty levels are going north, with debt, racing to the stratosphere.

If only the level playing fields, in the firms, would have been maintained, either by the regulators or by self-regulation of the industry, then such economic crisis, which is bedeviling the US, since 2008, would have been easily avoided. The important constituents, of the same, need to be in sync, for an atmosphere of music, in the life of people, in general. Then the despair among one category of Americans, which is demographically too large and too powerless, in current industrial relations scenario, would have been avoided. Industrial democracy, would have brought effervescence, to the lives of people and would have reduced inequality. At the same time, the top managers, would also have had nice quality of life. A nice attitude would bring sunshine, to the personal finances of the average Americans and their personal balance sheets, gradually would be liabilities free, over a decade or so, given a progressive outlook among firms..

The debt levels need to be low, with average Americans and they need to seek, not consumer loans, but loans with Return on Investment (ROI), which they be permitted to invest. In other words, they need to turn entrepreneurs, creating for example, surfeit of the tuition outlets for students, who are weak in science or math or reading or grammar, opening outlets, to teach yoga to the young, as well as the middle aged, in different slots of time, outlets to train people in painting or clothes stitching or knitting woolens or even educating the young on global affairs, to make them more knowledgeable or more outlets for architectural education, on home remodeling, or opening many boutique gyms, to help people lose weight or stay slim or even opening eateries such as ice cream parlors, burger parlors, which have the local taste flavor and not part of a huge a chain of eateries. This kind of loan could make teenagers, make their pocket money, middle age could make extra money and even the aged could leverage their wisdom, to make money, to feel good and also supplement, what they get from the US government, by way of the social security check. Focusing on ROI kind of debt, they would learn probably, to shun the consumption loans that increase poverty and its challenges.

13.2 US Compensation, With No Bonus No Annual Raises and No Health care benefits, Caused Rise in Poverty

With burgeoning of supply of labor, with no skills, due to diversion of those, who earlier worked, in manufacturing and then were left unemployed, due to off shoring of the jobs, in the 1980s, the employers found, their bargaining power increased, by exponential proportions, in USA and they suddenly started, bashing labor unions. If necessary, they did not hesitate, to even close certain businesses, where murmurs of complaints, against the management arose. They stopped giving annual raises, which were earlier a norm, in the 1960s and 1970s. Even the bonus was cornered by the management and not paid, to the workers, even if the firm achieved, good annual profits. These practices for those hailing from other democracies, in the comity of nations, appeared weird, because political democracy and industrial democracy generally, went, side by side. In India, the labor practices are very engaged, in big firms and they could go on strikes, if the benefits like annual raises and bonus, were denied, even if the firm makes profits. In several firms, in India annual raises and the bonus are offered, no matter, whether the firm profits or incurs a loss. The labor is given these benefits, before a management contemplates, to have it. Such inclusiveness, also helps in the work discipline, through the interface with labor union leaders. As bargaining power of the labor evaporated, with labor union bashing practices and the layoffs were, without notice and without reasons, in USA. A fear came to be an overarching feature, in American workplaces. Murmurs even to seek financial justice, could cost them their jobs. Once dismissed from the workforce, the American organizations, do not entertain any appeals, against the decision of the supervisor, even if his/her decision is not right. Even the colleagues, refuse to talk with him, who is dismissed, both formally and informally. He is forlorn, not contacted and his phone calls are not answered, even by his colleagues, with whom he may have worked, for decades. Such a dismissal, is known to come to people, for no great reasons, even if he/she worked in the organization, for over 18 years. So many cuts, by powerful employers automatically make employees poorer, as they have ceased, to possess any bargaining power, to achieve annual raises, even through negotiations, since the 1980s. A new paradigm has come into being, against the labor prosperity, since President Ronald Reagan, elected in 1980, took a tough stand, in favor of the management, which was overemphasized by corporate America, to undermine industrial democracy. As President of a multi trillion dollar economy, he would have lot of responsibilities and management labor relationship, is a small part of it. A few averments to discipline the labor, by President Reagan, appears to have been misused, by corporate America, to gradually plummet the compensation levels, by taking up cost cutting measures, as and when, some opportunities, such as offshoring, shifting manufacturing jobs abroad to China and India and going for accelerated automation arose. Rich thus became super rich and the poverty dawned, on the base of the economic period, besides unemployment spells, when all of their savings also came, to be eviscerated, because the family values, also do not permit a jobless sibling, to stay for a year or two, with another sibling, as is very common in India.

There is another trigger of falling into poverty in America, as the employed relatives, strangely do not welcome, unemployed close relatives and trust levels are low, even among the relatives, because of less family unity, more self-centrism and individualism Even in a marriage, if the husband agrees to welcome, the individualism of the wife, may come in the way and vice versa. So economy of scale, of available transportation, spacious homes with empty bed rooms, go begging, without being utilized, even in times of a close relative's financial challenges. This would have never happened in India, even with much smaller homes. An unemployed brother or a sister, would stay, for a year or so easily, until he/she is settled in a new job and no expenses even would be charged, by the employed sibling, during that period. In such a scenario, the debt is no more an option in America, but an absolute necessity. Debts are incurred, without even getting sensitized. Thus who borrows to the maximum extent, without paying any upfront amount, is accepted. Some even accept teaser interest loans or interest only loans, to be challenged heavily with peaking debt, in a few years. It is only postponing poverty challenges, for a few years.

13.3 Poverty Increased Due to Absence of Industrial Democracy

Conservative Government's support, to rich businesses, has distanced labor and the poverty increased. Between the two political parties in America, when the conservative party comes to power, which is intensely pro business and during their periods, the labor seems to have a very tough time, as entitlement welfare allocations, in the budget are decreased and sometimes even tax cuts are given, to the rich, reducing government revenue. George W Bush, the Republican President reduced the taxes, for the rich twice, which certainly hurt the labor. Businesses also turned inebriated, to cut costs and take away jobs abroad, more fervently than, during the times, when democrats ruled the nation. Strange was the initiative of the republican government, to give tax rebates, to those firms, which outsourced their jobs abroad. Not only the jobs of the local Americans, were taken off shore mostly, to India and China and some to East European countries, appreciating their IT talents, but even those firms paid lesser taxes, to the US government, which automatically hurt the schemes of welfare, to the poor. The moves were however reversed, during the 2010s, by President Obama's Government. Government can sometimes be pro-business and be indifferent to its consequences on the poor, as the poor are far less, engaged in the democracy in USA, unlike her counterparts, across the Atlantic in Europe and certainly far less engaged compared to, the labor, in the indusial democracy intense India. A tax rebate, to an outsourcer in India would have been, very difficult, whichever government would have been, in power, as the labor could have taken to streets, could have blocked traffic and could have exacted promise from the government of India that it would not hurt the poor, to help the rich. The State governments are known to fall, during elections, if the incumbent party, is pro corporate India and not so helpful to the rural masses, where poverty abounds relatively. In 2002, the Congress Party, which is traditionally known to be pro poor, came to power in the province of Andhra Pradesh, known for tech revolution and the political party that promoted the urban tech revolution, with many jobs from the US, lost the political power. The poor in India, unlike in US, hold levers of political power, appreciably. The pro poor Congress Party, has enlightened the labor so much, that even if the other party Bharatiya Janata Party comes to power, it has to adhere, to the same pro poor welfare schemes, to an extent, to stay in power in an environment, of peaceful democracy. Democracy is highly engaged and street demonstrations, like Europe, are normal and it even exceeds the engagement levels, of the European democracies. Courtesy traditions blazed by peace lover Mahatma Gandhi, by and large, demonstrations are peaceful non violent and are, focused on the issue, to make a representation, to the Government of India and to sensitize. Isolated pockets though could witness, little unruly mobs, which gets addressed, by law enforcement authorities, by preventive arrests. With industrial democracy gone, in the US, with burgeoning bargaining power of the business owners, the average Americans, are left with little option, but to accept the low hourly wage, keep quiet and then borrow under compulsion, wherever loans are made available. If he/she has to buy a car, reliance on auto debt, to the maximum extent, becomes a compulsion. Even to pay monthly bills, loans occasionally, to be paid in 3 to 4 years, may be an absolute necessity. Offshoring has hollowed out many towns, industries and allied industries, with no job in sight, increasing the intensity of poverty in USA.

With internet arriving in 1980s and computers, PCs picking up, on a large scale, with leveraging of talents that have risen, in some parts of the world, to handle American sub jobs, have been lost and poverty increased.

Less study of science, math, engineering and medicine, since 2000, when internet based video games, internet chats, email correspondence, text messaging from cell phones, individual cell phone talks and as a finale, social media one liner obsessions and making friends, friends of friends of friends ad infinitum, whom one has not met, not known but corresponding on lighter aspects, like weather, jokes, food, happening events in the respective towns, music and films, filled the minds too much, the space for academic rigor plummeted. As a result, the study of general affairs, which has limited or little application to life, dominated most universities and colleges for local Americans. Then the poverty increased, as these jobs were taken, by academic rigor capable, foreigners from India, China and countries of Eastern Europe.

With offshoring of manufacturing plants, jobs and allied industry jobs and near absence of studies of science engineering, math and medicine, the job left in the US economy fell, under the category of services, which belonged, mostly to the retailing industry, some in small retailing and some in giant retailing, which paid unfortunately, around minimum wages say $8 an hour. In the manufacturing sector, the employees were getting, 4 times about $32, thus reducing the standard of living and causing increased poverty, by a factor of four. In manufacturing places, an additional advantage, was that at least in the initial years, the American workers, could stay at home, with parents, for which there was some saving.

It is common knowledge that the manufacturing jobs, needed skills and they were specialized jobs, not everyone's cup of tea. It required trade education, in trade schools and a lot of hard training, in rough manufacturing atmosphere, with no air conditioned environment and naturally fetched higher pay. These firms usually had traditional labor unions, whose voice used to matter, even in fixing compensation, once in every 3 years, as has always been the case, in all firms in Germany, Japan and India. These were priced positions, which also offered pensions. Probably, it is the union's pressure, at which the firm, buckled to give pensions, to the retirees, as well as the health care, also to the retirees after retirement. I have never come across, any private firms in India, offering pensions, to the retirees and also health care, to the retirees. Too much exaction of long term benefits, to the employees, through industrial democracy, seems to have had a highly frightening and negative effect, on the firms, who came up later. They stopped health care, even during the job period and also retirement benefits, even annual raises and bonus. The shifted paradigm consisted of, expecting that the private firms, funded by shareholders, are basically meant to enhance on a regular basis, shareholder's value. The private firms probably felt that for them to offer pension to the retirees, was too much of an inclusiveness, which usually comes only, from the state owned enterprises and the government jobs only, in most countries. In India, the government jobs only, carry pensions and the private firms only pay, the current compensation and therefore those, who join private firms, have better saving habits, than the government employees and even the compensation in the private firms, is higher than a similarly placed government manager. US manufacturing firms, gave health care benefits during the work period, as well as after retirement. It also provided pensions and even family pensions. Heath care was due, to the spouse, even after the retiree died. Such was the ever encompassing inclusiveness, of US based manufacturing firms, like the Big 3 auto firms of Detroit. While the management jobs, in the manufacturing sector, went to the whites in the auto industry, most of the base of the economic pyramid worker jobs, went to the blacks. This created high middle class in USA. With one income, the families could send a few children, to university education. Of course universities, were also much less money minded, than they are now and the cost of tuition, was moderate, compared to the northern movement that it has taken, in the last decade. Without any student loan, the employees of the auto companies, could educate their children, in the universities for graduate education. This would reveal, how well off, the working class happened, to be in USA, when the manufacturing, was the mainstay of the US economy, when industrial democracy was in place and when the labor unions were relevant. The voice of the employees, in the manufacturing workplaces, headed and they carried the dignity, like they carry now, in India. In fact in case of nay injustice to the employees, the unions could be emotional and management, made an effort to cool them down, tactfully. Riding roughshod on the labor is out of question.

In the 1980s, the US observed that China's educational system, has caught on and had generated large number of science and engineering based graduates. It was also noticed that China's domestic manufacturing sector, has had picked up considerably and if they were proffered, by the support of the R&D of the developed world, along with injection of capital, even the Chinese firms, could make world class goods. Hence a number of manufacturing firms, found the manufacturing knowledge of China, pretty enticing. With President Nixon's ping pong diplomacy, duly assisted by Mr. Henry Kissinger, China was open to the idea of, expanding business relations, with US. Hence came the connections with government, foreign relations support plan in 1980s, to considerably increase the Foreign Direct investment. Thus China came to be the apple of the eye, for corporate America, to cut costs, cut labor costs, particularly and depend on China, to make goods. The result was shifting of manufacturing plants, along with jobs to China's eastern sea board, where infrastructure went up over the years, by leaps and bounds. Not only incumbent shifted the factory plants, but the new manufacturing businesses, instead of opening in USA, they started opening their businesses in China.

It was a scenario never known, since the industrial revolution in the 1600s, in Britain and Europe. It created a dichotomous situation, making the profits, go through the roof, for the firms. As a result, the compensation of the CEOs and the top management also started, taking a huge rise. An opportunity upped for top managers and even board directors, to go on foreign tours, which was business plus tourism, a scenario unmet in the past. So a slice of top managers, including the vice presidents and the CEOs, felt happy that they saw a leap in their compensation levels. Shareholders felt happy as the share prices also rose, by leaps and bounds, due to high profits quarter through quarter. But some constituencies, which were large, in number saw despair, descended on their lives. All of the owners of allied industries, had to close plants and dismiss workers. All of the manufacturing workers, whose jobs were shifted to China, saw their jobs lost. Hence the manufacturing cities, of USA, where the pockets of the businesses, the allied industries, the down towns, which used to buzz with life and happiness, saw a pall of gloom. Jobs disappeared, the plants disappeared, consumers stopped buying, shops were closed and the city wore a desert look. Gradually, ex workers started migrating, to the cities and state in search of jobs. Waiting for jobs disappointed them but it could be years. The black poverty rose suddenly, as most of the blacks, in these towns used to work, with some areas of manufacturing and they had a decent compensation. They had to now, be content with jobs, in the service sector. They were getting $25 to $30, an hour, for their specialized skills, which were not in need any more in America and they now got $6 to $8 an hour. South side of Chicago had lot of manufacturing jobs and only a small percentage, could be absorbed, in service jobs. Service jobs being general jobs, with no need for specialized skills, despite manufacturing specialized skills available, with black Americans, they were treated, on par with general candidates, and were offered, around the minimum wage. This was a huge come down, in their living standards, injecting poverty in their lives, as they were used to compensation of manufacturing, in which, US paid around $30 dollars an hour. In Germany, it could fetch as high as 39 dollars an hour. They were now poorer, by 4 times and did not know, how to survive. Poverty further increased, as there started, with about unions gone, a huge bargaining power of the employers. They showed their bargaining power, by asking the supervisors, to take mostly temp employees, so that none, could question denial of the long term benefits, such as health care. Supervisors, though affected by poverty of such decisions, as even they could lose their jobs and become a temp anyway obliged, with a lamb like attitude. He started distributing the hours to the temp employees, now for a week. Some got 4 hours a week, some 10, some 15, some 20 and some 35, all as per the dice that helped. Sometimes, he also played favorites. If he was not color blind, he could discriminate against the colored employees. If he was not region blind, a mid western manager, could give more hours to a Midwesterner temp and cut hours from the Latino or a white from the south. All of these divides started playing out, when there was arrival of droves of non-skilled employment, seeking jobbers. Sycophancy was enjoyed by the supervisors and as a lot of the temp employees, chaperoned around him, for few extra hours. In any other poorer economy, such salsa for extra hours and so much fragility of job tenure, is not seen. It naturally increased poverty in USA. Since anyone could be thrown out anytime, out of the jobs, the organization started devouring the middle income jobs also, as the need for supervision and training was not felt necessary, again a unique phenomenon never seem, across the Atlantic even. As the service jobs are unskilled and very low paying jobs, with offshoring of jobs, those who were in manufacturing jobs, now started searching for service jobs, thus burgeoning the jobbers, in the base category.

When middle-income jobs, again, due to high bargaining power, of the employers, started, evaporating, in US economic scene, those, who were working in these middle income jobs, had to toboggan, to searching service jobs, at the base. Thus number of average Americans of different categories, with current middle class jobs, also started joining this class. In these circumstances, the bargaining power of the business owners, went to the stratosphere, like the CEO compensation. Inebriated with wielding, so much authority, arrogance and ego began playing out, in the economy, with rising appetite, for more money, which could feed probably 10 generations, for the rich and super rich and made even daily meal and staying in a home, without home foreclosure round the corner, difficult for average Americans. Should this be the condition of average Americans, in a 14 trillion dollar economy, is left to the US Government and corporate America, to apply correction. Should this be called the plusses of democracy and capitalism, needs introspection, by the American intelligentsia? Is it the result of highly disengaged democracy of USA that so many Americans, are suffering for the quality and quantity of jobs, while public goods look magnetic and awesome, foyers of private corporate offices and the buildings look sometimes, out of the world. Imagine how charming do the casinos look, how so full of life are the sports stadiums, in every state?

An employee in USA, has lost so much, in the quarter of a century. In USA, today in the new millennium, they can be shown the door anytime, without showing any reasons and giving no notice. An employee could have a cup of tea, in the forenoon with the manager and in the afternoon by 3 pm, he/she may have been ousted, from the job and may have been asked to leave the premises. Hence in the 1980s, egged on by a book which stated, "Money greed is good," a lot of managements felt inclined, also to come on board, to be highly money greedy. Then President Ronald Reagan, the new President in 1980, from the Republican Party, was known to be highly pro business and the Government attitude, towards the labor unions, hardened. This attitude occurred, when a strike of the air controllers, took place during the first term of the Reagan Presidency. The President ensured that the airports functioned, with private executives. The incumbent striking employees, were asked to immediately join, their duties or quit the job. This move made a huge impact and the morale of the labor unions, precipitously fell in USA. Inebriated by the success of the management, and utter failure of the labor unions, the strike having failed, a new kind of scenario arose, in the US labor market. Suddenly, the management came to acquire huge bargaining power, against the labor and the labor unions lost the grip, over industrial democracy. Over the years, industrial democracy, genuinely enfeebled. Even in some organizations, such as Wal-Mart, the labor unions were legal, but the tools were designed, by the management, to prevent its formation. Any murmur about management's indifference, to labor, was detected by the management spies, on the floor shop and those employees, were asked to leave the job immediately. This created fear, among the employees that they could, be laid off, any time. Then came the tendency, among the firms, which were making good profits, to set a target of employees, to be laid off every quarter and every year, without any reasons. This was again, to reinforce the fear, making the employees that they were easily substitutable. Taking advantage of this fear, on a routine basis, same number of employees every year, came to be laid off. For example, in Wal-Mart that is the largest American employer, employing about 1.3 million employees, about 90% of employees, are discharged every year. Hence all of the 90% want to continue and be in the retained employees bracket of 10%. Hence they work sincerely and even extra hours, for whatever compensation is paid. The organizations took advantage of such fears, even in a gigantic foreign revenue, earning MNCs, with a global outreach, to plummet the compensations and the take home salary, for the employees. They stopped paying annual bonus, annual raises and health care benefits, except in senior categories. Retirement benefits, like that of the auto companies, were out of question. The lunch break plummeted to 15 minutes and any delay was financially punished. Every week schedule, came to be released by the manager, once a week and which days he/she had to come for, how many hours each day was juggled and informed. Hence the employees were totally kept on tenterhooks. Flexible labor market helped the management.

With compensation going south, at such a velocity, average Americans increasingly depended, on credit card limits, pay day loans and the like, to pay the bills. Had they been entitled, to better compensation, they could have paid their monthly bills, without resorting to hold, multiple plastic credit cards and without rushing to payday loans, every month. In contrast, an Indian employee is highly unionized, has a lot of voice, is respected by the management, is paid a reasonable salary, relative to the cost of simple living, gets an annual raise as a routine, gets an annual bonus, as a routine and is never laid off, unless he misappropriates funds. He enjoys permanent security of tenure and most retire, after full life of working. It is therefore no wonder that they do not have the debts, which their American cousins hold in plenty. Their saving rate is over 30 %. The industrial democracy, been in fine place, the management cannot ride roughshod, over the workers. Before faulting the poor for laziness or not saving enough or living beyond means, mind need to reflect the environment, in which the workers operates in an economy. If it is not one of sympathy, inclusiveness, kindness and with a thought of stepping into one's shoes and then simply faulting the poor would not, make them better in finances. With genuine kindness and inclusiveness, it is not difficult, to discipline the labor, the poor but the inclusiveness of the management, has to be genuine. Mother Theresa with a pure and kind heart, improved the economic conditions of many poor, in Calcutta and made them to feel responsible, about their lives.

That exhibits the scenario of affability and inclusiveness, in Indian workplaces, be it government, public sector or private businesses and least debt is visible in their balance sheets..

In the USA, even the hope that college education, would fetch high paying jobs, evaporated. For example, the college educated in Music, Theatre and Religion people in New York city, are now observed, to share an apartment, at the rate of 3 persons and a lot of these jobbers, with undergraduate in Theatre, Music academic disciplines are known, to address 3 to 4 jobs, in a day, to make ends meet.

A lot of American Students are demoralized, as there is no relationship, between promises made by the private educational institutions, about annual compensation boldly asserted and reflected in good font, big font sized attractive color brochures, made of silky cover page and the compensation, offered, in the real world, by the employers, after graduation. When the educational institutions, are seen breaking the trust, whom should the young trust anymore? Does that reflect, not only poverty of money, but poverty of self-confidence, leading to a poverty of nice life?

For a lot of the young, who aspire to go for higher paying jobs and fund their family better, they are hamstrung, by the challenges of the higher education, being very expensive. It requires, a lot of student loan, which on monthly basis, appears less relative, to the total amount, to be borrowed, for higher education. However, when every month that amount is deducted, it becomes hard, to make both ends meet. For those children, whose parents at least, are in better jobs, they can sometimes rely, on their parents, helping them informally to repay the loan, from time to time, when required. But those, hailing from single mother families or poor neighborhoods, where probably both parents work, in ordinary hourly jobs, the parents would be in no position, to help anytime, to repay the student loans. In such a case, confidence is far, from being available, for the student, to borrow student loans, because once he is unable, to pay the loan, the interest rates, could go up and he may find it still more difficult, to catch up, with student loan repayments. Usually these loans take away 20 years of peace, as every month, along with other bills, this loan has to be repaid.

With high school qualification, in current times, it is so hard to get a job and the jobs that come pay, so less that hiring a place, paying bills and maintaining a vehicle, becomes very difficult and poverty conditions, could arise, now and then. One illness could add to more debt, if the health insurance, is not paid by the employer. It is too expensive, to go to a doctor and pay for getting prescription medicines. Medicines would cost probably half the cost of consultation, with the doctor, where the doctor may spend hardly 5 minutes, to write the prescription. Thus poverty triggers in a rich economy like US, to a lower middle class person or even a middle class person, due to expensive medicines and expensive health care. He is aghast, when he listens, to the reasonableness of health care expenses, of Indian students that while in India, he could get a doctor's prescription, for a pittance. What a dichotomy that the American young are so challenged, with poverty, with a health care system, which has been allowed, to be so costly that it makes little sense. Hospitals and doctors make runaway money and stay in 6 bedroom mansions, whereas about 40 million Americans born and raised in USA cannot consult a doctor, when ill. Why an engineer brother, has to be content with 80,000 dollars a year compensation, where as the economic system, should allow the doctor brother or sister, a compensation as high, as 200,000 dollars a year, even if he is merely practicing internal medicine and he is not a surgeon? Why should such dichotomies, not be rationalized, to give better justice, to the American young, is very hard to comprehend. Some professions for no valid reasons, are pampered and paid very well in USA, while others are dumped, with hourly wages, no raises, no bonus and no health care. Those who have taken student loans, which they have to pay for 20 years, for studying Theatre or Music, in the New York city, are known to be addressing 4 part time jobs, to make a living that too sharing the apartment with 2 others, merely getting only room for the self, to stay appears too hard, on the young Americans. How could such a person, identify a spouse, to get married and raise children, with such measly compensation? Here, we are not talking, about a small town that could be job deficit, but we are talking of the metro like the New York City, which has a world renown. Here, we are not talking of the job woes of a high school dropout, in America, we are talking about the future of a college undergraduate. Should a basketball player and a soccer player or a baseball player, all males, should be making millions of dollars a year and then money for corporate endorsements and college graduates in liberal arts, should be so ill paid by the US labor market and yet, at the instance of the Corporate America, the labor market be kept, a flexible labor market, enabling the managements, to ride roughshod on the job seeking, young Americans? Does it make sense that those who had high school education, got nice cushy jobs sometimes, nice enough to run the family, with one income about 25 years ago and today even the college graduates have to work 4 jobs, to meet ends? Does it not reflect serious ethical issues and something seriously wrong, with the labor market? Should the government and corporations not sit together and address corrections and rein in the money greed, of the corporations? Sarbanes Oxley Act in2002, dealt with money greed, severely and sent well known CEOs, who were once on the cover pages of the national magazines, to several years of jail term and at least after some cleansing of the corporate America, CEOs in general, should probably have rolled back voluntarily, turning inclusive to society, having reined in their own compensations and money making obsessions? Treating the young job seeking Americans affably, could have accrued, at least higher goodwill. In 2014, the scenario should not have exhibited, such compensation woes and the job woes of this nature, at the grassroots. The higher education, is squeezing the young, with huge tuition fees and the quality leaves much to be desired, as it is run again, for money greed of the rich, with adjunct faculties, who in turn are insulted, by payment of measly compensations. The time has to come to insist private higher educational institutions, to be asked by the US government, to recruit full time faculties, so that the qualified graduates, acquire good knowledge and get high paying jobs, instead of undervaluing their degrees, which land the graduates, with joblessness or low paying jobs, enhancing the poverty in America. Secondly, if necessary, after recruiting the full time faculties adequately, let the universities recruit adjuncts, but paying them living wages and incentives, motivate then, to prepare for teaching. Paying the adjuncts measly wages, drives them crazy, to seek courses, to teach in several institutions, to pay their family monthly bills, thus tobogganing the quality of their teaching, or their facing poverty conditions. Why in a 14 trillion dollar economy, the intelligentsia should be living paycheck to paycheck, running around different schools, burning gas and commuting, to make ends meet? There are college graduates, many of them, from nice universities and some have even have completed doctoral degrees. In India, the number of adjuncts is few and far between and faculties are full time. They get compensation that enables them, to pay monthly bills, by Indian cost of living, which is simple and also to save adequately. India's personal saving rate is of the order of 35 %. If country with the GDP per capita, which is $1/16^{th \, that}$ of the US could run the universities, recruiting full time and giving compensation that even helps them to save 30 to 35 percent of the take home compensation and also subsidize fully the tuition for the students, should the 14 trillion economy, not keep faculties contented, with compensation and give wider access to all Americans, for higher education, at a very reasonable cost.

Current system in America, of keeping higher education also, in the realm of private industry, has probably, done more harm than good. This system is allowing shareholders, to make runaway money. Allowing top managements, to make runaway money, and bedeviling the students, with huge student loans that keep them, busy paying back these loans, for 20 years makes little sense. The US government would do well, to subsidize higher education and even taking over private educational institutions, to run as State Universities. Let there be utilitarian infrastructure, for these centers of higher learning and not huge extensions being undertaken, to the incumbent buildings. Let the architecture be turned green, with less air-conditioning and less lighting. Let there be far less open lands, to add beauty to the eyes but rationalizing the savings of the students and savings of the faculty, would make education serious and accessible, to tens of millions of the young Americans, who are now, for want of ability, to repay student loans, though meritorious, are remaining, out of bounds, of higher education. Money is spent to construct posh dorms, with great architecture, but burdening the students, with 20 years of repayment of loans and sprucing up architecture of the school buildings, does not make the young happy. Marriages break in the west, as many spouses find it hard, to pay the bills, to which student loans is a huge liability. Some go to better schools and get higher monthly bills, to repay that makes the problem worse confounded. Spouses look at credit scores and the amount that is left after paying the bills, while marrying as well as during the marriage and it is not easy, to keep the marriage, with such financial challenges, compounding the national economy's economic problems further.

The cumulative effects, of all of these results, in the poverty enhancement, arising from the load of heavy student loans, of even the college educated. Why could government not scrap farm subsidies, to giant corporations, like Monsanto and Cargill and big farmers, which are funding, the rich people and institutions that make huge profits and also have international presence and divert that amount of subsidy, to subsidize higher education, like India pays for higher education in science, medicine, engineering, math and liberal arts? Poorest of the poor, in India, gets full subsidy, for higher education and they come up very fast in life, achieving, the socio economic mobility.

Among the average Americans, it is not the money greed, but the living standard greed, which is heavily challenging them. Psychologists working with insurance and banking agencies, keep informing the loan underwriters, how the loan seekers are feeling. With talks of politicians that the poor also should be entitled, to home loans and egging on the poor, to be home owners, average Americans many of whom, have either no education such as those who came to America as illegal immigrants, are in dire straits to go for buying a home. They are induced to borrow, at a high rate of interest, as their credit scores may be poor, saying he./she could pay interest only now and then they could come on board later to pay the principal portion of the home loan.. Then there are others, who stay in slightly crime infested areas and they are badgered, by the realtors that they could buy a home borrowing loan, to shift, to safer areas and they are attracted to borrow. Further, some are given to ego stimulation. To such of the Americans, the realtors state that as an university educated manager, he/she deserved a more spacious home, in a high end neighborhood and the home prices are likely, to go up in about 3 to 4 months time and this is the time, to make a final decision, to buy a nice home

With government's benevolence and general amnesty, some illegal immigrants from Latin America, become citizens. Among these citizens, a lot of them acquire education and aspire to buy homes. The pressure from the realtor, is so suave and convincing that the university educated, also gets into this net of lending. Adding all of these lending numbers, he makes money, to keep his family happy, as he earns incentives, for extending loans, which in America, is termed selling of the loans. How a realtor talks with a client, could make a difference. The expressions have the potential, to either elevate or enervate people's moods, as per the versions of the psychologists. When the lenders tell a borrower that debtor is borrowing a loan, it is a negative mood triggering expression. When home buyer is told that he is buying the home and buying a loan for 15 year period, it sounds more soft and convincing. All of these tricks are played out, by the mortgage industry. However, in US economy, these were not played out in moderation, but were played out at a breakneck speed, in the new millennium, which landed tens of millions, into terrible woes. Some got into heart ailments, some died and others treaded to psychiatrists, for mental ailment treatment. Finally lot of them, lost their spouses, a bizarre thing that happens, in social realm in USA. Thus housing industry battered, so many families, to live in poverty. Many close relatives started living, like a joint family of India, to make savings, or to break even family expenses. One feels happy that Indian joint family, is at least impressing Americans, in times of severe recession like that of 200 7/ 2008.

Selling some product, at a high price, then through speculation, raising the price and supporting the consumer purchases, by easy debt has become a practice. These are leading to bubble formation, every few years, which economists call boom and then the bubble bursts to bring about recession. Through these booms and busts, the new riches are created by few and a lot of Americans, sink into poverty forever. This is artificially proffered, though in economic, circles this, is stated to be natural, in capitalism and market conditions.

We are increasingly witnessing ill effects, of being awash, with debt in America. It will be interesting, to analyze the factors that are making the average Americans, borrow in a casual manner and then suffer from inability to pay the debt, in time. Many of them are landing in the financial mess and poverty. The very nature of financial definition of debt, for the banks and their executives, who know the profession of finance, more than the multitude and their ceaseless efforts, to improve the balance sheets of the bank. Bank's balance sheet puts the debt of the average Americans, on the asset side, because the amounts that are lent to the loan consumers are receivables to the bank. Hence more the lending, more the assets on the balance sheet, of the banks, which appears, to improve the financial performance of the banks. Further, there is a huge density of banks in

America, about 9000 in number, which is hard for the Fed Reserve, to keep an eye, as to how be the quality of their lending. The number of borrowers and the amount lent, as explained go to the asset columns of these 9000 banks and they look good. In contrast, the balance sheets, relating to personal finances of average Americans, who are borrowing under compulsion of poor wages and other exogenous factors, are also oblivious of the damage, they are doing to their balance sheets. They are financially illiterate in most cases and they do not even know how to read balance sheets properly. For them, it is hard to comprehend that the loans are battering their balance sheets, because all of their loans are shown in the liabilities column, of their balance sheets. They are unaware that to improve their own balance sheets 9000 banks, are making the balance sheets of tens of millions of Americans, look ugly and financial situation of US economy not looking so good. As the level of GDP and GDP per capita, may look very nice, in the eyes of the foreigners, to appreciate but financial challenges of the individual Americans, from paycheck to paycheck challenges them. Even the middle class executives borrowing from payday loans, on a monthly basis, with no savings, either in the capital markets or in the banks, have been spreading the feelings of despair, in many pockets of America. In the nutshell debt, has been disastrous, and they need to rein in.

Chapter 14

Illegal Immigration and American Poverty

Developed countries are challenged by poverty, inflicted by the immigrants and developing countries escape the same. As more jobs are available in the developed countries, and their infrastructure is world class, some people from the infrastructure deficit developing counties are attracted to migrate to the developed countries.

At the same time, there are many in the developing countries, who are emotionally rooted in their counties, no matter how poor are those countries, their minds never think of migrating to the developed countries. They are happy in their countries, never thinking of settling down abroad. Some of them, who find infrastructure deficit too much to cope and are attracted by the glitters on the TV, when they tend to watch developed countries, they plan to immigrate. Some educated immigrants migrate to the developed countries, to pursue higher studies and research in their academic field.

Among the immigrants, there are 2 categories of people, who are magnetized by the developed world. Those who are educated and wanted to go a developed world to better universities, for higher education and once they are educated abroad and find compensation levels, converting them into currencies of their home country, they tend to like to take up a job. They are able to send cash remittances, to help their parents and sibling's education. This gives them, a kind of pride and satisfaction from immigration. While they miss their home country, being away from the close relatives and their high school mates, university mates and find a kind of dilemma, but glitter of the developed world, such as nice roads, shopping malls and cleanliness of the urban areas, they find them, as a contrast to the home country. Gladly staying abroad becomes a second habit and they could permanently stay back in the developed world, visiting their home country, once in few years. Parents keep missing them and wish they would someday come back. But their hopes are mostly belied. They spend the last days of their lives, with moist eyes, to be close to their children. As long as their health permits, they visit children, located in the foreign country, when children send air tickets and gradually aches of the body turns, too intense, to be able to take long journey, across the oceans. Despair comes to them that they would intently look up to those little windows of time, when their children come. This is a huge challenge to the emotional parents, of the developing countries of the east, where emotion intangibles are too high and family values are too strong. Sometimes, the parents find one after the other, all of their 4 children are helped by one child, who went abroad first, to go abroad, leaving all of the separate rooms, for the adult children, their parents had constructed. The home in India thus becomes empty with all the 4 children lost to the foreign destinations. Then the home appears too big and their failures to keep their children in India, hurts them, when they see the big house, empty, except themselves, built with the hope that the joint family will stay. Then they quietly shift to a smaller apartment, selling the big home.

Phone calls come from the adult children settled abroad. They are happy to hear their loved children's voice, but that does not substitute the feelings of the mothers of the developed country destinations, who are aware that their children probably are couple of hour away from them. It's about feeling, not proximate and lies in the realm of psychology.

The immigrants, who are educated, add indeed a lot of value to the economy of destination from pursuit of research in educational realm, in medical fields and in engineering. As they are financially disciplined, they live well and they do not add any poverty dimensions.

Another category of immigrants are those, who are not educated ably, have gone to school but know farm work, know factory work and could work hard, at the manual level. As no scheme of their immigration is available, in the developed world, they come in a haphazard manner, taking lot of risks mostly through borders, which are long and hard to guard. They carry not even passport or any other category of identity. They do not carry even the birth certificate, to know how aged they are. It is also not known, if they had criminal records in the country of their origin..

Among these illegal immigrants, geographically many countries, may be pretty close to a developed country, but their desire to come abroad illegally, could be few and far between whereas few countries may be too impassioned, to be a part of the developed environment. For example, Latinos come to America as many as a million, every year, for over a decade and law enforcement cannot regulate their arrival. They simply walk into America, almost like an evening outing and settle down. Basically small and medium enterprises, who are keen on cost cutting and are too driven by money greed, fearlessly employ these illegal immigrants, which is against law. If only these businesses would have been ethical, not to recruit the illegal immigrants, their numbers would have never swelled as without employment, they would have been forced to return to Mexico. Not only the businesses, recruit the illegal immigrants in vacancies, strangely in a flexible market, it is not uncommon for them, to save money and address cost cutting, to recruit the illegal immigrants dismissing the local Americans. This has been hurting local Americans, as they cannot work at the low wages, for which illegal immigrants work, with the employers. Without any papers, they also take up gardening work, home cleaning work and at eateries in the kitchen, to clean the dishes initially and then work as a server and finally as cooks too. Blames cannot be only laid, at the doors of the illegal Latinos from Mexico, as citizens in America illegally, in very large numbers absorb them, in employment, unfortunately replacing the local Americans. Local Americans are too calm, not to resist or demonstrate. In any other economy, the dismissed locals could have been, on the streets to demonstrate. They have been lapping poverty, quietly with patience and it has been rising every year from, this rigor of the illegal immigration.

The illegal immigrant leave their spouse and children, back in Mexico. They come to USA work and sometimes take off, to visit their family in Mexico. They spend little on themselves, as a part of their thrift habits and live well within their means.. Those families from across the border in Mexico come to USA in droves and they live alone in shared apartments. In a 3 bedrooms apartment, about 12 to 15 persons may be staying treating not even a room but a mattress as their own, occupying about 55 square feet per person. They live in shared apartments, with families, living in low cost economy in Mexico. The companies pay them too less and therefore they come on board to work, at much lower hourly wages, than the local Americans, almost one third of the American wage. This kind of living, in a shared apartment, creates poverty conditions in America. They move about in markets, eateries, know no English and they have not even gone to school, which give the impression of their being part of a poor economy. When their population reaching tens of millions, certainly tantamount, to import of poverty into America, in terms of the lack of education, lack of knowledge of English, both written and oral English, in terms of the dress they wear or manners they exude or the rented living standards of the all of which reflect poverty and this number would rise, as the flow of illegal immigrants increase, over the years. The face of America, could fast change, at least in some of the southern states.

While the work ethics of the Latino immigrants, their punctuality and reaching the work deadlines, in a calm disciplined manner, deserves appreciation and to that extent, the individuals, who employ them, get quality work output. But since they hail from poor families in Mexico and are barely educated and do not speak English, they are likely to continue, as an underclass for decades. As they do not possess papers, the locals occasionally, are likely to threaten them, to be content with much less wages, which would impoverish them, in the years to come. As the competition for them, also is on the increase, because of continuous flow of similar immigrants, the supply of labor for similar general kind of unskilled jobs, are also likely to increase, which would perpetuate the poverty of this underclass. Though their children, if they pay attention to the studies and come up in life, they might escape the challenges, of their parental and familial poverty. Since their parents and siblings, would continue to stay in the home country, he desires to financially help them through cash remittances also, would make their family budget, in USA still smaller. Thus due to illegal immigration into USA, on such a large scale, two dimensions of poverty is arising, one due to joblessness and wage competition to the local Americans and secondly through the immigration, the poverty of immigrants is getting imported into USA to constitute a new underclass. As the Latino immigrants, are family oriented and usually have 4 to 5 children, the demographics of the US, would change drastically, the with a blacks and the Latinos, constituting a large group of minorities, and added together their total population in 25 years could almost match the majority population, which may have some political implications, in a democracy, if the voting pattern takes a racial color. Much would depend upon the political leadership, to be inclusive, to the major minorities such as the blacks and the Latinos.

While the next generation of the uneducated immigrants, might come up well, to integrate with the economy, but incumbent illegal immigrants are likely to act as vertical. They cannot update in education and they will have to be content with, base level manual jobs. This base of the economic pyramid in America, is likely to expand significantly and this appears to generate an inescapable poverty, due to lack of knowledge of English language and also school education. However, religious homogeneity is one factor that might help them integrate better, whereas that advantage is not available, to the European countries as immigrants are from African countries and they could be from other religions too. In Europe, the challenge of illegal immigration and related poverty, is much smaller compared to USA in terms of the numbers, though they come from different countries. They also live in segregated neighborhoods, which are poorer and infrastructure is far less, compared to the general neighborhoods. These are pockets of poverty, which also coincides with some criminality. Occasionally, riots are known in Europe, engineered by the minorities, when they feel hurt or feel slighted, and get frustrated due to poverty and joblessness, due to lack of proper education.

In USA, one does not notice any riots by the immigrants, as neighborhoods are better relative to European minority neighborhoods and law and order is strictly maintained. Having known that black immigrant youth, gets incarcerated, from time to time the Latinos are cautious to maintain peace and remain afar from crime. Sometimes they indulge in crime and are booked under laws and even slapped with jail sentences too.

US could have acted prudently, not to allow so many millions of illegal immigrants, because that is fraught with conditions, which could characterize, not only incumbent increase in poverty, but a flow of poverty, for decades to come. This was avoidable 20 years back, when NAFTA was designed and gave the illegal immigrations a kind of informal courage to come to USA and work illegally. A lot of areas, which were a part of Mexico, in the early 20 century got annexed to USA and a lot of population of the border states of USA have naturalized American citizens, who were initially of Hispanic origin. It is this population which has also played some role, in augmenting indirectly illegal immigration, from Mexico. As illegal Mexicans find comfort, when they see people of their origin, well settled as naturalized Americans, for generations in the border states. This tends to embolden them to come to USA. Further these areas were once a part of Mexico, also gives them kind of identification to the border states when they illegally arrive.

American Business classes have developed a lot of comfort, with illegal immigrants, like in a feudal set up feudal landed gentry, would like to have a lot of workers, pampering them, asking only a low wage and living fine, with poor living conditions. These feudal feel happy as long as, they live in mansions and they are served by people loyally, though they may be living in poor conditions in the neighborhoods. Such feudalized conditions are likely to happen, as tens of millions, have arrived and millions are wanting, to arrive in USA, from a developing country, where they see already challenged financial conditions.

Chapter 15

Slavery, Burden of History and Poverty

A lot of poverty arose in the world, during and after industrial revolution, at the initiative of the European naval powers, causing a lot of agony to human beings, who were from poor countries. One feature of the slavery, was not to identify the poor in Europe such as France Germany, Eastern Europe, Balkan countries, Switzerland, Holland, Scandinavia where there are under classes and poor people too. Probably if some slave catching contractors, would have been identified, in the European countries, alluring them, with good financial inducements, they would have helped slave trading companies of Britain, in pursuing the European poor, to become slaves and go abroad to work, on farms. In all of such cases, initial steps are to be taken, to give a rosy picture, to the poor that they will be better off and in case of their refusal, to comply to go abroad, the contractors were known to forcibly catch them and make them board the ships, in congested conditions. Probably, it was racism, to exclude the white poor people of the European countries, this time, during the industrial revolution and only concentrate on the west Africa. Slave traders did not collect slaves, from South America also though, there were many poor people there, in South America. In the 1700s and 1800s the British company pretty much focused, on collection of slaves, from the West Africa, to collect the slaves, then board them, in the most congested conditions. The slaves were constrained, by space, to a small sitting chair, where they had to sit for days, until they arrived at the destination. They were oblivious of the uncertainties, which they would face, and the back breaking hard work, each one of them would be asked to address, on arrival at the destination. Further, who would be the master and whether he would be kind or cruel also crossed their minds. Where would they have to live and work and how far would the workplace, be from the destination, were unknown to the slaves.. Being uneducated and illiterate, they lost their identity forever. They did not know the name of the place, they were heading. Since they did not know, how to write, they could not even contact, anyone from their country of origin, for want of a postal service, to their countries in the 17 th century and they were lost to Africa, lost to their country and lost to their villages and relatives. They were never to return, as the travel in those days, was so difficult and expensive, which they could never fund. They were collected from different tribes, whose languages, were different and they could not communicate, with each other, except probably in sign languages. Some were collected from different countries and interaction though Africans from different countries were near absent. They could only talk probably, in the sign language. Some water and some food used to be distributed, in heavily congested ships. Some could not withstand the shock, got into sea sickness and died. Once a slave died, he was merely lifted and thrown, into the sea and all the others saw the behavior, meted out to their fellow deceased brethren. They were severely hurt and frightened. As they were chained, they could never protest. Their supervisor, was a British and he asked them, to keep calm. They also feared that if the supervisor got angry on someone, latter could be thrown alive, into the high seas. Such was the plight of the people, of countries, from where the British decided, to collect the slaves. The slaves were in this situation, for no fault of theirs, as they were not criminals. Some while coming had to leave, their wife and children behind and suffer in agony the separation, from their families. Some were collected with wife and children and if a family member died on the ship, they were thrown unceremoniously, into the high seas, as though it were some rotten fruit or rotten vegetables. Human were treated, in an inhuman manner and the slaves came to anticipate, how heinously, they are likely to be treated, once they reached the destination of high seas travel, as William Wordsworth says "child is the father of the man; morning shows the day".

This is how Britain, which was for international community, the leader of the industrial revolution, having produced engineers and scientists and it was known to manufacture myriad goods, treated the poor people, from other parts of the world, to inflict agony and extreme poverty. These were not undesirable gangs or pirates, but respectable business owners, who took to this business, to make profits and also gave shareholders their share of profits. Historians tell us that the merchants of London happily invested, in this firm and so did the Mayor of the London and other cities and numerous Sheriffs, who were to overview law and prevention of crime in London. London, which was the well known city to the world and people wanted to go there, for higher studies, in its premier universities was astonishingly organizing this slave trade through its 1000 year chartered company, chartered by the queen, the sovereign, which took investments, from the elites of London. Even the noblemen, indirectly endorsed and participated in the slave trade, by investing in this firm. For those, who oversaw administration, during that period in Britain, could there be anything more nefarious, to perpetrate such agony, on a segment of humanity? Britain never had to pay any reparations, for such heinous conduct. International community never asked Britain, to pay reparation, to those countries, on which such inhuman actions, were perpetrated,. Neither did Britain ever volunteered, to accept the mistake and apologize, to the world. Confessing crime and seeking apology, are essential ideals of Christianity, the religion which the British follow.

On arrival at the destination, the slaves were auctioned, to the waiting buyers of the slaves, who would buy them, to enrich themselves, and take them, to their outhouse, for them to live and help them on the farms, in the farm work. They were individually, put on a higher pedestal, for people to watch and bid. Successful bidder, was permitted to pay the price, to the company representative, enchain the slaves and take them, to his home. Those slaves, who had come with families, thinking they would live together, as slaves, with the same master, were thoroughly disappointed. The families were separated, men, women and children were auctioned separately, to separate slave owners, who took them away, in different directions, a scene of very sorrowful parting of families. The family members were not to see each other, again in their life time. Husband went in one direction, with one master, wife was sent, in another direction, with another master and the children were taken, as slaves, with the third master. Thus ended the family of the slaves and they became singles. Here people became single, not through separation and marriage break up, as it is common, in the west today, in the new millennium, but despite the sense to be together for life, the slaves turned single, then in salve trade in the 17th century, by an external force of a rich man's desire, to make runaway money, selling slaves globally. Planters in the West Indies, also bought slaves, on the shores of the ships that reached West Indies. Cotton planters in Southern USA, bought them form American destinations. Latin American slave buyers bought, the African slaves, from the destinations of slave carrying ships, in countries of Latin America.

People from Africa, were taken to different parts of the world, to make them slog, to produce sugar in West Indies, tobacco and cotton in southern USA and generally to work on the farms, in Australia and other places.. Indirectly, the British firms, dealing with slave trade, were spreading diversity in the world. The diversity that is talked about so much, in political speeches in the USA, as something that is good for America, came about, because of the arrival of African slaves, who were to work, on the farms in America, Latin America Australia, Western Indies and other places, while the white land owners relaxed. Strangely, there were no indents, for the slaves in Europe. Hence we do not notice diversity, so much in Europe, as one notices them in America, Australia, even in Latin America, and overarching presence of the African origin people in the West Indies and of course in the USA and partly in Canada.

With slave trade, British economic system, went heavily backwards. Usually, when we think of the developed world, we think of the free trade, being done, by paying in global currency, which until the global war, for many centuries, was the pound sterling. The purpose of issuing currency, by the central banks of the developed economically educated nations, was primarily to place, the barter system, in the back burner, with payment by currency, not only in domestic trade but also in international trade. At best, the metals, like gold and silver, were used in trade. But it is bizarre that the British will come up with, a nefarious innovation in trade, among nations. For buying sugar, and tea from the West Indies, the British started exchanging them, like a barter system, with the slaves, they had collected from West Africa. Hence regularly this barter trade, went on, between the West Indies and Britain, buying sugar and spices, in exchange for the salves, the African slaves from West Africa or even interior Africa, of the sub Saharan area that they had collected to be sold, in substantial number, to the West Indies farm owners. Could there be anything, sadder, than the indignity inflicted in this fashion, on the humanity in the world? It probably never occurred to the Mayors, Sheriffs, wealthy merchants of London and the noblemen that the posterity would view their nefarious activities, with contempt later. Even current generations of the British, feel ashamed, about their ancestors and many openly acknowledge, the indignity that they inflicted, on hapless people, in their times. Whenever a heinous crime occurred, in a period, it has to be viewed, in current times, for peace, in isolation and never need, be attempted, to be linked to the incumbent generation of today. Behavior of incumbent generation and that of the earlier period, will have to be viewed in isolation, while judging humanity or a race. In a particular period, an activity could be shameful, nefarious and highly condemnable, but that activity for gain or prosperity or laziness of the wealthy, need to be seen, as madness, in one area of activity, such as behavior, towards other races, because in several other areas of activity, that race could have made rich contributions, to themselves, to their nation, or to the foreigners and even the international community. For example, all of the inventions that have shrunk time, taken in human activities, be it manufacturing of cloth, transport, food production, surgery and the like, is being enjoyed by the whole world, who received without much expenses, the transfer of this knowledge. Further, a lot of the modern innovations, in engineering and medicine, have occurred in Europe, which also has a queer distinction of having, exploited foreign people, through colonization, imperialism and extraction of raw materials, at a pittance, to enrich themselves, through industrial revolution.

Once the slaves, reached the farms, in southern USA, the farm owners put them presumably, into a tight work schedule. Their supervisor woke them, at 5 in the morning, took them all, to the farm, allocated responsibilities and then they returned, from the farms, at the sunset. Sunrise to Sunset was the time, these African slaves had to slog. They were from different language areas. They could not speak, with each other and even foment a rebellion. They turned disciplined and maintained quiet, while they worked. At the end of the day, they were too tired, to just go to sleep and then again start the morning work schedule, next day. They stayed huddled, in a congested hall, the minimum that would suffice for them. They ate the food, supplied to them, which was barely enough, to keep their body and soul together, the scholars write. Whenever the work target given to them was unmet, the supervisor picked on, a couple of slaves and lashed them. The cries, the shrieks and the tears of the lashed slaves, frightened the rest of the workers, to make them work harder and achieve the master's economic prosperity. The productivity of the lands increased, with very hard labor of the slaves. Their positions remained the same, for decades and they were never released, until they were found, to be sick or weak, with hard labor and the master decided, to sell the slave to another master.

A crude joke on humanity, could be seen, when outside the homes, of the Southern Americans, a writing boldly displayed for pubic perusal "Furintures and slaves are in good condition. They are for sale." The women worked as maids, in the home of the master and the men worked on the fields. Women were fine nannies and took good care of the children, of the master. When their mother was relaxing, reading books or even partying over lunch with fellow ladies, she played the nanny to the children. The slaves had no freedom, to pray alone. They were to pray, with supervisor's guidance, together. They got converted into Christianity and gradually the children, were given Christian names. Even incumbent slaves were given Christian names.

As a social group, when slavery was abolished, courtesy nobility of Mr. Abrahams Lincoln, the kind and humane President of USA, in 1867, in the middle of the ninetieth century and a little earlier by Britain had in her colonies in 1813, it brought relief to those, who were enslaved. The blacks in Africa, may have felt happy that captivity, which was so hard on their brethren, was gone, but all of those aspects of slavery that included a lot of humiliation to the slaves, also indirectly robbed, the self confidence and happiness of the people, in Africa, who felt sad and sullen that as a social group, they were ill treated so severely, in such an inhuman manner, merely because they were black in their skin color, lived on in their memory and in the memory of next generations. A burden of history, not only made blacks in America and other countries, ruled by the whites, but it severely hurt the psyche of the blacks in Africa also, who felt humiliated, disgusted and insulted that some of their brethren, even lost their identity. They did not know, which country did they came from, which city or village, within a country, they came from, as they were disentangled, for their own ethnic or country social groups.

While talking about their poverty, one cannot forget that while imperialism was hollowing out their minerals at a throwaway price and while they were made to work, in very hard way, getting pittance as wages. The African countries, lost their money to the colonial masters, who in turn did not set up, schools or universities and institutions of democracy and totally neglected the infrastructure. All of the preliminaries that make democracy and development happen, were denied to Africa, by the colonial rulers. The infrastructure, the educational institutions, the bridges and the roads, needed for trade, the semblance of a national capital were never developed in African colonies.

With burden of history, of colonization, imperialism and above all slavery, undoubtedly has inflicted lot of wounds, on the African continent, compared to other continents, by people of lighter color. Whenever they go for the bilateral aid and for the multilateral aid and attend meetings, to seek funds, debt, they might be reminded that those who exploited them, are to give them financial aid now, on their request. The members of the intelligentsia, are aware that whatever economic disadvantages in the two world wars, occurred in Europe, it was a result of the fighting between countries, belonging to the axis powers and allied powers, though the war was started by those belonging to Axis powers, such as Germany and Italy. As the Germany was the aggressor in the second global war, the Germans were made to pay reparations, for the damages, which occurred to the physical infrastructure of the victorious countries, such as Britain France and Russia. Occasionally the Africans, feel that for all the slavery and exploitations of mines in Africa, during colonization, no reparations from the colonizers, were asked to be paid to the countries in the African continent. The colonial rulers rolled back, making the African countries, independent but thoroughly fleeced them in money and raw materials.

In addition, the cost of environment pollution, due to extraction of raw materials, with not even rudimentary pollution control measures, further affected adversely, the productivity of agriculture in Africa.

The international community, expecting that the African countries, will bounce back, as nations, seem to be living, in a mega fool's paradise. Even building the educational institutions and infrastructure takes decades and it was being addressed. Local competencies, in science, math and engineering, were also developed, to an extent, with teachers from India in all of the schools in Africa, subjects of academic rigor such as Physics Chemistry Mathematic and Commerce, being nicely taught by the Indian teachers. Gradually professors in the university, who were expatriates from colonial master countries, drawing their salary in dollars, were sent back. They were gradually replaced, by the local African professors. But in terms of prosperity, thousands of miles, have to be scaled, till its semblance becomes visible.

As the psyche of the people, of Africa were bruised immeasurably, to the maximum extent, in addition to negative inflictions, by the developed world, the aspect of capturing slaves, shipping them wherever they wished, and making them slog, duly, keeping them enchained as slaves, with no compensation, for all the hard work. Even here, the international community, didn't pay any reparations, for the indignity caused, to the people of the black skin of the African continent. It is a queer coincidence that migrants from European countries, who colonized and exploited resources, in Africa also did not pay the value, of the mining that they undertook. They also refused to pay proper wages to the African labor. In addition, they bought the slaves from the African continent, to make them work on their farms. They even punished the slaves, on any shortfall of daily deadline, in the farm work, with physical torture of the farm workers. Extracting labor from the African slaves so heinously the American farm owners continued to get themselves enriched. They exported the farm produce, such as cotton and tobacco, to other counties, profiteering in a big way besides earning huge quantities of the foreign exchange. With no reparations, no apology, no repentance, coming from those, who made the impoverishment happen in Africa, in this manner, one can imagine, the dent in African self confidence. Half the progress, in a country takes place, with institutions, self confidence of its people and with a positive environment. On the top of it the IMF talking incessantly about regime corruption non repayment of debt and non compliance of Structural Adjustment Programs (SAP) insisted by the IMF, all the more complicated economic development in the African countries

In this backdrop when officers from IMF, hailing from European countries, ask the current African regimes, to cut subsidies, in many cases and fully stop subsidies, in others, how much of a hurt feelings would it cause, one can gauge. Then, while extending little loans, when the IMF again acts grandmotherly and insists the implementation of the cost cutting SAP program, under the supervision of the IMF, which tend to severely hurt the poor and the middle class substantially, it tantamount to rubbing salt, on the wounds.

But for the institution of slavery, ever having being brought on this earth, the two social groups, the whites and the blacks, probably would have attended the IMF meetings, while in an atmosphere of amity, cooperation and happiness, which is currently missing, due to such slighted burden of history. If African officials, who attend the debt seeking meetings with officials of the multilateral institutions, are more sensitized, about the humiliations, which the black slaves would have met, from the whites in America and about the mal treatment, meted out, by the developed world, through colonization and imperialism, the meetings could have been probably less of a success in receiving the loan assistance.

It is nice to hear, the world leaders, like Mr. Nelson Mandela, who in his speeches, reiterated that history should not be remembered, while living one's life of action. In fact the TV talk show host Winfrey Oprah, at the Commencement Ceremony address in 2013, at the Harvard University mentioned that she never thought about history in her life. If lot more African leaders, would have preached, the amity and about forgetting history, probably the white and black cooperation, in economic development, would have reached much higher and qualitative levels. Probably, the future of the African countries, would have been much brighter. Even now, to stamp out poverty from African nations, the scars of slavery and imperialism need, to be forgotten and a new era need to dawn, where as absolute equals, the leaders of the African nations, work with the developed world and multilateral institutions such as the World Bank and the IMF confidently, asking for debt reliefs, wherever necessary and certainly, not borrow to pay interest on loans. That is so debilitating. Living within means, by African nations, would hold them a great deal, to reduce the debt and improve their national balance sheets, with better financial performance. It is mentioned repeatedly that the government officials and the politician, in places like Nigeria's national capital, live in runaway life styles, with government providing them with Mercedes cars, every few years. It is a common knowledge that the capital of Nigeria has more number of the Mercedes cars, than any other city in the world. The civil servants also live in mansions, provided by the government. In contrast, the civil servants in India lead a simple life and they have been provided with cars, until recently, which are manufactured in India and cost about $4000 dollars, equivalent of Indian currency. The homes provided, by the government, to the government officials, are by no description, mansions. They are simple homes, with a small garden and is on a plinth area of an average of 1500 square feet, with no fancy embellishments. Looking at the top, the multitude also learns to live, a simple life and that improves their balance sheets, their saving levels and they can with education and hard professional or trade work, a simple life, not afflicted by poverty. I feel that if confidence level of African youth improve, along with dropping of the students drop out rates, the officials and the businessmen could motivate them, to erase the memories of slavery and colonialism. In that situation, the African continent may deal with poverty levels, with more confidence and reduce them substantially. With focus on education, institutions, democracy, hard professional work, inclusiveness to the poor, entrepreneurship and intra nation and intra neighbor trust building, the continent of Africa could soon see sunshine, in the realm of development, in about two decades. Life of simplicity and a fervent nationalism, in each of the nations, may have to be garnered, by strong and committed to people leadership and attempts have to be ceaseless to have a strong national ethos. Tribalism and it s unnecessary adherence will have to give way for the larger cause of national prosperity. that at the social level only, one could be local, but in the rest of thinking, the thought of the nation, need to prevail, with centrifugal forces, absolutely at the back burner. Countries that act sometimes supercilious with African nations and even ruled on them as colonial masters were no different from African nations in the character of their divisiveness such as Germany and Italy, few scholars probably know. But for the national strong leader like Bismarck German unification would have probably, not occurred in 1870. Until them Germany was divided, into more than 30 ethnicities and tiny political jurisdictions, with significant differences among them. In Italy too, the structure of politics was similar, heavily characterized by divisiveness. African economies, if through national development council efforts, could iron out ethnic differences and create a national ethos, strong like that of the Germans and Italians developed after German unification and Italian unification, then prosperity in African nations could not be a distant economic and political dream.

Unfortunately, the black leaders in America, with the exceptions of a few, try to bring up the topic of slavery, time and again. Then the young are repeatedly reminded, about the burden of their history. A small difference, with a white friend, on the playground or in a school brings back, the burden of history. A rude talk by a white professor, faulting the academic assignment of a black student, could hurt the feeling of the black student, unnecessarily though. Pinpricks of some racist white home owners, refusing to give the home on rent or to sell a home, merely because the client, is an African American and talks like an African American accent could, breed ill feelings, in USA.

The whites, try to get the comfort, stating that slavery has not been a racial or skin color thing. they sometimes aver that even in ancient times or the Middle Ages, the richer people of lighter color, took slaves of lighter color, all the time. They give examples of the existence of slavery the ancient civilizations of the Egyptian, the Persians and the Greeks. In Greece in ancient period, whoever came to work, on fields from adjacent nations were called slaves and no citizenship, was granted to them. For example, in the ancient times, in Greece the slavery existed and those who worked on the farms, from other republic islands, and were staying in Athens, were termed as slaves. They had no right, for example, in Greece, to elect officials and the Chairman of the City Councils. Whenever the Egyptian or Persian or the Greek emperors went on a war that consumed many years, as the territories for conquests, was expanded, the conquest usually coincided, with plundering the city, on a large scale, capturing a lot of men and women as slaves and enslaving them.

Though undoubtedly it is weird that the, British, who without any war or conquests, started a specialized firm, to trade in slaves and adopted undesirable methods, to capture the Africans labor, by force and boarded them into highly congested ships, terming them as slaves. In earlier periods, of history, no information about nefarious trading of the slaves information, is forthcoming. Neither were the slaves drawn from on race or one geographical region alone. Nor were they known to be ill treated, with lashes, for not reaching the work deadlines. They were not hideously poor too, huddled, in small congested rooms. They were not denied, the right to live privately with wife and children. In a way earlier slaveries, if it could be said, there were no heinous cruelties, as are found in the the slavery practiced by the British in 17ty century.

As the slavery, in the USA was abolished in 1867, one would think that agony of the blacks in America would have come to an end. It was far from relief. It is astonishing that even after the abolition of the slavery by President Abraham Lincoln, successive Presidents did not take steps, to give them the citizen rights of voting. Voting rights continued to be denied, to the blacks for decades after decades, This denial of voting rights gave an opportunity to the whites, to perpetuate different kinds of economic and social discriminations, though the blacks, could not be compelled to work, with the southern farmers, on a permanent basis, at their terms and conditions. The slaves once freed, left their masters and started moving north, particularly went to the East and Mid West, where the heinous discriminations of the Americana in the South, did not exist. Some masters in the southern USA, illegally tried to keep, slaves, by imprisoning them in chains and their practices though intermittent, went on for few decades, even after the abolition of slavery. While the farm work slavery was over, there was hardly, any other kind of employment, in which the blacks could get jobs. The manufacturing was picking up and the railroads were underutilizing quite a few projects. In these two areas, the blacks were recruited and they proved the worth of their hard work. In the Midwest, the blacks in manufacturing, came to occupy a niche, through their hard and sincere work.

The blacks, free from segregation, in transportation and also while they walked along with the whites in the market places, they found mid west and east much more friendly. When the blacks were denied voting rights, until the first few decades of the 20th century, they felt very frustrated. They had nowhere to go, as they did not know, which country they came from, in West Africa. Only option they had, was to exact their rights, from the white regime. Dr Martin Luther King came to the scene and mobilized the blacks, to fight for their rights, the voting rights for the blacks. The issue of voting rights was already there and Dr King leveraged this issue, to ask the US Government, to give justice to the blacks. He led marches in different southern states and talked about peace and non violence. He made himself to believe, in the great truth and non violence principles, enunciated by Mahatma Gandhi. He told the masses that he was impressed, with non violent method, adopted by the revered Mahatma Gandhi, who brought national independence for India, from the British rule. He dreamt that one day, the blacks and whites would live, in an integrated environment, where black brothers and sisters and white brothers and sisters, will hold hands and march together, for the nation. Voting rights were granted to the blacks, as a result of the civil right movements, led by Dr King., Dr King was honored with the Noble Peace prize. In that address, he mentioned India as his inspiration.

Chapter 16

Famines in India: Caused by the Negligence of the British Rule

Famines were caused due to natural calamities, the neglect of the relief works exacerbated the problem. When people were famished and dying, the state expenditure, was ordered to be cut by the British authorities. This was like rubbing salt, on the wounds of the locals, increasing famine stricken poverty. Keeping the prices of the grains high, when zamindars and moneylenders, in normal times were allowed, to collect usurious interest rates, for their extraordinary gains, tantamount to allowing the famine stricken people to die.

Viceroy's talk of cost cutting, on relief measures and keeping money for Afghan War, to contain Russian expansion to India, and thus allowing famine, to increase and allowing the Indians to die in droves, were highly unethical. Disallowing help from Britain and America to send relief, to famine stricken places, was so wrong. Exporting grain, as per the million ton target, to Britain during the famine times, was heinous. The export of grain at a time, when any part of India, was facing severe natural calamities, such as drought, the least the government, could have done, is not to export food grains, to Britain. Government should have provided extra grains, to calamity affected pockets of India, as an inclusive measure, to save the lives of the people. Instead, sticking to the annual target of exports, of grains to Britain, was ludicrous, to say the least, by the British administration. For example, major famine occurred during 1896-1897, preceded by a drought, in Madras Presidency. The districts of Ganjam and Vizagapatam, were the two severely affected areas, in this famine of 1896-1897. Astonishingly, while people suffered from starvation, during this famine, the government followed the policy of total inaction and called its stand, as the policy of laissez faire, in the trade of grain, a term popular with market ideologues. To exacerbate the problems of people further, mindlessly, the export of grains to Britain continued, throughout the famine. Could anything be more bizarre than, this mode of government action in a colony?

The drought conditions, prevailed in Bengal and Odisha, in 1866. Policies of laissez faire were resorted to in this earlier famine also by the British administration. The harbor in Odisha became inaccessible after south western monsoon, which came, in the way of the much needed food, to be imported, though food could reach Bengal. The British Secretary of State for India, Lord Salisbury, took no action in this matter, for two months and a million people died. Even the viceroy Lord Lytton was also indifferent to the sufferings of the drought affected people in Odisha. Lord Salisbury could not escape the blame for inaction, in a food crisis in India. Some British citizens such as William Digby agitated for policy reforms and famine relief. Astonishing though it seemed, during all of these famines, different constituencies of Britain, reacted differently. Sometimes, it is the Secretary of State, who took the famine issue casually and sometimes such a routine approach, dawned on the Viceroy of India and at other times, the British officer in charge, on the field, reacted callously. As a result of any one of these events, the famine hurt the people severely. There was lack of consistency and coordination among different layers of British administration in handling the relief work in Indian famines. There were also occasions, where the British citizens alleged neglect and raised their voice and desired the British government to help the famine stricken people in India. The heavy casualties of the peasants from famine was caused, among other factors, due to neglectful attitude of the British government and for adopting the weird policy of laissez faire, at a time when people were dying of hunger and disease, due to famine conditions and severe natural calamities.

Another bizarre move of the British government, was to enhance the taxation, at a time when the Bengal famine was ravaging villages and people were dying in droves. This unfortunate tragedy, was visiting Bengal, despite the fact that Bengal was the most proximate province to Calcutta, the British capital in India. This famine occurred in 1870. This also coincided with the time, when labor was ill treated right in the city of London, having very little housing and most living in heavily congested smog ridden and smoke ridden environment of overcrowded slums. About 10 persons occupied one room in the London slums. They did not have proper toilet facilities and suffered from heavy water supply scarcity, precluding most of these poor Britons, from taking bath even once a week. The clothes were unclean as rarely washed and due to alcohol consumption

231

they smelled badly, according to the chronicles of the contemporary British historians. The London slum conditions, in the late 19th century, gave a very dreary look, with people moving about barefoot and the children in dirty clothes, playing in the dust. If Victorian poverty was, acute in famine stricken areas, in India, the Victorian poverty was also writ large, in the dreary slums of London, where a lot of people stayed, due to industrial revolution. They came for job hunt, in industrial areas and got trapped either receiving low wages or remaining unemployed, for considerable time, living with their parish people. In any case, it was community living with very little privacy. The baths were also community based. It is not as though the base of the economic pyramid in London was treated any better, but in India it was a question of life and death, in the famine affected areas. Yet the insolence of some of the British officials, sometimes of the Viceroy Lytton himself came in the way of famine relief.

Lord Lytton and Lord Ripon dealt with people, in two different ways. Lord Lytton was indifferent to the sufferings, of the people in India. He talked about Sir Adam Smith and the importance of market, which according to him, on its own volition, could solve the problems, rather than any need for the government, to intervene, in the play of the market. He was forgetting that Adam Smith's theory of competition and market, was given a go by and forgotten, when the British imposed heavy tariff, on the Indian textiles and the Indian goods imported into Britain, to protect the British textile industry. As a result, a policy of protectionism was adopted by Britain in respect of imports of goods made in India. The British government in India adopted free trade, to import British goods and British textiles, free of customs duty, losing whole lot of revenue, for the people of India and also trying to kill the industrial infrastructure of India, specially Indian textiles of world renown. This was a huge hypocrisy, noticeable in Lord Lytton's governance, in dealing with Indian famines. Lord Ripon was just the opposite, of what Lord Lytton stood for. Lord Ripon was known to be a humane and kind viceroy. His attitude to people was one of benevolence. His policies were liked by the people and he could endear himself, to the Indians in general. He dealt with natural calamities in India, with a kind heart and he was therefore appreciated, by a lot of British people also, who wanted the famine stricken people, to be helped always by the Government in India. Florence Nightingale, with a very kind heart to India, praised Lord Ripon and she kept in contact, with him all through, his viceroyalty and thereafter. Lord Lytton was antithesis of what Lord Ripon stood for. If Lord Ripon prevented poverty to inflict the peasantry in India, Lord Lytton's actions brought, the tsunami of poverty and loss of enormous human capital that if taken care, would have added value to the rural areas.

Through his indifference and looking the other way, people starved, due to famine. To rub salt on the wounds of the Indians, he would aver, from time to time, supporting his policy of laissez faire, non intervention in the in the markets of Indian economy.

In regard to 1876 famine, Lord Lytton, felt that the relief would make people, in Indian rural areas, shirk their work and despite loss of crops and famine conditions, he went to the extent of saying, "Let the British public foot the bill, for its 'cheap sentiment,' if it wished to save life, at a cost that would bankrupt India,". There were suggestions, to reduce the price of the grain, at least, so that the famine stricken people could, buy food grains and satiate their hunger and escape death. In response, the British Viceroy Mr. Lytton ordered, "there is to be, no interference of any kind, on the part of the Government, with the object of reducing the price of food." His instructions went to the District Officers, to "discourage relief works in every possible way." He stated, "Mere distress is not, a sufficient reason for opening a relief work."

There was a lot of suffering, accruing from the famine in 1876. This famine was very severe and broke out, in Madras. Lord Lytton's administration, again believed that laissez faire policy would suffice, leaving the solution of the problem, to the market forces. But market forces were not, to be saviors of those, suffering from hunger, due to scarcity of grains. According to reports, about 5.5 million Indians starved. Lord Lytton was forced, to rethink and he took a sensible step of abandoning the laissez faire policy and brought government help. Lord Lytton established the Famine Insurance Grant, a system in which, in times of financial surplus, 500,000 Rupees would be applied, to famine relief works.

British Viceroy, Secretary of State and the people in Britain felt that the past performance of the governmental measures were inappropriate as the government in India had not come up, with proper design of a policy, to address famine relief. Strange as it may look, but no such design of a famine policy, was undertaken and it is no wonder, that when the famine in 1943, struck Bengal in India, the Government was taken unawares and found itself highly unequal to the task. About 3 million Indians died of hunger. Such a devastating famine, being unaddressed properly, after 190 years of the British rule, speaks plenty, as to how the finances of India were spent, on the British administrators, on their retired life, on waging wars, to protect and expand British interests, in the world, for quelling rebellions in remote colonies, taking the help of the Indian army. Several investments in London infrastructure, were met from the Indian budget and above all, huge wealth were annually transferred to the crown. A part of the transfer of wealth from India was kept by the crown for itself, and remaining funds were spent on development of Britain, including implementing schemes for the welfare of the British poor, even in normal times. Even in normal times when there was no famine or scarcity of the food grains the poor laws in Britain, protected the poor. Florence Nightingale pungently said that India did not have poor laws, even when inflicted by natural calamities, where as Britain and Europe had poor laws, even in normal times.

During 1896 famine, in India, about 4.5 million people were, on famine relief. British Viceroy Curzon also "cut back rations that he characterized as "dangerously high," and stiffened relief eligibility, by reinstating the Temple tests."

In the 20th century, the frequency of famines in India plummeted and there was lull kind of relief for the peasantry, for about 4 decades until 1943, when Bengal famine devastated the country. It was a dangerous famine and millions died, for want of food. The second global war, was raging in Europe and Britain's financial condition, was so precarious that it had to heavily borrow, from the USA, in addition to the funds that President Roosevelt of the USA, arranged under Marshall Plan, for European reconstruction, after the war. It was around this time, when Bengal famine gobbled, about 3 million lives, another 2 million Indians died in the Second Global War, fighting on behalf of the British, from among several millions, who fought in the second global war The British government appreciated the Indian soldiers and officers, for fighting the wars, very gallantly and valiantly. This caused poverty, though, to the deceased, of the war widows, whose families were not compensated, for the loss of life of their husbands. No family pensions were granted to the Indian war widows, though their counterparts in Britain, had pensions for life.

Between 1.25 to 10 million people died, in India, due to the famines. The famine during World War II, led to the development of the Bengal Famine Mixture (based on rice with sugar). This would later save, tens of thousands of lives, at liberated concentration camps such as Belsen. Keeping the famine relief, as cheap as possible, with minimum cost to the colonial exchequer, was another important factor, in determining famine policy. These famines, were typically followed by various infectious diseases, such as bubonic plague and influenza, which attacked and killed a population, already weakened by starvation. The Bengal famine of 1870 and its devastation, accentuated all the more, by concurrent enhancement of the taxation. Such moves taught the British administration a lesson and they took the precaution thereafter. The successive British governments, did not add to the burden of taxation. As a result of the famines, occurring at a close frequency, a Famine Commission was appointed, by the Government, which came up, with a series of government guidelines and regulations, on how to respond to famines and food shortages, called the Famine Code. There was prevarication, during the time of Lord Lytton's tenure as Viceroy and the famine code was approved, when his tenure ended and he was succeeded by a liberal minded Viceroy, Lord Ripon. The famine code came to be passed in 1883.

The intelligentsia, has come up, with reasons, of so many casualties, during the occurrence of famines, in India. They gave their objective findings, after thorough studies. Development economist Jean Drèze studied the Policy configurations, before and after 1880, when the Famine Commission was set up and observed that the pattern of occurrence of the famines in India, shifted. In this connection he stated, ""A contrast between the earlier period of frequently recurring catastrophes, and the later period, when long stretches of tranquility were disturbed, by a few large scale famines" in 1896–97, 1899–1900, and 1943–44." According to Drèze, the "intermittent failures" were caused, by four factors, namely the failure to declare a famine (particularly in 1943), the "excessively punitive character" of famine restrictions such as wages for public works, the "policy of strict non-interference with private trade," and the natural severity of the food crises.

The Temple's tests, to reduce the financial expenditure, on relief measures, rather than extending timely relief, of reasonable quantities of food grains, was an extremely uncaring and indifferent step, which negatively affected human lives, during the famines, particularly during the Bengal famine of 1943. Thinking of trade more than suffering of the human beings, due to famine, was too harsh a way, to deal with a food crisis that naturally caused millions of deaths. About 3 million deaths occurred, in the Bengal famine of 1943.

Given the will of the British Government, the Bengal famine, could have been addressed, much better, had the Secretary of State for India and the Viceroy taken important measures. There appears no justification, for the death of 3 million Indians, in Bengal, during the famine in 1943 and also millions of deaths in Madras and Odisha. The recommendations of the Famine Commission in 1880, urged to build railroad network, intra India, as opposed to inter port. Had these recommendations, been carried out, as India had by the 1940s, the new railroad lines, to facilitate the flow of food, to famine-affected areas, the famine relief could have been tackled much better in early 1940s. But the relief managers, did not leverage, its British rail facilities, to make grains, reach the famine affected areas. The severity of neglect of relief work gets reflected, in the observation of Mr. Mike Davis, who also endorsed the availability of rail network, to make succor reach to the provinces of Bengal, during famine in 1943, but that rail network was instead missed, according to him. He stressed, "The newly constructed railroads, lauded as institutional safeguards, against famine, were instead used by the merchants, to ship grain inventories, from outlying drought-stricken districts, to central depots, for hoarding, as well as protection from rioters".

At a time of severe food scarcity, after declaring famine, in any part of the country, the least the Government should have ensured, was not to export food to Britain or any other country. This minimal step, could have been taken, by the British administration. Presumably, since the Government does not appear, to have been sensitized enough and attitude of the power, was not one of inclusiveness, in general, no steps were taken, to stop or reduce exports. The food, which could have been diverted, to the province of Bengal, to address huge scarcity of food and famine in 1943, was allowed to be exported to Britain.. This appears absolutely heinous and on the top of it, the then British Prime Minister Mr. Winston Churchill kept on making sour observations, in a bad taste.

Jean Drèze (1991) also endorses the same view that food meant for the succor to famine, was diverted to exports. He said, "The necessary economic conditions, were present, for a national market in food, to reduce scarcity, by the end of the 19th century, but that export of food continued, to result from that market, even during times of relative food scarcity." According to the Irish economist and Professor Cormac Ó Gráda, "priority was given to military considerations, and the poor of Bengal were left un provided for".

After the fall of Rangoon, rice from Burma, could not be imported, easily to assuage, the suffering of famine affected people of Bengal. Thus one of the factors that led to the famine was, the cutting off, of the supply of rice to Bengal, during the fall of Rangoon. To the Japanese, this was only a fraction of the food, needed for the region. Reserving lands by the British administration, to raise cash crops, to be exported for traded goods, required in Britain from China and other countries, such as as opium, then jute, indigo exacerbated the food scarcity during the famine. Strangely the British Government in India recruited labor from areas where it was cheap and moved them by railways to the areas where it raised cash crops to use the cash crops in exchange for the goods that Britain traded, with other countries. The labor in cash crop plantations were not only paid lower wages than the market but also kept in bondage to raise cash crop farming productivity by the British Government. All of these moves of the British Government, led to higher prices of the grains. Here again the neglect and culpability of accentuating the famine conditions, by the British administration cannot be ruled out.

Lord Lytton desired to clamp down, on the "out of control" expenditures that "threatened the financing of the planned invasion of Afghanistan, "and towards this objective, he deputed the Lieutenant Governor of Bengal, Sir Richard Temple, to South India, as plenipotentiary Famine Delegate. In 1876, about the famine in the South, Lord Lytton expressed indignation, at Buckingham, for making "public charity indiscriminate" in Bellary, Cuddapah and Kurnool, where one-quarter of the population was employed, on public works, such as breaking stones or digging canals.

Temple was briefed by Lord Lytton, to follow frugality and make out a case, for much reduced expenditure, on the famine relief measures in Madras and he appeared inclined to come with an idea, to be in the good books of the Viceroy and also India Office, in London. He got clear signals, from London too, that it was not the job of the British administration, to keep rural Indians alive, in India, in Madras where challenge from famine in 1876, was severe. Thus guided both by India office in London, as well as by the Viceroy, to exercise least government intervention, and allow the market forces, to solve the famine problem, he showed an approach, which was very market oriented."

His non intervention, to provide relief to famine affected people, in Madras in 1876, not without the adequate and effective guidance, from both London and Calcutta, Temple's reputation became, one of drastically rescuing the relief, by carrying out some tests on the labor, to know their eligibility for relief. He became to "Indian history what Charles Edward Trevelyan, Permanent Secretary to the Treasury, during the Great Hunger (and, later, Governor of Madras), had become to Irish history, the personification of free market economics, as a mask for colonial genocide." The culpability of neglecting starving population, in famine of 1876, falls on Mr. Temple. However, his culpability is only reduced, to the extent that he was effectively instructed, by the Viceroy to save money on relief, no matter how many lives, were lost in the famine. It is hard to comprehend, how the Viceroy and the Council of India after British empire was benefitted from British rule, for over a century in India, could be so negligent of their fiduciary duties and be so inhuman, to human beings, no matter which part of the world, they came from. The Colonial Government, was a Government, based on law and Britain was known to be a place, which cared for human rights, rule of law and principles of natural justice. It is hard to imagine, how Queen Victoria, who in the same year, declared herself the Empress of India, could allow such inhuman treatment, to the hapless peasants in Madras. The instructions of the Vice regal authority of Calcutta, brings such heinous attitude, to sharp focus. Although Queen Victoria in her message, to the Imperial Assemblage had reassured Indians that their "happiness, prosperity and welfare" were the "present aims and objects of Our Empire," Temple was briefed by the Council of India as follows: "The task of saving life irrespective of cost, is one which, is beyond our power to undertake. The embarrassment of debt and weight of taxation, consequent on the expense soon, become more fatal, than the famine itself." Likewise, the Viceroy insisted that Temple should "tighten the reins," in regard to famine in Madras.

It was really heinous what Temple addressed, merely to keep his bosses, in good humor. It could be termed blatantly inhuman. In a lightning tour of the famished countryside, of the eastern Deccan, Temple purged, half a million people from relief work and asked Madras to follow, Bombay's precedent of requiring starving applicants, to travel to dormitory camps outside their locality, for labor on railroad and canal projects. The able-bodied adults and older children were refused work, as per his instructions, within a ten-mile radius of their homes. To be eligible for relief, a certificate came to be necessary, that they had become indigent, destitute and capable of only a modicum of labor."

It is the same Lt Governor Temple, who did marvelous work of relief, during the famine of 1874, when the casualty, was as low as only 23. He took effective steps, to get additional quota of rice, from Rangoon and fed those affected by famine, in Bengal. Locals were happy and appreciative of the British administration's kind gesture, to provide timely relief and save lives. But Temple was faulted, for the expenditure that he had to incur, to save lives in Bengal famine of 1874. It was the only truly successful British relief effort, in the nineteenth century and might have been celebrated, as a template, for dealing with future emergencies. Instead, the London office charged Richard Temple, for the "extravagance" of allowing "the scale of wages, paid at relief works, to be determined by the daily food needs, of the laborer and the prevailing food prices, in the market rather than by the amount that the Government could afford, to spend for the purpose." In public, he was lambasted, by The Economist for encouraging indolent Indians, to believe that "it is the duty of the Government to keep them alive." Senior civil servants, in London stated, as informed by Lord Salisbury that it was "a mistake to spend so much money, to save a lot of black fellows."

A lot of damage, to human relations occurs, when such racial divides, tend to smear a famine relief policy and such remarks also leave scars and burden of history. It is highly unbecoming for educated civil servants, to be so indifferent of the human plight and speak, such rough language. Such supercilious and arrogant attitude, of the British administration and instructions from London, not to intervene and help during famine adequately is reprehensible, when millions were dying, from famine and hunger. Such policies, only point to an attitude of extreme indifference and one can therefore gauge, if this be the attitude, at the time of such severe famine, how indifferent could have been the British Government, to make revenue extortions, from the poor peasants of India. It is no wonder that the British and the world historians write, so critically about, the exploitation of the Indian peasants, by the British rule, keeping the zamindars, on the one side and the moneylenders, on other side, to fleece the peasants, allowing these two negative constituencies, to merrily exploit their own people, the peasants and make money, besides comforting the British exchequer. How selfish and money greedy, were the British people, in the regime at that time, though there were private benefactors and people in Britain, who criticized the famine policy of the Government. Several well meaning British doctors, officials and public leaders of the contemporaneous times, were pungent, in their criticism of the British indifference though.

Digby, the medical person, was highly aggrieved, at the way, the health of the peasants, were handled, under the instructions of the Viceroy and Lt Governor of Calcutta. Dr. Cornish stated "Apart from its sheer deficiency, in energy, the exclusive rice ration, without the daily addition of protein-rich pulses (*dal*), fish or meat, would lead to rapid degeneration". He also brought forth the information, to the notice to convince Mr. Temple, "Indeed, the Lieutenant-Governor, was undoubtedly aware, that the Indian government had previously, fixed the minimum shipboard diet of emigrant labor, "living in a state of quietude" at twenty ounces of rice, plus one pound of dal, mutton, vegetables and condiment". Dr Cornish was emphatic that such a small diet of only rice, suggested by Mr. Temple, could endanger the declining health of the famished peasants and might bring casualty. But Mr. Temple was only concerned, probably to rejuvenate his image that he could comply with his bosses, even if the instructions, were not right.

Mr. Temple declared "the famine under control." Digby sourly responded that "a famine can scarcely, be said to be adequately controlled, which leaves one-fourth of the people dead." Exactly as medical officials had warned, the "Temple wage" combined, with heavy physical labor and dreadful sanitation, turned the work camps, into extermination camps. By the end of May, horrified relief officials in Madras were reporting that more than half of the inmates were, too weakened to carry out, any physical labor whatsoever. Most of them, were dead by the beginning of the terrible summer of 1877.

When we think of the indifference to people, dying in millions in famine, one finds it hard to understand, the ambivalent attitude of the British rule in India. Interface of India, with British colonization, was one of ambivalence, but the fact remains that rural India was heavily impoverished, during the British rule of about 200 years.----

British, to consolidate and expand their rule in India and keep long term control, as it was the jewel of the British empire, went extra hundreds of miles, to educate and recruit Indians, to run the administration. It even recruited educated Indians, in the British firms, enabled them to go abroad, for higher education, hob-nobbed and socialized with elitist Indians. The British did not fail, to develop the city of Calcutta and the surroundings, besides Madras and Bombay, setting up numerous English medium schools, in the metros, giving Anglican Indians access to some clubs and occasionally, playing golf with them. The British played the divide and rule policy by encouraging some Indians, whom they educated in English medium, in the newly set up city schools and pumped arrogance in them, to look at their rural brethren, with indifference and not without ridicule. It also opened engineering and medical colleges, besides opening big well equipped hospitals, in the cities only. In aesthetics, the British contribution got reflected, in naming the city hospitals, after the British royalty. Investments in replicating British architecture, was made liberally, constructing National Museum, District Museums, District Libraries and Memorials, but the focus was only, bigger municipalities. The British introduced railways and the city of Calcutta in 1890s, looked as pretty as London and its water supply and sewerage systems were well invested, in addition to Bombay and Madras also. The British thoroughly pampered, the middle class and the rich in India, another tool to keep multitude of the poor suppressed and indifferently treated by the other two economically well off classes. This pampering created a divide between urban India and rural India. Strangely, the rural India was fleeced way too much and the accomplices, were the rich zamindars and moneylenders, who joined the British, in exploiting their own people, at the quiet and clever behest of the British. Rural India was recruiting ground, for the army that was sent abroad, to fight and several millions died, with no family pensions, being paid to the wife, of the deceased. Wars were fought abroad, for the Empire and not for India's interests, but strangely funded by India's exchequer.

The British officers were paid compensation and perks, way too much and after return, to Britain, they availed life term pensions, at the expense, of the rural India's fleeced wealth. A huge amount of money, was transferred to the Crown and it was invested to build English infrastructure. Poverty thus in British India, did not trot or canter, instead it galloped, for decades and for about two centuries. The British period saw the fleecing of rural India, never known in the world history, at any time, leaving mass poverty, as described by Prof Galbraith, the American economist from Harvard

University. Since the educated were pampered, who lived in urban India and they were into writing books, very little of the British exploitation of rural India, has come to light.

British liked the positive attitude, of the middle class and leveraged them, to experiment democracy, in India setting up institutions that have been, a boon to India's governance with rule of law and principles of natural justice. The British gave India, extreme poverty of rural India, but from the back door, it also helped India, build its marvelous democracy, which brought about solid change, in the rural India, after its independence. Rural India now produces educated, university educated people, as no rural parts of the world. India prides itself of having their people, serving in the medical, engineering and IT fields, not only in India, but throughout the developed world, its farmers and agricultural laborers feeds, a nation of 1.2 billion people, without relying on food imports. The poor people in India are a contented lot, smiling on small jokes, caring for children and sacrificing for them, caring for the aged and even eating, after the parents, have been served meal, living in a joint family, under the same roof, served by the same kitchen. They do not miss out, on caring for animals, who are tied in the courtyard, of their homes. City visits are a fun and they go to cities, for at least, on a monthly visit, in coaches that a state government provides, charging then very small amount. There are about 60,000 coaches in one province. If the State of Illinois, USA had about 60,000 coaches, plying every day, one can imagine, how many trips in a month, an American would have undertaken, from Decatur or Springfield or Peru or Hinsdale to Chicago. It is the price of the gas and for some people, lack of personalized vehicle or inability, to drive long distances, due to age that preclude, a weekly trip to Chicago and take a walk by Chicago river.

Poverty, viewed by others, appear severe, in certain pockets of India, despite millions being pulled out of poverty trap every year. But for those, who are a part of poverty, they say it hurts them less, because they are used to the life of simplicity and austerity, as the religion and culture of spirituality, preach them. It is the two hundred years of imperious British colonialism which severely neglected rural development in all its aspects including education. Rabindranath Tagore aptly mentioned in the later phase of life in the late 1930s, "Today for various reasons villages are fatally neglected. They are fast degenerating into serfdom, compelled to offer to the ungrateful towns cheerless and unintelligent labor for work carried on in an unhealthy and impoverished environment. The object of Sriniketan is to bring back life in its completeness into the villages making them self-reliant and self respected, acquainted with the cultural tradition

241

of their country and competent to make efficient use of modern resources such as tractors for the improvement of their physical intellectual and economic conditions."

In India, from times immemorial, the life of a sage, is to wear an unstitched long cloth, sleep on the floor, eat very simple food and preach spirituality, from neighborhood to neighborhood. People look up to such personalities, with enormous reverence in India, especially in the rural India, as much as the Americans, like Rockefeller and view him, as an ideal in America.

Indian sages, receive global reverence. An idea can be had, from the fact that about hundred thousand people, from all over the world, significantly from the developed world, assemble, to celebrate birthdays, of some of the sages in India, all the way travelling, to his hermitage in rural India.

India's poverty that accumulated, after being slapped for 200 years, by the British rule, in India's democracy, found substantial reduction in half a century, due to extreme patience of the poor and optimism of the democratic governance of the nation, after its freedom in 1947. Democracy can do wonders, with little national patience, which a nation, with multi millennium heritage, could handle pretty well.

India saw a lot of poverty, as the British governance in India, after 1857, among other poverty generating tools, is stated to have also pursued a policy of divide and rule. India from times immemorial, has learnt, to welcome different ethnicities, into its fold, allowing them to happily settle down in India. When the Jews were defeated, by the Romans, many of them as early as 2000 years ago, arrived in India and settled down in Kerala. Jesus Christ's disciple, in his own time, arrived in India and many Brahmins got converted to Christianity. Thus Christianity arrived in India and was welcome, before even arrived, in today's predominantly Christian World, of Europe. Such has been the antiquity and rich cultural heritage of India. When the Arabs invaded Persia and proselytized the Zoroastrians to Islam, those Zoroastrians, who were not converted to Islam, left Persia and took happy refuge in India, initially in Bombay and then from Bombay, they also settled down in Bangalore, Hyderabad, Pune, Indore and Ahmadabad. Even today, they follow their own ancient religion of Zoroastrianism. This tradition of cosmopolitism and religious inclusiveness has been the overarching idea of India from times immemorial. Rabindranath Tagore who was conferred Nobel prize in literature in 1903 stated, "I have, as you are no doubt aware, worked all my life for the promotion of racial, communal and religious harmony among the different people of the world". He further added, "I had set my face against all claims of narrow and aggressive nationalism believing in the common destiny and oneness of all mankind".

In consonance with his assertion of cosmopolitanism and unity of mankind Tagore wrote to Mahatma Gandhi in his letter dated 1th May 1933 stating, "I appeal to you for the sake of the dignity of our nation, which is truly impersonated in you and for the sake of millions of my country men who need your living touch and help to desist from any act that is not for the rest of humanity."

Islamic rulers knew about the cosmopolitan nature of India's culture and confined their rule around the national capital of Delhi and the peripheries. The rural areas, by and large, were, left to enjoy their autonomous character, merely collecting annual revenue. That is how, the social and economic structure, of the village republics, in India have been in place, during the entire Islamic rule and there were no occasions, of Hindu Muslim clashes anytime, during the pre-Mogul and Mogul rule. However, the violence against the local population when invaders came, cannot be ruled out.

Before the Parliament of Religions, was convened in Chicago in 1886, the Mogul King Akbar had convened a conference of people of all religions, where the Hindus, the Jains, the Muslims, the Zoroastrians and also the Jesuit fathers, who were Christians attended. This Parliament of Religions was convened in Mogul Emperor's palace, to undertake deliberations, on spirituality and it was named Din-i-Ilahi. Akbar started a spiritual movement that promoted peace and it was named Suleh Kul. Thus the idea of unity of religions, which started with the Vedic concept of Sanaatan Dharma, in ancient times, about 10,000 years ago, also was continued, during the medieval period, as convened by the Mogul Emperor. During Asoka's rule, Kanishka's rule and Harshavardhana's rule, India's religion of right path, spirituality and peace was propagated as Buddhism, preached by Gautam Buddha, and it received universality in China, South East Asia, Mongolia, Sri Lanka and even Afghanistan. Though Moguls came from Central Asia, they made India their home and no money was ever transferred to Central Asia, collecting taxes from the peasants in India. Both the Hindus and the Muslims, found it strange, when a foreign company, with monopoly of trading powers, started raising army, making treaties with local royalties and sending their troops, to provide security to the local princes, against their own peasants, in case of a revolt by the peasants. A wedge was attempted to be driven, between the local princes and their peasants, by injecting a fear, in their minds that their peasants could rebel against them. The company even waged wars and looted the wealth of the local princes, by siding with one royalty and waging war with another, with an intention to play the favorites, among the princes and driving a wedge, between the royalties. Even annexation of territories, was not uncommon, after skirmishes. During the company rule, which was absolutely bizarre, as a company, could never be sovereign, a doctrine of lapse principle, was introduced by Governor General Dalhousie in 1850s, providing for taking over, of the royal prince's jurisdiction, to rule if a male heir was not born, to the incumbent royalty. This move irked the royalties, both the Hindus and the Muslims. Presence of the skin of beef and pork, in grenades, to be used in the army, infuriated the Hindu and the Muslim soldiers both and the mutiny was joined, by the frustrated peasants, who were taxed very heavily and also by the Hindu and the Muslim royalties. All of these groups nominated the last Mogul Emperor Bahadur Shah Jaffar, as their leader. The company officials were unnerved and nervous. They felt that a strong military action only, could quell the rebellion. The company very urgently, raised big army; from places, where the mutiny and the rebellion had not occurred, which was Punjab, the Hill Districts and the South India. The battalions, led by the Brahmin officers and those from the North India, were immediately disbanded. This was the beginning of divide and rule that started, with the army.. Queen Victoria declared herself as the Empress of India and took over administration, of India from the East India Company. She wrote a long letter to the Governor General, asking him to ensure that the Hindus and the Muslims are not to be allowed, to be close to each other. Attempts should continue to create and perpetuate divide, to keep the British rule, strong. Such clear directions, coming from the crown, to the Viceroy of India, encouraged the divisiveness in India.

The Viceroy started receiving separate parleys, representations from the Congress that represented all in India and the Muslim League, representing only the Muslim cause. Emboldened by the British governance, the members of the Muslim League were occasionally, critical of the Congress and Mr. Jinnah was sometimes critical, about the fact of Mr. Gandhi, was speaking for both Hindus and Muslims. He desired him, to confine talking only about the Hindus and not for the Muslims. During the second global war, when the Congress declared Quit India slogan, asking the British, to grant Independence to India, Mr. Jinnah and the Muslim league, kept silent, without offering any remarks. Mr. Winston Churchill, somehow found Mr. Gandhi too Indian and too ethnic in all matters, including his very simple dress, in which he had attended the Round Table Conference, in London. Mr. Churchill could not bring himself, up to appreciate the demonstrations, the bonfires of foreign, cloth, the civil disobedience especially, when as the War Prime Minister of Britain, he was very busy, participating in the Second Global War. He found Mr. Gandhi, asking for independence very untimely, when the War was devastating the buildings, the factories, the academies of the Allied Powers, of which Britain was an integral part and when the British treasury was challenged with, huge deficit of finances. The financial deficit of Britain necessitated Mr. Churchill, to request President Roosevelt of USA, to lend money to Britain. The war was taking, a huge human toll, running into millions. Mr. Churchill distanced himself, from Gandhi and he developed a liking for Mr. Jinnah, a western person, in style and manners and certainly dressed, in suit and tie. Mr. Attlee of the Labour Party, coming to power, who during his election campaigns, had promised, to grant independence to India, made India's independence happen urgently, as soon as the second global war came to a close in 1945. But the beginning of division, that letter of Queen Victoria created in 1857, continued to make, the divide of a national family of citizens that was united for 900 years. All of the violence that unfortunately occurred, accompanying the partition of India, would have been completely avoided, had this divide, not being created by the British.

India would have not been, so impoverished, at the end of the British rule and it could start, at a much higher level, of per capita income. In India's case, the tendency to divide, was exported from Britain. Whereas in countries like USA, where burden of history, by southern cotton farmers, practicing slavery and all of the bad stories of the poor blacks, suffering, from very hard farm work, being lashed occasionally and being sold putting them, on auction, stating that the furniture and slaves in good condition, for sale, created the divide, which attenuated the overall prosperity, and widened inequality, between the haves and have-nots.

Divides within the nation, which is homemade, in this case, has certainly taken a toll, on its overall economic prosperity and higher standards of living, besides better job situations. Several articles that are published about the US economy, entitled great divide, would have never come into being. All of that money, released from, lack of need of crime control, incarceration and abandoned properties, in poor neighborhoods that can serve no purpose and the like, would have released huge money and that could be available, for subsidizing public school education and higher education, for both blacks and whites. Inclusiveness efforts are now top down, with affirmative action moves, but the bottom up divisive tendencies, unfortunately makes the divide, a reality and it certainly has financial implications, and loss of overall prosperity. The gap between the rich and the poor, as a result have been going up, for over three decades now in America.

In many Latin American countries, the huge inequality that happens, between the gated communities of the rich, the middle class and drug infested crime infested slums, blight the economy, though they are middle income countries. It is the egoistic attitude of the rich, which all scriptures guide to shun, locks capital unnecessarily, with some families and never allow the same, to be circulated, to help the poor in the slums, at least once in few years. It delays to pull a, large number of them, into mainstream. Some positive moves, could bring the poor, to have a lot of gratitude, for the well off, removing the mistrust, between them. Such an approach has the potential of speeding goodwill, which could get monetized, in a big way, to bring prosperity, in a ubiquitous manner.

Today, the CEOs in India, take about 10 times more, compensation than the base level worker and this number is 550 in USA. Imagine, if the CEOs in USA suddenly get this spiritual brainwave, to emulate India and take only 10 times, compensation, instead of 550 times, how much capital would be freed, in each organization, to bring distribution of better compensation, even including health care benefits, for all the employees. How much goodwill would get monetized, in USA, if the CEOs tend to show, such a caring and inclusive gesture, shunning their ego and arrogance, would be anybody's guess. Inclusiveness makes, wonders, in economic prosperity, whereas divisiveness increases, crimes incarceration, loss of morale among minorities, lack of education and tobogganing poverty, afflicting them.

Chapter 17

Remedial Measures: Reduction of Poverty

17.1 Higher Education, Subsidized by Government Reduces Poverty and Brings Prosperity

Government plays an important role, in higher education, making it within the bounds of common man, at a young age and student loans are an unknown commodity and do not bedevil the finances of young Indians, for years on end, as it bedevils young Americans until the late middle age. Even the doctors in USA, who are well paid professionals, cannot escape it. Due to student loans, they are unable to even own a house until mid 40s, when they are likely to be debt free. Even those pursuing legal education, are burdened with huge student loans. President Obama acknowledged that 2 years before, he became the President, he and the First Lady were paying student loan installments, every month. Such has been the sad state of student loan affairs, in America and that makes social mobility of those, living in low and medium end neighborhood not possible. Thus the multiple generations, lead the same life of meeting ends with difficulty, unlike in India, where economic mobility every year, pull people out of the low end to candidates, who would be able to lead a much better living standard, through the permit of slogging in higher education, which is heavily subsidized by the government. There is a lot of scope, for America to make higher education very cheap, in terms of fees, to be paid, only if it could cut down on policies of tax cuts for the rich, social security for the rich, medical for the rich, which on the face of it look bizarre. President Obama has been paying focused attention, to helping the community colleges, to function better, where many courses, could be taken, with much less tuition fees, by students staying with ther parents only. Waiver for those courses, could be taken in universities, including IV league universities. There is a commonality of thinking, discerned, here among the public policy makers of India and USA.

India uses talents available in mansions, small middle class homes, as well as from small mud huts, without discriminating in fact, acting in proactive manner, to help children, from very poor families, to become officers, managers, architects, attorneys, engineers and doctors and recruit them on priority and asking corporations to lift the poor young and the poor children. The MNCs seem to have learnt turning GDP per capita blind, to recruit talents from abroad, from India and China, from where whole lot of its doctors engineers professors in the universities and in recent decades software professionals are drawn. Offshoring and outsourcing that have happened, in a span of about 3 decades, beginning in 1980s, resembles the inclusiveness of the Indian governance, to those deprived. However in recent years a bad element of money greed, from cost cutting has spurned its image and people have been criticizing offshoring and outsourcing. Then the Government in early 2000s, in the US giving tax exemption to those, who outsourced jobs, have been found to be heinous, to the locals besides being unethical and brutally ridiculous. It is no wonder, there is lot of opposition that heads developed in recent years against the US government and the US Corporations neglecting locals, in the jobs, while proffering up talents from India and China. This is fairly understandable. These actions, have been overdone and pursued, at the expense, of the recruiting the locals. If there is so much talk, in US about work family balance, those who matter, such as the Government and giant MNCs need to maintain balance, recruiting the locals and scouting the talents abroad, instead of mindlessly pursuing outsourcing or recruiting foreigners way more than the locals, in the process impoverishing job scenario, in USA and creating a huge middle class, in host economies, where already the size of the middle class is higher than the total population of USA.

While learning from the inclusiveness of the Indian governance, the steps that the US took should have been such that only murmur could have occurred and not screaming. US steps invited screams from the average Americans, from Congress to get the jobs back to America and stop offshoring and outsourcing. A balance between the 3 actions would reduce poverty in America, arising from lack of well paying jobs of young average Americans for years. It is a shame that there are cases, where those finishing bachelor's degree are compelled to work, to survive in the US economy, as bartenders. quixotically sometimes, in downtown Chicago land and New York One would see captions with people, asking for alms, stating "I am a graduate, lost my job and unemployed for 30 weeks, please help." Family having distanced itself, from individuals, on the social plane and government encouraging outsourcing and driven by the cost cutting greed, to earn enhanced profits incessantly, the corporations are recruiting foreigners, where the American graduates would go, if not hitting the roads, in major city downtowns. Should in a situation like this, as a part of corporate social responsibility, the corporate America, should not have clear cut goals set, to address poverty reduction in a big way in USA? Should it only be the responsibility of the US Government alone? Should the family not rise up to the occasion, to help the young Americans, who have slogged to achieve a degree, whereas the elder generations enjoyed higher standard of living, engaged themselves in vacations, domestic and foreign, just completing a high school, as all of these cost cutting measures had not polluted, the minds of the corporate sector and because Government exercised right regulation? Should the media need to self introspect, what harm, have they caused, to the social structure, which neither stands today, for child care nor for helping the young, when they face financial crisis and are too eager, to send the aged to old age homes, instead of making them live with the family who should be nursing them.

The Indian aged always live, with the care of their adult children. Children find one of the parents, receiving them affectionately; responding to resolve their doubts in conversations, helping them with home work, allotted by the school, which is rigorous and offer homemade nice hot food, when the children are hungry. The young could rush home in India, whenever they have a crisis and they continue to be helped, as kids for eternity. Could US learn from India, now in the realm of social values and norms to make life, more interesting, less challenging and less anti depressant dependent?

17.2 Democracy With Institutions Reduces Poverty

Institutions offer justice and welfare, as they govern as per the rules and the laws, made by an elected body, at the national and sometimes at the sub national levels. Three major institutions that characterize a democracy, have been executive, legislature and judiciary, each acknowledging their duties and not ever treading the boundaries of duties, of each other. If by way of inadvertence, one institution embarks on moves that cross the boundaries, it is known to rollback, as soon as they realize and also, when appealed by the affected institution. Political and economic power in a democracy, is peacefully transferred, at the end of usual 5 year term and free and fair elections are held, by a National Election Commission, with its provincial branches, to elect the law making body, at the national and in some cases, at the sub national levels. Democracy functions, under the overarching compliance of a country's constitution, which is valued the most. Even oaths of offices, to the head of the government and its cabinet members, reiterate that those taking oath, will function, as per the constitution. Constitutional provisions, offer a brilliant guidance, to rule of law and principles of natural justice. In India, whenever constitutional provisions are violated by party, writs are filed to provide justice, under article 226 of the constitution to the High Court and under article 32 of the constitution to the Supreme Court. The tools of poverty generation, among people that are available with the affluent is to pay measly non living wages, to the workers, to keep the labor in the bondage, not selling certain merchandize, to some social groups, out of social discrimination and not providing goods, on the basis of race and color, are brought pretty much under correction, through the process of democracy. For example, in South Africa, when Mahatma Gandhi was an attorney and suddenly on a night, when his wife was to deliver a baby, he approached the hospital, which refused to offer the service, as he was of Indian origin and because he was not a white. Mr. Gandhi mentions, in his autobiography that he helped his wife Kasturba, to deliver the baby boy, at home, as delivery services, were not available in the apartheid dictatorial regime in South Africa. Such a bizarre denial of services for a child birth, could have never taken place in a country, governed by democracy. In this case, no poverty conditions ensued, but in a lot of cases, when the governance is discriminatory and looks the other way, without following the rule of law, an array of economic and social injustices, could occur, enhancing poverty of the incumbent poor and causing poverty to those, who are yet not termed, as poor. In India, minimum wages act is to be followed both in agriculture, industry and services, as per the laws of that land. Workers in industries, have a right to go on strike, if their legitimate demands are not met or the management turns haughty, not to come to the negotiating table. In India, the security of tenure, is given to the manufacturing units that are maintained, as state owned enterprises and the Government departments, which gave the workers voice, against managerial excesses and their financial malfeasance sometimes and supercilious and unilateral innovations, in business, in the directions, where the future could be bleak, though top managers could benefit. The labor unions, tend to keep a watch on management practices, especially when it is fraught, with money greed and indifference to other constituencies. A lot of the tools of inflicting artificial poverty, on social groups that are different and against those, who are already suffering from poverty, could be avoided, in a democracy, Such nefarious moves that are capable of being avoided in the environment of political and industrial democracy, could be perpetrated incessantly, causing agony, to the multitudes, in dictatorships, unless the guidance of the sages and the leaders, are followed, not to fear, as the fear itself, is the enemy of human life.

The gap between the rich and the poor, in wealth and income, also shrinks in democracies, compared with economic scenario in the African dictatorships. In democracy, the craze of political leaders, to rule is limited and they are happy, to transfer the political power, in peace, when elections elect other political party representatives.

17.3 Institutions such as, executive, legislature and judiciary, with checks and balances, reduce poverty

Most African economies and quite a few South American and Central American countries, are given to dictatorships. Dictatorships, on most occasions emanate, from the army coups, which they justify, saying that such a governance provide political stability. Once having achieved power, the army general, rarely want, to relinquish the political power. Benevolent and incorruptible dictatorships, could be a shade better, than those having deficits, on those fronts. But generally, the force that is behind the general, who occupies political power ensures that members of the armed forces, are very comfortable, with high salaries and perks and the President most comfortable. However, this system rides roughshod, on all of the institutions of democracy, such as the judiciary, the legislature and the executive, drawn from the legislature. The decisions are rarely based, on the requests of the people, as interface with people, tend to less and bottom up feedback, is also highly limited. The receptivity, of the government, would be minimal too.

If by chance, the dictator, is given to corruption or high corruption and he is given to aligning, with countries that may be war mongering or the ruling government of a civil war torn country or belonging, to an ethnicity, which is ill poised, to many other ethnicities, in that nation, then the administration, could cause a lot of poverty, by the injustices inflicted. Such spread of poverty, courtesy a dictator could happen, in the domestic economy, as well as some other economies, of the global economic landscape. If a dictator desires to implement, a public policy or an array of public policies in favor of the rich, to enrich them further and want to neglect the poor, no recourse of justice, becomes available, to the poor, as in many cases, a dictator could continue in power, for over several decades.

Hence for reduction of poverty, to be achieved and also to see political freedom, the best course of action, for the people is, to strive to install democracy, in the country, a system known, as nice all over the world, as is based on the checks and balances and the freedom of expression and thought.

17.4 Sheltering Industries to Reduce Poverty

There is a undoubtedly a cost, of sheltering industries, in an economy, which gets reflected, in higher prices, of goods and services. If the industries are sheltered, for many years, they could turn arrogant that the Government, is with them. Then they may not invest, in innovations, in the Rand D and they may even not maintain, the quality of the products. Besides, they may also hike the prices, sometimes abnormally, to gouge more profits, from the customers. It could also turn into an economy, heavily populated by the monopolies, in each industry. The monopolies, with their not so desirable moves, could impoverish the consumers, with inferior standards of living.. One industry could even, be having just one firm's monopoly. It may even set its production targets, unrelated to the capacity of people, to pay for the goods and services. Sometimes, the monopoly business firms, could disallow competition, even from new entrepreneurs, by managing relationship with the Government, taking license for additional capacity, so that no domestic competitors arise, in that industry. The bane is that sometimes, these monopolies, take licenses, for additional capacity, but they do not set up, production facilities, for years, adversely affecting, to meet the demand of the consumers.

However, sheltering industries, for a limited number of years and for limited number of decades, when the country has recovered, from exploitation of indigenous industries, by a foreign political power, may even be prudent, as it happened in India, for decades of import substitution, inward orientation and sheltering the industries. Such moves could be beneficial, to the home and also help economic landscape, to get consolidated. Maturity could come to the industries and professional competencies could get chiseled. Managerial competencies, also reach to a level, where global competition, can be met, with global firms, on a level playing field. India saw the competencies, rising well namely managerial, professional, legal, financial etc, to a level, when global firms, would not be able, to hurt the local businesses. It was at that time, India opened and liberalized its economy, to foreign direct investment and the opening of branch offices of the foreign businesses and the foreign banks, that too, in a limited manner, mostly in the urban locations. Even then, the non alcoholic beverages businesses suffered in India and so did the breakfast item, cornflakes industry, as in these two consumer products, the level of ad expenditure, by the MNC s were, way ahead of the local firms and with newness of the foreign products, the novae rich people, in India, who with a slavish attitude, to the west, took on quickly, for no valid reasons, to consumption of goods of the foreign firms. Consumption of Pepsi and Cola, besides being a sweet beverage, to relax was an index of fashion, for this category of people and it was kind of, adopting Americana. Similar was the situation with cornflakes, made by Kellogg vis a vis Mohan Makin. Inducement, of one time good money, to the local businesses, also made them, to sell their firms, to the MNCs, but this usually could have a negative effect, on competencies, such as professional, entrepreneurial, managerial financial, and even legal and hence needs to be shunned, by the emerging economies and developing economies, to sustain economic growth and economic development.

For nations to prosper and reduce poverty, managerial, professional, financial, legal, entrepreneurial and administrative competencies, need to be built, over time, say few decades, after achieving independence, from a foreign rule of economic exploitation, by sheltering the indigenous industries, to prevent them, from going into oblivion, stressed heavily, by sudden opening of an economy and allowing the MNCs, to operate in the local economy. Once these competencies are built and the industries consolidate, gradual opening of economic boundaries and allowing FDI could result in substantial reduction of poverty and rise in prosperity, in such nations. This approach require patience of the national leaders, to achieve economic prosperity and also ability, of not being confused, by the badgering of the MNCs' attempt to own the local firm. It also is the result of, the home countries, in the developed world, to make efforts, for the MNCs, to be encouraged to own firms in the host economies/countries, quickly instead of losing time.

What steps need to be avoided, to help reduce poverty of developing countries, by the international community?

Not buying too many goods and services, from one country, as it indirectly enriches its reserves needs strict avoidance. Not buying too many goods and services, from one country, the US and the countries of the developed world, would not only reduce poverty of the major buying nations, but also of numerous other nations, where the buying by the major nations would be diversified. US, by buoying too many goods from China, has indirectly denied other nations, to thrive their exports and has denied them, thus a huge opportunity, to reduce their poverty. The amount of buying of goods and services that US does from China, if those imports would have been diversified, at a minimum, from another 25 countries, the latter would have come up, by increasing their export revenues. Those nations, by increasing their exports revenue, would have increased investments, in their respective economies. The poor in those nations, would have seen a lot of sunshine.

Not relocating manufacturing or service operations, solely in few countries, would have similarly and indirectly helped many other nations, to reduce poverty, in their jurisdictions. Numerous countries, after decolonization, are pinning their hopes, on cooperation, from the developed world, to enrich them and they have kept seen their economic conditions flat. If US would have diversified its FDI decisions abroad, to set up manufacturing plants in about 25 countries, those economies, would have also seen manufacturing expertise of the economies going up. Those economies would have also seen, the skills of its labor, reach global standards. Those economies would have also seen their youth, getting better paying manufacturing jobs and also their educated human resources, would have been appointed, as managers and supervisors, in those economies. In addition to China and India, so many countries, probably would have been discussed, by the intelligentsia worldwide..

Not lending too much bilateral aid, for selfish reasons, to extract mineral resources, from those countries, by paying bribes to the few unscrupulous politicians or few military generals, who may be ruling the country and giving highly unfair value, unfair to his countrymen value, for the natural resources extracted.

From strategic point of view, some economies may be more important, than others. But from poverty reduction point of view, worldwide, the richer nations would do well, not to help the dictatorships, because on the face of it, a dictatorship handles poverty, with much lesser efficiency, than a well functioning democracy. Hence the US and other developed nations, may do well, for poverty reduction, to avoid giving bilateral aid to the dictatorships. In fact, a lot of bilateral aid, received by the dictatorships, is misused to suppress ethnicities, in African economies.

Not insisting on too much SAP, the IMF will do well. Multilateral institution, like the IMF and the World Bank, need to be just, to the poor economies, which have unfortunately seen a lot of downsides, due to inappropriate expansionist policies, of the developed world nations. Keeping this burden of history, in mind, the IMF will do well, not to insist on the SAP, and if at all, the SAP is necessary, to implement SAP, with a human face. Such a step would reduce poverty, in the target economies.

Not insisting on removing subsidies, in areas of job availability and job growth would have the potential of poverty reduction The donors need to be relaxed, in extending aid, by not scuttling subsidies, without which, some economies, would be hard to run. Occasional subsidies to agriculture or to a public sector industry, is unavoidable, keeping the requirement of politics in mind. Subsidies are partly economic and partly political, even in the developed world and that has to be appreciated, if poverty reduction, in the official debtor countries, is a priority. Economic stimulus packages, given by the US President, bailing out the US players in the Economic and Financial Meltdown of 2008, Savings and Loans Associations and the institutions and LTCM, in a strong economy, a market oriented economy like the US, need to be, kept in mind, by the World Bank and the IMF.

The governments of the countries especially developed countries may do well, to give some incentives and also disincentives, to see that, the firms diversify, into a portfolio of societal goods, gradually rolling back from manufacturing arms for developing countries absorption. Government could give the incentives with timeline say of 5 to 10 years, to roll back, from armaments sale and asking them, to scale back, such sales to close it according to the timeline. This would be a huge help, to contain and close the civil wars sooner and also to indirectly bring more peace and power decentralizations to the provinces. in countries mostly in Africa, where dictatorships prevail. Governments of developed world, can play a nice indirect role, to the reduction of poverty, in the arms buying nations, mostly of Africa. Asking the armament industries, to roll back, from selling the arms, to the poor country dictators and fighting factions of the poor countries, in the waging of civil wars would help reduction of poverty in a big way.

Not waging avoidable wars, in weak countries, with less military force, would also help those economies, to continue with their programs of poverty reduction. While the standard deviation, in the incumbent military prowess, among 195 nations, cannot be avoided, but countries possessing more military power, need to be less inclined, to wage wars or to give threats of war, to receive some economic concessions, as per the norms, laid down by the United Nations and also the ethics of international relations. Wars from powerful countries could harm, the targeted nations and disturb the reduction of poverty steps, taken by the weaker nations, for years.

The richer countries not insisting economies to liberalize and invite FDI, in the name of competition, saying competition is good, would also be helpful to reduce poverty of nations. Innovation in domestic businesses and supply of varied goods in the economy and giving the consumers choices of the goods, to select from a portfolio of goods, based on quality and price could also help reduce, poverty challenges.

The richer countries not insisting the poor countries, to introduce capital market liberalization would do well for them, in the pursuit of poverty reduction. There are some countries, where unlike high finance industry, full of unregulated innovations, in the Wall Street of USA, the finance industry, would be too weak, to handle abrupt swings, in its functioning. While Government may not have any intention, to cause harm, to the host economy, but Wall Street has enough number of investors, big investors. These investors could invest, in the market voluminously and turn nervous, sometimes unnecessarily, to suddenly withdraw capital, from the economic liberalizing economies, of the developing and the emerging world. These investors never care for, even their own brethren in the US or the EU, as to how much they would suffer, if they roll back their investments, from the Wall Street. To expect that they would have a heart, for people in host countries, who would be impacted by sudden capital withdrawals, of the foreign investors, is expecting too much.

Then to proffer local investor's wealth, asking the financially weak economies, to liberalize their economies, need to be avoided, giving their financial experts time, to give their counsel, to their Government, so that poverty, arising from sudden withdrawal of the capital of American investors, may not destroy their economies. The Asian crisis of 1987 is a case in point here and one knows, how a number of economies, known for very good economic performance for decades, suffered, because of too much capital, entering their stock markets, which suddenly left at a very short notice, such as Thailand, Malaysia, Hong Kong Singapore and Indonesia.

There continues talks in the air that as US and other countries of the developed world, are major shareholders, in the IMF and the World Bank and the US is the largest shareholder, it influences the lending, by these 2 world institutions. The US will do probably well, to act in a fashion that this impression evaporates, from the minds of the international community, so that these institutions, could play a more meaningful role, in the reduction of poverty, in the developing world and emerging world, based on mutual trust. The reduction of the poverty, in many of these nations would then occur, by confidently availing, a number of good loan facilities that the World Bank and the IMF, have to offer.

17.5 The Moves of the Developed World, to Make a Difference in Poverty Reduction, in the Developing Countries

US and the developed world, need to be involved in fair trade and not only free trade. By fair trade, one would mean genuinely, to follow what Sir Adam Smith had to say. Where a good can be conveniently be made, without any help, from any quarters, including Government subsidy, only those few nations need, to be patronized for importing that particular good instead of misallocating resources, to make those goods, individual nation wise and not believe in the free trade. Secondly, when an array of goods, are available for sale, by a nation which wants another nation, to open up its economic boundaries, to see that their poverty levels do not go up, only such of those nations, need to be pursued at least some smaller array of goods are made. In addition, the countries where goods are not capable of being made, the developed nations need to examine, which goods could be competitively made, in that nation, if technical expertise, training to those educated nations and capital is organized by a group of well established firms.

The multilateral institutions need, to be more fair, giving fair representation, to economic scenario of the world, in the last 50 years. Merely saying Asian countries, will lead global economic growth, in another 40 years, is not enough. It is widely felt that now, in the new millennium, IMF, World Bank and WTO, need to be more representative, of the comity of nations, rather than power play, in the hands of those countries, which were in the vanguard, after the world war 2.

Globalization of economic operations, need to tap only the talent that is in deficit, in the home country. They are but not to indulge, in ethical malpractices, of identifying countries, where environmental and safety standards, are relaxed and liberal, relative to the home country. Investing in such host economies, neglecting investments in the home countries tend to destroy environment in the host economy and also leads to ill treatment of the labor, in the host economy. Due to higher brand equity of the developed world, working with a foreign firm, is considered a prestige and the labor may be ready to work, with low wages, in the host economy. Firms located in the developed countries, driven by moves of the cost savings, pay the workers, in the foreign investments, in their foreign locations, far less wages, which are more or less, aligned to the cost of living, of the host country. It needs to be remembered, by the offshoring and outsourcing MNCs, that cutting costs in this nefarious manner, denying employment/ jobs to their brethren, in their home countries, bring their downsides and their nation's downsides in the medium term. These firms only tend to gain, in the short term, at best a few years but lose heavily, on sustainability of business success.

17.6 MNCs, to help reduction of poverty, in the home and host countries, need to only recruit talents, from abroad, when local talents are genuinely, not available and also, in the medium term, attempt to generate talents, within the nation.

The ills of colonization, whether it was made, by the ancestors of the current citizens, of the developed world, in a proactive manner, or it was the making of only few selfish regimes of that time of the developed world, has been a stark reality. The fact remains that a lot of political and economic exploitation, has gone on, ruling the country, to maintain status quo. Many of them were denied, by the colonizing developed countries, agricultural growth, industrial growth, primary and secondary education growth, in the rural areas, rural development, to the disadvantage of the colonies and its people. Average people in the colonies, had to bear the burden, of the excessive taxation, collected by the colonial regimes through the local landlords known as Zamindars.

Colonial exploitation, is now, a common knowledge, as a result of the serious academic researches, in the developed world itself. The objective and frank academicians, came up, with conclusions, of their studies that the colonial regimes, impoverished the colonies, thoroughly, to enrich themselves, for decades, Even the struggles for independence, took a heavy toll, when the energies of people, got diverted to fight, for independence, for decades, than building the nation, with rising GDP, which developed world had the opportunity, to pay attention. As the colonies, were a part of the European industrial revolution, the mother country businesses also enjoyed, selling their products, to the captive markets, of their colonies, which they ruled. Some of the Colonial regimes tried even, to decimate the industries in the colonies, to beat competition to the mother country, by arranging to raise tariff walls, against their goods, in the mother country, which were popular, with consumers in the mother country, by pursuing protectionism.

It is the same protectionism, with which they were, ruining the developing countries, the colonies for several decades, they disallowed the colonies, after independence to adopt protectionism, once the colonies, became independent. They badgered their newly formed governments, to shun protectionism instead and they used, the route through the IMF and the World Bank. These institutions, which had the responsibility to maintaining the balance of the global economy and were, at the least expected, to be fair to all the countries, instead, started acting, in a partisan manner, as representatives and mouth pieces, of the developed world. Such moves of the multilateral institutions, also accentuated poverty in the developing countries.

To help nations, reduce their poverty, their actions were expected to be, highly objective and not influenced, by their major shareholders. A body of technocrats, to say the least are expected to remain fair and depoliticized. Elaborate reforms now would be needed, in the IMF and the World Bank, most of which, now has to be self motivated and the developed countries, may have to leave, these multilateral institutors alone. Some of the economically well performing countries, of South East Asia, are voluntarily shunning especially the IMF, because of their biased structural adjustment programs, at a time, when they should have advised, expansionary monetary and fiscal policies.

A lot of the poor countries are asked, in recent decades, by some of the emerging economies, with promises of far more aid, to shun the IMF and the World Bank, expressing their ire against them, due to unnecessary conditionality, being insisted, even for small dosages of credit. Compared to the small credit received, the conditionality imposed, on the poor nations, especially by the IMF, have been extremely costly and hurt the common people, during the Asian crisis during 1997. Unemployment rose and people suffered, with financial distress of the Himalayan proportions, whenever IMF slapped the debtor nations, with rigorous conditionality, with little positive results, once SAP implementation was over. In the developed world, in similar situations, strangely the opposite policy was pursued by the IMF. Prof Stieglitz, the Nobel laureate in Economics pointed out that while IMF dealt with countries, like Argentina, in similar situation as in Asian crisis, with the opposite prescription. IMF suggested to Argentina expansionary fiscal and monetary policies.

Their playing into the hands of the developed countries, especially to bail out the west based big banks, from their loans, turning sour, the IMF continued to dump loans, to the Asian nations, asking them, not to default to the banks, while people on the streets, agitated without jobs and without food. This indifference to help Asian crisis afflicted nations, created loss of international credibility of the IMF.

In the new millennium, their language is highly defensive, stating that they have realized their mistakes, in not according right advice, during the Asian crisis of 1997, to the East Asian nations, Russia and Mexico, which faced crisis and bounced back, in a few years. They need to be highly objective and help nations in crisis times, with a kind heart, especially for those nations that have suffered increase in the poverty of the masses of the farmers, during the colonization days, to maintain balance, in the world economy. Even bilateral aid need to be given, to reduce poverty, clearly realizing that a lot of poverty, in the developing economies, even now, were due to the wrong policies of the colonization regimes, in regard to their former colonies, which they ruled, for many decades, transferring huge quantities, of the annual wealth, to develop the infrastructure, in the mother countries. It was a zero sum game, for which a kind attitude of lending, both bilateral and multilateral, may have to prevail, for a century, if the poverty in the world, has to be reduced.

As much as it is good, to stay in a neighborhood, where people of by and large similar backgrounds and living standards stay, though the mount of wealth, in the form of gold, securities such as stocks and bonds, investments in real-estate domestically and globally and he like may have, a huge standard deviation. Similarly, though national wealth may be high or low, but it looks nice, at least to live in a world, which visually does not look very different, in terms of the basic cleanliness, living standards, possession of private goods, such as availability of water, electricity and the like. This will be possible, with a benevolent lending, with very little interest rate and some waivers of the loans, every few years, having a meeting, not in Paris, but in Kenya, Nigeria or Zambia or Ethiopia. Kindness comes, when decisions are taken, living for few days, surrounded by people of the debtor nations.

Chapter 18

Conclusion

Poverty of nations their causes and cures have been addressed in the chapters of the book. The study concludes that poverty has an element of ubiquity. Some countries face poverty though, more than others. Different countries address poverty challenges, in different manner. All of these aspects have been examined, in the book.

The study found that the dictatorial regimes tend to accept poverty, in their countries, as unavoidable. Some continents in recent centuries, have witnessed more poverty than others. Distribution of poverty, within a continent, is pretty similar, except a few exceptions. Some countries are found to be exceptionally rich and others are exceptionally poor. Hong Kong and Singapore are exceptionally well maintained city states, with high living standards, better educational facilities and better physical hygiene. Most of their credits are earned, by the local regime's efforts of dynamism and nice foreign relations. The countries that witnessed the industrial revolution and acquired techniques of the mass production of goods and services, using free trade include the US and EU, countries such as Australia, New Zealand and Canada. Industrial revolution individually, in these countries and whole hearted cooperation, among industrially developed countries, brought them prosperity. To exploit foreign markets, for industrial goods, produced by different nations, these nations were well heeled, in consequence of learning from each other. Hypocrisy of asking foreign markets, to follow Smithsonian free trade and at the nation's side, adopting protectionism, had the potential of sheltering, their nascent industries and making them earn runway profits. For many countries, this policy meant the demise of industries, in many economies, such as India and killing artificially competition that Smithsonian economists preach and value.

The study revealed that the Colonialism and imperialism, practiced, due to military and naval superiority, gave Europe and the America a huge edge, over the colonized countries. Colonized countries, were bled to transfer enormous wealth, to develop infrastructure in Britain and other countries. The developments in the colonies, were severally neglected, including education. Banking, finance, industries and the cheap army was recruited, many a times, to wage wars for economic prosperity. Such a gross inequality developed, during colonial and imperial expansion that expecting it to go away, in few decades, is to live in super fool's paradise. It is no wonder that some countries in Africa, are borrowing to repay the interest on loans. The countries that saw the Industrial revolution first, developed specializations, to make money, through domestic and foreign trade, with captive colonies. Lack of adequate currency was occasionally felt, even by Britain and she did not hesitate, to revert back to the ancient European barter systems. The liquor and hogs were used freely, as a barter medium of exchange, for the goods and services, among states, within the country and even for inter country free trade. In USA, even in 1700s. Britain went a step further, to use opium, as a medium of exchange, with the Chinese. Britain traded a ghastly war against the Chinese, who refused to take opium, as barter. Countries of West Indies, were convinced to take slaves, as a medium of exchange, for exchange to buy sugar and tobacco, for Britain. Such was the heinousness to capture slaves, from Africa and use them as medium of exchange, for trade with the West Indies countries. The poverty received a quantum jump, in different parts of the world, along with the nefarious practice of brutal racism, spread of abusive racial vocabulary, among educated as well as uneducated segments of human society of the west, In the 1700s, as the colonization of African continent, was played out. Poverty of this nature arising from deliberate harassment, of target races, the obnoxious practice in Britain, where an entrepreneur desired to start a monopolistic business, out of human exploitation. They got a firm chartered in England, with a charter, issued by no less than a person, other than the Queen Elizabeth of Britain, the agenda of which, was to trade in the slaves. They were to collect slaves, paying some pittance, to the mediators from Africa and then transport them, in rough conditions to the shores of Europe, Americas and the West Indies. These serfs were then auctioned, to the farm owners, to work on their farms, free of cost, all life and price for owning the slave for a lifetime, which was paid, by the slave buyer, was a result of open auctions, like furntitures and other home artifacts. While the British government abolished slavery from Britain and its foreign dominions in 1817, still the slave trading British firm, in an inebriated manner, kept on supplying black slaves, all over the world, on payment. None of the developed nations, protested as they were befriended, with each other, as partners in partitioning the world, for colorizations. Even after abolition of slavery in 1865 by President Abraham Lincoln, some slave owners illegally and criminally, kept the slaves imprisoned with them. Some slave retainers were booked under law and others managed with the cops.

An idea can be had as to how much the slave ownership, to work on the farmlands and farm houses, was taken casually, with little or nil sensitization about the sufferings of the slaves, that many, who even fought for their freedom in USA, from the British control, had several slaves, working with them. President George Washington, the first US President had slaves back, in his home and country. When the US constitution was adopted, the founding fathers did not have the guts, to adversely comment, on the evil practice of slavery. After having been freed, the slaves left the slave owners and moved to the north and north east. In employment, some got absorbed in railroads, some in manufacturing and others started to move to south of Canada. Some moved to Canada, which welcomed the war immigrants. While being enslaved, the blacks were hardened in life, but their wages were low and therefore their economic conditions remained, in the trenches, for decades. The countries of origin of all of these slaves, were robbed of the human capital, when the monopoly firm bought African slaves, to be deported to destinations of slavery, paying pittance. These countries in Africa, from where slaves were pulled away, in large numbers, lost huge manpower and economic productivity to an extent, mentally incomprehensible. Simultaneously, those who traded in the slaves made huge money, to prosper themselves, their government and also their infrastructure. The American South farm owners, who raised cotton and tobacco, the cash crops, paying no wages, with farm labor, made huge money, through the product exports. They lived lavishly with maids and servants, in huge mansions that continues to this day.

The British went a few notches extra, to make solid money. Money and money, appeared to have obsessed them in 1700s. They seem barely to have thrown humanity to winds, without hesitation to exploit people, of colored races, both mentally and physically. The Africans were captured and put in ramshackle ships, with hardly any space to sit and they were sent, to slave buying destinations. They quickly grasped internationally, in which shores, the cheap or no wage labor, would be needed, for industries and also for the farms, for increasing agricultural productivity and also for bringing more farm lands, to farm use.

Unlike the cost cutting money greed, of the current MNCs, a monopolistic British firm, in the 1700s, came up with the idea of extracting labor, in foreign lands, by brutal force, by importing labor from the poorer countries, at a price to the slave trader. For free trade and promotion of trade, for capturing markets abroad and for setting up colonies in foreign lands, Britain faced competition, from other similarly placed racially aligned whites regimes of France, Germany, Italy, Spain, Portugal, Holland. In the nefarious economic activity of slave trade, to increase wealth of the white race dominated countries, to increase the wealth of the recently industrialized countries, there were no parallel and no nefarious global or regional contractor came up to compete with slave supplying firm of Britain. Thus the uniqueness of Britain, to make quick and solid money would in the world history be the British example alone. This firm instead of being castigated in Britain, found supporters in the City Mayors and Sheriffs and Parliamentarians of London, who bought this company's shares. This company's shares were traded, in the market and the firm owners paid, dividends, to the shareholders. Shareholding and stock market left to it, could be so brutal, so inhuman, and so unethical and racist in ideas, could be be hardly comprehended. Even Queen Elizabeth of Britain, owned these stocks, of the slave trading firm. The firm was given shamelessly, a charter of 1000 years, by the then Queen Elizabeth and the British.

Probably next to the industrial revolution, next to the rising of naval power, unusually in some countries in Europe and the Americans and colonization, next to the militarism and imperialism, the next most ghastly tool of poverty increase, in numerous countries, was the slave trade. The slave historians suggest that the slaves were overworking, in perpetual fear, as every day, their supervisor took shirts away, from some labor and lashed them, leading to cries and shrieks, from the African labor. These shrieks and cries, were a reminder, to the rest of the African slaves that any attempt, to foment rebellion or reduction of forced labor or any laxity in daily work schedule, will invite similar lashing. Exasperated by such heinous practices, to the black slaves, Mr. Abraham Lincoln, as the President, passed a law in 1856, abolishing slavery. This law gave an opportunity to the black slaves, to claim wages and in case of nonpayment of wages, they started fleeing in droves, to the north of America. Still undaunted, some farm landowners, imprisoned their slaves and exacted work, free of charge, until the police booked the criminal cases and booked cases against farm lords. The freed slaves in USA, found themselves, without jobs for months and they had to acquire new manufacturing skills to be absorbed, in industries., the Blacks in east, northeast and the like, in the late 19th century. The poverty was made to embed itself, so badly in these African slaves, in collusion of the slave trading monopolistic firm, ship transportation companies and mean Sothern white landlords, that for them thinking, anything other than only poverty, became incomprehensible. Poverty for them became a way of life, for multiple generations. Even today, this they feel poverty, is in the kind of neighborhoods, they stay.

Poverty in a village town or a city, in a backward economy, is a combination of both endogenous and exogenous factors. As reported above, the exogenous factors, predominated the scene, but the role of endogenous factors, cannot be ruled out.

The scriptures, be it the Bible, the Old Testament and the New Testament the Geeta and the like extol poverty and regard the poor people, as blessed. While efforts, to reduce poverty in society, may have gone on, with bottom up and top down measures, from time to time, from centuries to centuries, but famed leaders with confidence, talking for planning to reduce poverty or remove poverty, is a phenomenon of the current times, such as 20th cnrtury.

Mr. Nelson Mandela, in a public meeting, in 1954, before his political party, ANC, to seek freedom for the blacks was banned, by the white regime and before he was imprisoned in criminal charges he averred that poverty is an artificial phenomenon and it can be removed, given proper measures, being applied. The Africans in South Africa, had to wait for 40 more years, to see the poverty reduction of Africans, being played out. Indira Gandhi's training in Shantiniketan, a school set up in the rural area, by the Indian Nobel prize winner in literature and then she, while studying in Pune, led a simple life, sleeping on the floor, along with poor students of labor castes, with whom she had cultivated nice friendships, prepared her, for a life of sacrifice and devotion to the poor. When she became the Prime Minister of India, after her father's demise, she followed into the footsteps of her father, believing in the socialism. The study delved into her actions, to remove poverty with a solid slogan Garibi Hatao, which in English, would mean Remove Poverty.

She knew that her father, though a congressman, used to, now and then, air pro poor views of socialism, since his visit to Russia, in the 1920s. He had also released, a small pamphlet, talking about plusses of socialism after Nehru, the leader of India's national movement to free India, from the British. As a Prime Minister of India in the 1960s, when she found, the private banks in India doing precious little, in the realm of innovation, such as micro Return on Investment type of schemes, she was very disenchanted, with the Indian banks. Her repeated requests, to the banks, to focus on lending, to the rural poor and also indifference to financially helping the prospective job makers, to set up micro rural industries also fell on the deaf ears. She repeatedly asked the Indian banks, with urban headquarters, to proactively help the farmers and financially assist the rural industries, for which the private bank response, was nil. Then she overnight nationalized 14 private banks, with clear mandate, to help the poor, help the rural India. She issued ordnance, duly signed by the President of India, to be placed before the Parliament later, when the Parliament had to meet. The study reveals that reduction of poverty, in a country, is not a small challenge even when, most people are, in the "not so rich income brackets", as financial institutions, though small, in number, could play a highly negative role, impeding improvement, in the living standards of the poor. Indira Gandhi, the Indian Premier and Margaret Thatcher, the British Premier were political contemporaries and possessed a commonality, in their personalities of assertiveness of character. She was known, as a tough Premier like Margaret Thatcher of Britain. She took removal of poverty, as a challenge and made huge economic progress, in their lives, education and self confidence levels. The Poor and labor castes, in the villages in India, who had limited voice, during the entire British period of about 200 years, came to change the governments, through elections and the voting power, in the new millennium. People hailing from the poor families in India, were found everywhere, since the early 1970s such as administration, police, judiciary, medicine, engineering, research and their business entrepreneurs, hold quarterly conferences, in financial capital, Mumbai, in one of roof gardens of the five star hotels. At the same time, they litigate to exact their fundamental rights, granted by the founding fathers, in the constitution of India. The same banks, which Indira Gandhi, who was the Prime Minister of India, for over 15 years, functioned, in a disciplined manner, during the laxity of financial discipline, exhibited copiously, by the American British and European banks, including huge investment banks. At a time, when 150 years young Lehman Brothers, the US based investment bank, an American icon failed and when the Bank of America and the Citibank, needed immediate liquidity and had to be finally bailed out, by the US President. All the banks, which were nationalized by Indira Gandhi in 1969, were making waves, earning profits, quarter through quarter. They were also doing roaring financial business. Mr. Paul Krugman and Mr. Joseph Stiglitz, the Noble award winning economists, in no uncertain terms greatly appreciated the Indian banks and stated that they have so much to offer, in learning about the global banking, including US based banks.

The political reactionaries and conservatives, the well grounded rich, found it too innovative and played games in politics. She had to formed a new congress party, duly adopted a new political symbol for the new political party applying to the National Election Commission of India and participate in elections. Her party won, with a thumping majority and she again became the Prime Minister of India. Backed by a huge popular mandate of people, she proclaimed her public policy, as Garibi Hatao "Remove Poverty." President John F Kennedy, in early 1960s, had a heart for the poor and he worked closely, with the Vice President jobson. When President was assassinated in 1965 president Johnson started a scheme entitled "War against Poverty' In America.

There have been discussions in the book, how well organized are the village poor in India, relative to other parts of the world. They are appreciated, internationally, as they deal with their poverty, in an independent manner, without even the poor laws in place in India. Florence Nightingale a development scholar of India, besides being a Queen's knight, for ennobling work in Crimean war, appreciated the Indian poor, because they manage their poverty, without too much reliance, on the Government as India. She mentioned that unlike in Britain and Europe, where poor people are covered by poor laws and get government assistance, as soon as the poor need them, even in normal times whereas in India, the poor has to go, without poor laws, even in times of the natural calamities.

The study also revealed the attitudinal plasticity, in the way the poor welfare, is viewed by the political regimes, in different nations. If political regimes are dictatorships, be it civil or military, the poor receive little attention, in development. In a democracy, the poor receive attention, only when the developed economies do not have the availability of the dopes. Wherever dopes are available, despite being illegal, the poor get drawn towards it either in consumption or in crimes both of which peep poor where they are. In democracies where liquor is available in plenty at a reasonable rate and the density of the bars sports bars neighborhood bars are very high and rising, even in democracies the poor receive less attention for their welfare.

In a democracy when people are so busy with casinos entertainments of films and 24/7 TV cheap liquor and cheap food the poverty reduction in society is pretty afar. City sport in numerous urban locales and T shirt industry food industry souvenir industry being smaller levels of accelerated reduction of poverty is possible, when the regime introduces a number of welfare schemes and thee is bottom up enthusiasm and trust that given the excitement to emulate those higher economically, like In countries where social system is obsessed with divides open as well as non transparent such a as caste divided India and racially divided a number of countries.

It is strange that some social and economic systems, leave aside, an effort to reduce income inequality and reduce poverty. These systems seem to want the same, economic gap, to continue or even rise. One would think that probably relish the idea that the let the poor address work which is inferior to that of the white man's jobs is quietly and covertly liked by many in the majority. In US social and economic system, while the poor are made to see material comforts better than developing countries, but socio economic group mobility, educational group mobility, equality of educational and economic opportunities and in achieving homogenized social and economic environment of localities, much has remained to be done, even after about 5 centuries now of togetherness. Those came to America from other countries, to migrate legally on their own volition with graduate education from their own poorer countries. They would have done so well, relative to the colored brethren, the blacks, who are living side by side, for over 5 centuries now. Children of such black nationals, who have studied, in US based universities, seem to face much more vicissitudes, than the children of the Polish, the Indian, the Japanese or the Korean immigrants. For the latter, the jobs are far easy to come and far difficult to go, with money available, for upfront investment, it is easy to buy homes, in exclusively white neighborhoods, without reluctance from the homeowners, to sell properties to them.

The study also examined the poverty conditions, of the migrants, who voluntarily went to work, on European farmer owned farms, in the countries of West Indies and also South Africa and never could return, though they were, to return in 5 years, as deliberately no travel arrangements, were made by the farm owners. The promised wages were not paid and the wages paid were so meager, that ir could barely to keep the body and soul together and live permanently on the farm, working for the white farm owners and when body ached, they had to be on their own, in small homes in segmented poorer neighborhoods. Poverty lasted for life for them, though no harassment, exploitation and violence ware perpetrated, as it was done with slaves in USA for decades, particularly in south of USA, where cotton and tobacco, were grown in plenty, which needed more farm labor, hence the slaves were bought.

Even the Indian labor slogged and enriched the landowners, by leaps and bounds and latter traded domestically as well as internationally, lot of money. But the farm owners got into the habit of deriding even voluntary labor from India, calling them coolies. In the developed world people, intra interface, among themselves, in recent decades, a trend has generated that a bad student who is disinclined to study, is not permitted to be pulled up, by the school teachers, The parents in America rush to fault the teacher, if a derogatory remark against their child, is uttered in frustration, by the American teacher. While the child makes merry, doing no homework for weeks, or merrily writes all wrong answers, in response to the home work, the American parent give the impression that they have no time, to even ask their children, to study seriously, as in most cases, they are overzealously protective, of their children, in the name of sustaining their self confidence. These are trends noticed, in few decades now, in the western countries. Similarly, a man who is overweight /obese cannot be commented as such, in the school, in the college, in the workplace by any colleague, as an advisory note, by the bosses or even onlookers. All of these protections for the fat person, are provided in American law now, passed by the law making bodies and they are administered by the police. No one has time to pause and think if the obesity could be serious in its implications for the self and even for the nation when tipping point in overweight and obesity is reached in a few years ; how soon he/she is discharged from work due to inefficiency, arising from obesity or if his/her promotion overlooked and if the airlines are finding at least 4 to 5 obese passengers, in every flight, in every airline out to help them with difficulty, take a seat in the plane. It is not even commented how in some hospitals the surgery doors had to be remodeled to be able to carry stretchers carrying obese Americans for surgery. Precluding society, to call a spade a spade could endanger economic scenario of individual Americans and also th4e economic scenario at the Washington level as driven by high and rising obesity in America, US government at the national levels, could see their debts snowballing and budget deficits reaching high proportions, endangering the living standard and quality of those Americans, who are yet to be born.

Instead of reducing the existing poverty, one notices that by such "looking the other way altitude, "also insisted under law, to make no observations, is harmful for the US economy. Once Malcolm Gladwell's tipping point reaches in regard to the obesity of the Americans, the hesitation/shame for having turned obese has the potential to vanish, denting the future of US economy. Then if more and more Americans voluntarily, leave jobs, to lead a comfortable sedentary life, a lot of health conscious disciplined Americans, would feel highly frustrated because bailing out individuals and institutions go on in America pretty liberally no less than in Scandinavian socialist countries though the expression socialism, is avoided and market forces and competition, in the US economy are incessantly talked about. All these bailout take place in America, at the expense of all of those, who are disciplined enough to eat in moderation, drink in moderation, walk significantly rather than leading a sedentary life, of driving around, even in the neighborhoods and who watch TV, only for limited hours and do not hog pop corns and unlimited coke, at the cinema theater, every other weekend. There are American people, who would never go near, the tap of unlimited coke, and neither would they go to a buffet restaurant, with a spread of 72 items, treating the provider of food as trigger for ill health. For all the discipline that whole lot of Americans and the westerners conjure up and make it a way of disciplined life, have to pay out of their pockets, for many others who not only turned heavily undisciplined, about their health, but also perpetuate it, with no cutting of weight for years. and finally become the cause of their poverty and then the cause of the poverty gradually of the fellow citizens, who have to pay for initially obese people's denting of economic productivity. It is strange that a lot of Americans have little or nil sense of gratitude, to the US establishment, for having created fine conditions of living environment that are afar from poverty in visual terms, such as nice roads with dividers, nice highways, neat and well maintained rest rooms, on the highways, food courts on the highways, nice illumination in the city squares some state universities for higher education and certainly a free elementary and high school education. Not only the US, as a nation provides so many comforts, to its citizens, unknown in most parts of the world, it goes multiple steps further to dote on its citizens to have a go go life with unlimited coke, 70 items spreads of buffet, gas guzzling SUVs to be used even for multiple trips within the locality, issuance of multiple plastic cards unrelated to any eligibility, free emergency medical services, at the hospitals and for many of the irresponsibility of conduct, of day to day life, by the citizens, when heart ailments and obesities, mount in the society, no regulatory advice or economic disincentives or higher taxes, by way of economic disincentives, are resorted to. With so much of doting, on the citizens, is it any wonder that the personal saving rates have plummeted in 25 years to almost zero; the borrowers cannot even put up upfront of 5% cost of the car and the house, when their parents used to easily put up upfront, to a tune of 25 to 30% upfront, while borrowing. Is it any wonder that Americans in their 30s are turning heart patients? Is it any wonder that balance sheets of average Americans are loaded, with high volumes of debt, including student loans? It is for the readers to judge, as to which constituency needs more correction, self introspection to extricate America from such challenging poverty conditions today government or the citizens with so much infrastructure being added by the government and so many sops provided, to please voters and citizens with the lack of prudence, inviting highly challenging poverty conditions on to themselves and their national economy. even casual advice comments from friends acquaintances are not permitted under law. People are refusing to recognize that with inaction and dismissals in the workplaces, due to heaviness, their individual productivity, in the work, is becoming warped. Ailments for a large number fat people, could skyrocket the Medicaid and medicate expenditure to stratospheric heights. All of these events, in few decades would accumulate, to make individuals poorer with heavy debts, pending and even governments seeing huge budget deficits, to care for numerous obese,

While addressing or referring or even lightly joking members of the same race today are not called fat, not called obese, not called dumb, thus totally avoiding, calling a spade a spade, but people from other races, are very casually inflicted with insults and humiliations calling people of Indian origin Coolies as they volunteered to come as farm labor for sugar plantations in the West Indies and South Africa. It doesn't matter if today's generation, of such people are intelligent, go to universities and after acquiring degrees, work in foreign and domestic firms. Today the per capita incomes is higher than most whites in these countries and so are the educational levels. Many of them are well paid professionals, such as accountants, doctors, engineers, bio technologists and live well with nice homes and personalized transportation. But they are sill referred as coolies. Fat men and super fat men and women, saunter around, with no shame in US, drawing no derogatory comments, for being fat and super fat, no elderly advice is forthcoming. A dumb student in the class cannot be referred, as dumb, as it is said to reduce a child's self confidence, as per UD based pedagogical research. So much superfine feelings have been developed for their own racial people, considering how they would feel. Calling a black a negro, became a general practice, when in fact the majority population farmers organized the rime of arranging to pull them away from their homes, then illegally, criminally, unsociably and unethically were deported to slave needy countries.

Even the Indians, who joined as farm labor, were not spared, from the insults, being heaped, through negative comments and this calling of names, went on ceaselessly, for the last 200 years. I am told that even in 2000s, the West Indies citizens, who are of Indian origin, feel insulted, when they are referred as coolies, by the white landowners and white others as coolies, both in South Africa and the West Indian sugar plantations. This type of reference to call labor coolie, in a supercilious manner, was never declared illegal, in their legislatures and even to this day, they are reminded that their ancestors came as farm labor, 4 to 5 centuries ago, no matter if they are today cricketers, golf players, doctors, engineers, lawyers, chartered accountants, business hotel and restaurant owners Casually the people of lighter skin, in a derogatory manner, keep referring to Indian home neighborhoods, as coolie neighborhoods, coolie shop, coolie restaurant and the like. When social cleavage, is perpetuated by people of lighter color, how could there be any attempt by them, to improve their economic status and reduction in poverty. Reminded of poverty of their ancestors, by light colored people, how are they allowed to dissociate themselves, from the concept of poverty and acquire self confidence, to be money makers and job providers?

Indians in Durban, Transvaal, and Johannesburg, after 4 to 5 generations are still referred, as coolies, reminding them that their ancestors in 1800s, came to South Africa as coolies, the farm labor. If such references are not lack of civility, what else could be termed uncivilized, no matter how highly placed professional a name caller could be. Such human indignities are constant reminders of the plight of their poor ancestors. To solve the problem of poverty, such subtle derogatory remarks, have to be flushed out, by the institutions like the International Court of Justice. Prime Minister of India would be fine, to address the Chief of the World Bank and the Chief of the IMF and also the Chief Justice of International Court of Justice, Hague, to erase the coolie expression, from the lexicons of the West Indies and South Africa.

The dichotomy of not calling, a fat American a fat American and calling a doctor of Indian origin, a Coolie, drawing on the names on events that occurred in 1800s, when the British permitted Indian labor, to undertake journey to the West Indies and South Africa, to earn wages and return after 5 years. As they could not return to homeland, due to money greed of their employers, not to pay them, living wages and not to organize return travel to India, as promised by the employers and the British government.

How the case was dealt with by prosecution and how evidence was adduced and how frequently the adjournments were taken to punish the guilty is reviewed with police officials, on a regular basis. Finally how many cases were convicted and how many acquitted is taken serious cognizance of. This has triggered enough fear, among such members of the forward castes and there is lot of deterrence, not to call any names to the labor castes. India can offer a lot of learning to the global powers, where such name calling, racial slurs go on no matter, how high is the GDP of such an economy. Looking the other way will allow such nefarious activities raising the poverty levels of some segments of population in many multicultural counties.

Every year, in India, a few recalcitrant forward caste fellows, undergo jail sentences, of about 6 months. The punishment of 6 months imprisonment, is mandatory and once the offence, is proved, against the perpetrator of human indignity, there is no escape, from jail sentence, for all the accused, no matter he/she hails from a respectable family, whether he/she is university educated or he/she works as professionals, such as architects, lawyers, doctors and the like. Calling people and professionals of Indian origin as Coolies, in the West Indies and South Africa are obnoxious practices, which should be erased, with similar legislation and implementing law, very strongly, both in South Africa and in the West indies, nations. It is high time, such obnoxious words of social humiliation and human indignity evaporate, which would indirectly help, such countries, reduce poverty considerably and introduce a high level of inclusiveness.

The developed world people whose ancestors colonized many countries are probably, ignorant of how, they used to be derisively refereed by the Indians, when the British ruled India. They would not feel happy, if they would know, how derisively, they were referred. But that expression died out, as soon as the country got independence and progressed so well, with cooperation of development agencies, of the World Bank, the IMF and their country administration. Similarly, expressions like Coolie, should have been forgotten long back. When in these countries, the people of Indian origin, were insultingly referred, they should have acted legally and politically, to make other race of lighter color, to refrain from such derogatory comments against people of Indian origin. Such cheap social practices, need to be brought, by those adversely affected for justice, to the law enforcement authorities.

Government also has to have, lot of self regulation, so that its political power hunger and its war mongering, do not come, in the way of reduction in poverty. Further, the government would need to run democracy, offering themselves to elections, for new Government, with a periodicity of 4 to 5 years, duly giving freedom of thought and expression, but not frivolous license, as it is in India and the developed world today. Government need to be very inclusive, to include many of the ethnicities in Africa and castes and linguistic groups in India, so that their ethnic and caste and linguistic prides dilute and national prides boom. Government in Britain, has failed to maintain, the inclusiveness, in their cabinet and also parliamentary committees. It has also failed despite, demands of several decades, to give autonomy, to the elected local Governments and elected chiefs of the provinces, reporting of course, to the national government The referendum in the Scotland, was very close in October 2014.

Some ethnicities are richer than others in Africa and so are some castes, richer than other castes in India. Thus interethnic marriages could not only eliminate dowry, but also could bring about economies of scale and better standards of living, as an outcome of inter ethnic marriage. For this purpose, the past tradition of millenniums, of distinct identity of tribes in Africa and castes in India have, to be gradually forgotten. No ridicule of older generation, for their social customs, would make changes happen and changes have to be in place, appreciating the feelings, of all the constituents, involved. While government may increase financial incentives substantially, for inter ethic and inter caste marriages, even the corporate sector also need, to offer financial incentives, for social changes. While this idea may receive some acceptance, among people of the same skin color and same religion but skin color and religion for millenniums, could have been very important factors, for settling marriages. if human identity as one sees even now in the new millennium, how haughty some people of lighter skin are, for no achievements of theirs, except the skin color, on many occasions.

The study also revealed that child poverty in USA, which is high and rising especially in the inner neighborhoods of Chicago New York Los Angeles and the like then a lot of attention America has to pay to proffering up institution of marriage. with no seminars workshops being held in universities or communities such a lions clubs rotary and Jaycees clubs on the immense value of the institution of marriage on TVs never mentioning about get back to basics get back to living in marriages would keep the status quo of child poverty continuing with severe challenges of adult poverty of after the adulthood. Heavy sacrifices will have to be met by the young men and women to live in marriage and then give birth ti children and al both parents raising the children within the boundaries of marriage to enable children to acquire good education good values and good ethics. It is a huge dichotomy that though USA, is a 14 trillion dollar economy, in its jurisdiction tens of millions of children, live in abject poverty/ frustration, with only one parent, with no home discipline, due to their parents. Many families decimate their companionship in marriage having decimated the holy institution of marriage, ordained by God. Then they make experiments, of inter gender interaction, calling by different names such live in, multiple dating, parallel dating, instead of serial dating of the past, keeping the dating very fast sometimes 2 weeks and then refusing to take calls for no valid reason. Like flexible labor market the marriage dating seem to have no rules followed. For example dating cessations take place, with no advanced notice and giving no valid reasons. It is just not receiving calls rudely. Poverty reduction for those who are poor in such a social malaise would be near impossible. In such social practices which the western countries are calling liberal social practices the reality of poverty of children in this manner are embedded. It has to be viewed by the western countries in the economic sense more than social sense.

Without a huge comedown from show off attitude and without living beyond means with incessant borrowing would the US be able to fetter poverty of the American poor. Switching to a simple way of life, smaller cars and public transportation reduction, the reliance on would cease in some decades, in the US, a necessity and not an option any more. Writing has been clear on the wall for 25 years now.

Similarly if the labor in workplaces have to receive living wages to reduce the heavy needs of borrowing now, they have to get their annual bonus and annual raises and health care in a routine manner. To make these financial plusses happen the labor corporations have to forget the days of union bashing and the like coercion and the government need to sit together and revive industrial democracy so that hands of the management are tied and they are disallowed to indulge in runway expenditure such as astronomical CEO compensations, frequent executive/first class air travel, renting huge suites for CEO's personal recreation, unbelievable figure of severance packages and all of the shameful misdemeanours.

Without a strong industrial democracy, the job uncertainties will continue, to wreck professional and family life and average Americans have to be engaged democracy, to prevail upon government to make businesses pay decent compensation health care long term benefits of some sorts. Temp revolution of job recruitment, has to roll back and even disappear, for sustainable reduction of poverty.

Government need to keep level playing field, between retailers and suppliers. In a market economy, offers of goods with low price model, could only, be offered based on pay stubs, only to those, who are at the base of economic period, not to the millionaires, as then for the millionaires, the goods and services sold at low prices always low prices, at the cost of the financial suffering of tens of millions of employees/workers of the poor suppliers. The poor employees of firm and suppliers form India and abroad and their employees, now are made to slog for measly wages not getting appropriate living wages that too for middle class rich class and super rich class to enjoy goods ai a heavily subsidized rates. here we see an highly unethical event of transfer of wealth from the poor to the rich and super rich in America.. This restriction needs to apply to Wal-Mart Carrefour, Target Ratnadeep and More chains in India where offer of goods need to be offered to the base of the economic pyramid to reduce rich power inequality. Progressive taxation, for very big business, need to be introduced, so that monopolistic tendencies, curb injustice in democracy and capitalism.

References

Altman, Daniel," Managing Globalization, Dealing with the Global Food Crisis." International Herald Tribune, May 6, 2008

Bhagwati, J., "India in Transition- Freeing the Economy." 1994, Oxford University Press, New Delhi.

Bhagwati, J., "Is India's Economic Miracle at hand?" June 9 1985, New York Times

Banerjee, V. Esther Duflo, "Poor Economics: A Radical Rethinking of the Way to Fight Global Poverty"

Collier, Paul "The Bottom Billion: Why the Poorest Countries Are Failing and What Can Be Done About It."

Collins, Drayl, Jonathan Morduch, Stuart Rutherford, Orlanda Ruthven "Portfolios of the Poor: How the World's Poor Live on $2 a Day"

Colvin, Geoff," Making Health Care History: The Next President will have a Fighting Chance to Defeat the Lobbyists and Reform a Broken System." Business Week, June 9 2008.

Dandekar, V. M., "Indian Economy Since Independence." Economic and Political Weekly, April 23 1988, Vol. 23

Dickens, Charles, "Great Expectations"

Das, G., "India's Growing Middle Class." Global Development, Monday November 5, 2001.

Dinavo, Vangu Jacques, "Privatization in Developing Countries: Its Impact on Economic Development and Democracy." Greenwood Publishing Group, 1995.

Ehrenreich, Barbara, "Nickel and Dimed: On Getting by in America ."

Edelman, Peter, "So Rich, So Poor: Why It's So Hard to End Poverty in America."

Frank, Catherine, "Indira: The Life of Indira Gandhi." London: Harper Collins, 2001

Galbraith, J. K. "The Affluent Society." 1987, Penguin Group.

Grow, Brian, "Hispanic Nation; Hispanics are an immigrant group, like no other. Their huge numbers are challenging and assumptions about assimilation. Is America ready?" Business Week, March 15 2004

Hog, J., "The Rise in Asia." Foreign Affairs, July/August 2004.. Long, Jeff and Christi

Hall, Ben, "France Eyes Curbs on Executive Pay." Financial Times, May 30, 2008, P2.

Howe, Irwin, "The Other America: Poverty in the United States by Michael Harrington,"

Jalan, Bimal, "India's Economic Crisis: The Way Ahead." 1993, Oxford University Press, New Delhi.

Kennedy, Michelle, "Without a Net: Middle Class and Homeless (with Kids) in America."

Kolodco, W. George, "Russia Should Put its People First." The New York Times, July 7 1998

Kozol, Jonathan, Savage Inequalities: Children in America's Schools

Kozol, Jonathan," The Shame of the Nation: The Restoration of Apartheid Schooling in America"

Krugman, Paul, "The Myth of Asia's Miracle: A cautionary Fable." Foreign Affairs, November 1994.

Lareau, Amette, "Unequal Childhoods: Class, Race, and Family Life"

Lall, S., "Building Industrial Competitiveness in Developing Countries." 1990, OECD, Paris.

Leavitt Greifeld, Bob, "America cannot Afford to Drive Away Talent; Many US Companies

Lloyd, John, "Who Lost Russia? The New York Times, August 15 1999.

Mazumdar, D., "Import Substituting Industrialization and the Protection of the Small Scale: The Indian Experience in the Textile Industry." 1991, World Development, Vol.19 (9).

Minhas, B. S., "Rural Poverty and Minimal Level of Living: A Reply." 1971, Indian Economic Review, Vol. 6 NS

Myers L. Bryant, "Walking With the Poor: Principles and Practices of Transformational Development"

Orwell, George, "Down and Out in Paris and London."

Palkhivala N. A., "We the People- India, the Largest Democracy." 1991.

Parsons, "Campaign 2008; Take Responsibility, Obama Urges Fathers; At Southside Church,

Payne Ruby K. "A Framework for Understanding Poverty Pendersen, Dige, Jorgan, "Explaining Economic Liberalization in India: State and

Society Perspectives." World Development, Vol. 28, Issue 2, February 2000, PP 265-282.

Rai, Saritha, "India Looking up." International Herald Tribune, May 28 2005.

Rivlin, Gary "Broke, USA: From Pawnshops to Poverty, Inc. - How the Working Poor Became Big Business."

Robinson, James, "Why Nations Fail: The Origins of Power, Prosperity, and Poverty by Daron Acemoğlu, James Robinson"

Spagat, E., "Proctor and Gamble to Outsource About 80% of Back-Office Work." Wall Street Journal, June 14, 2002.

Sachs, D Jeffrey, "Resolving the Debt Crisis of Low Income Countries." Brookings Papers on Economic activity 1:257-86. Economist Conference October 17 2002.

Sachs, Jeffrey D, "The End of Poverty."

Singer, Peter The Life You Can Save: Acting Now to End World Poverty by

Shipler David K, "The Working Poor: Invisible in America"

Srinivasan, T. N. and Pranab Pradhan, "Rural Poverty in South Asia." 1987, Columbia University Press, New York.

Spagat, E., "Proctor and Gamble to Outsource About 80% of Back-Office Work." Wall Street Journal, June 14, 2002.

Steinbach, John, "Of Mice and Men"

Steinbach, John;" Grapes of wrath."

Stephen, Huyler "Village India." 1985, H. N. A. Brans, New York.

Stiglitz, E. Joseph, "Price of Inequality." Venkatesh, Sudhir, "The Underground Economy of the Urban Poor" Princeton University Press January 1st, 2009.

Vernon, Raymond "Economic Aspects of Privatization Program." 1987, The World Bank, Economic Development Institute, Washington DC.

Vickers, John and George Yarrow "Privatization and Natural Monopolies." 1985, Public Policy Center, London.

Waidmeir, Patti, "Home Baked Solutions to Illegal Immigration." Financial Times, June 13 2007, P12

Wilson, Q, James and Peter Skarry, "Line in the Sand: A Return to Fundamentals on Immigration." Wall Street Journal, May 18 2006, PA14

Witte, G. and N. Henderson, "Wealth Gap Widens For Blacks, Hispanics, Significant Ground Lost After Recession." The Washington Post, October 2004, pp. A11.

Yunus, Muhammad, Alan Jolis, "Banker to the Poor: Micro-Lending and the Battle Against World Poverty."

"CEOs Rewarded For Outsourcing." Associated Press, September 1 2004

"Spain and Immigration; Still they come, A new route, but an old problem." The Economist, May 13 2006 P61, 62.

"As US population swell, so do problems." USA Today, July 10. 2006

Arizona Governor Signs Tough Bill on Hiring Illegal Immigrants." International Herald Tribune, July 3 2007

"Annual Reports, Reserve Bank of India Economic Surveys." Ministry of Finance, Government of India, Various Issues.

"Budget Speeches of Union Finance Ministers-Various Years." Ministry of Finance, New Delhi.

Blunt Words on the Importance of Family." Chicago Tribune, June 16 2008 Section 1, P4.

"China's Middle Class is Booming." Daily Policy Digest, International Issues, Thursday, January 24, 2002.

"Judge: Wal-Mart Violated Minn Labor Laws 2 million times; Minn Judge rules against Wal-Mart in employees class action suit." myfoxtwincities.com, July 2008.

Ministry of Finance, 2007, Economic Survey of India, 2006-2007, New Delhi.

Rely on Inventors, Scientists, Engineers and Academics, who are Foreign Born but US Trained." Financial Times May 30, 2008, P9.

Reserve Bank of India, 2007, Handbook of Statistics on the Indian Economy, 2006-2007, Mumbai, India.

"What America Must do to Compete with China and India; The Sheer Brainpower in Both Countries Gives Them an Edge." Business Week, April 22/29 2005.

About the Author

Dr. Subhrendu Bhattacharya, a senior bureaucrat, an administrator, a policy planner and analyst has been associated with economic development and implementation of welfare schemes in the state of Andhra Pradesh, India. In his role as a policy planner he advised the state government on wide range of policy issues from poverty reduction to universal education. As the financial planner he implemented of World Bank and other bi-laterally aided development projects and facilitated economic liberalization in the state and during the author's tenure as the chief executive certain state run corporations witnessed the process of economic liberalization and privatization.

The author holds a PhD. in Economics besides MS. in Finance, Physics and History. His recent work has been Globalization and a Shrunken World published in 2011.

www.ingramcontent.com/pod-product-compliance
Lightning Source LLC
Chambersburg PA
CBHW030422290526
45786CB00001B/87